Céline: The Novel as Delirium

CÉLINE: THE NOVEL AS DELIRIUM

By ALLEN THIHER

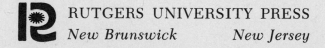

RUTGERS UNIVERSITY PRESS
New Brunswick   New Jersey

Grateful acknowledgement is given to the following publishers for permission to publish excerpts from Céline's works in the original French or in English translation:

The Bodley Head, Ltd.: *Death on the Installment Plan; North.* Chatto and Windus, Ltd.: *Journey to the End of the Night.* Editions Gallimard: *D'un château l'autre; Entretiens avec le professeur Y...; Féerie pour une autre fois I; Guignol's Band; Mort à crédit; Nord; Normance; Le Pont de Londres; Rigodon; La Vie et l'œuvre de Semmelweis; Voyage au bout de la nuit.* Holt-Blond, Ltd.: *Castle to Castle.* New Directions Publishing Corporation: *Death on the Installment Plan; Guignol's Band; Journey to the End of the Night.* Seymour Lawrence, Inc., and Delacorte Press: *Castle to Castle; North; Rigodon.*

Library of Congress Cataloging in Publication Data

Thiher, Allen, 1941–
  Céline: the novel as delirium.

  Bibliography: p.
  1. Destouches, Louis Ferdinand, 1894–1961.
2. Mental illness in literature. I. Title.
PQ2607.E834Z9   843'.9'12   77-185394
ISBN 0-8135-0717-0

Manufactured in the United States of America by Quinn & Boden Company, Inc., Rahway, New Jersey

Contents

Acknowledgements

I should like to express my deep gratitude to Germaine Brée, who started me on this project at the University of Wisconsin. I am also greatly indebted to Roger Shattuck for a detailed reading of a first version of this study and to Paul Fortier, who was kind enough to send me the useful concordance of *Voyage au bout de la nuit* that he did at the Institute for Research in the Humanities at the University of Wisconsin.

The English translations provided in this book are intended to be fairly literal renderings of the French texts in order to facilitate a direct knowledge of Céline's style. Ralph Manheim's excellent translations, and others, have, of course, been consulted, but the final wording is my own. It may be noted that the French originals vary slightly from edition to edition, no doubt due in part to the difficulties of deciphering some of Céline's manuscripts.

Céline: The Novel as Delirium

Introduction

Immediately after the Parisian physician Louis-Ferdinand Destouches, better known as Céline, published *Voyage au bout de la nuit* in 1932, Trotsky observed that Céline had walked into great literature as other men walk into their homes. He went on to say that Céline would not write a second book with such an aversion for the lie and such a disbelief in the truth. This dissonance would have to resolve itself. The paradox Trotsky so clearly perceived did not, however, resolve itself, and Céline's work stands as a monument to the dissonance, rage, and madness that such a paradox could generate and generate unceasingly for thirty years. When Céline died in 1961, he was still at work on one more novel, *Rigodon,* in which he continued to pour forth his vituperation against the lie, against all lies that blind men to their misery.

Yet Céline never really offered any belief in the truth, that is, in any truth beyond the recognition of man's horrible necessity to grow sick and die and of the an-

guish that accompanies that recognition. Perhaps it is
inappropriate to speak of truth and falsehood in Céline's
case, for his novels propose a form of discourse that lies
beyond the realm of normal verification and beyond the
paradox that springs from the antithesis of lie and truth.
His novels are, in essence, discourses in the delirium
that springs from his intolerable awareness of human
misery; and as discourses in delirium, Céline's novels
are an inexhaustible source of truths and countertruths.

From his first to his last novel Céline's work can be
compared to a journey, or, more precisely, to a flight that
leads into the night of existential, metaphysical, and,
finally, historical darkness. There are momentary flickers
of light in this night, such as Céline's lyricism in
Guignol's Band or the joy he finds in the dance. There
is also his anti-Semitic polemic, the outrageous pamphlets that constituted an insane effort to bring illumina-
tion to the night. *Voyage au bout de la nuit* first sets
forth the theme of flight into darkness and thus serves as
a kind of preface to the entire body of Céline's work. It
is a preface complete in itself, yet it points beyond itself
to the journey that ends in the disaster of Céline's last
novels in which he narrates pseudohistorical "chronicles" of his flight across Nazi Germany.

Céline's flight into darkness is more than a physical
or even literary journey, for his works trace a descent
into a night of another sort, one in which the light of
reason has been extinguished. This snuffing out of the
light of reason means quite simply that Céline's journey
leads to the darkest reaches of madness. Céline's novels
present extended travels into the delirium of men,
things, history, of existence itself. Madness is his favorite metaphor to explain the nature of being. Hallucina-

tion is his favored mode of perception. Or as Céline himself put it in a letter to Daudet in 1932:

> Vous connaissez certainement, Maître, l'énorme Fête des Fous de P. Brueghel. Cela est à Vienne. Tout le problème n'est pas ailleurs pour moi...
>
> Je voudrais bien comprendre autre chose. Je ne comprends pas autre chose. Je ne peux pas.
>
> Tout mon délire est dans ce sens et je n'ai guère d'autres délires.[1]

> (Certainly you are familiar with the huge Carnival of the Mad by P. Brueghel. It is in Vienna. The whole problem is right there for me...
>
> I'd like to be able to understand something else. I don't understand anything else. I can't.
>
> All my delirium is like that, and I hardly have any other kinds of delirium.)

Though no painting by Brueghel bears this exact title, Céline's comparison shows both his way of interpreting reality—to the point of projecting his own title on a Brueghel painting—and his awareness that only a Brueghel-like vision of madness will ever be the stuff of his novelistic worlds.

This book proposes to follow Céline's journey into his worlds of delirium by setting forth a comprehensive introduction to his novels and polemic while offering an analysis of their fundamental structure and themes. His journey begins with *Voyage au bout de la nuit* and, in terms of sheer verbal power, progresses through *Mort à crédit* to culminate in *Guignol's Band* (which includes *Le Pont de Londres,* the concluding part of *Guignol's Band*). These three novels are Céline's greatest accomplishment as a writer, perhaps because he wrote them before he fled Occupied France and underwent imprisonment and exile. *Guignol's Band* is the least known of the three, since the first part was published during the Occupation and the second part posthumously. It merits the same critical attention that the first two novels have received.

Céline's itinerary leads not only to the creation of *Guignol's Band* but also to his anti-Semitic crisis and the publication of three works of delirious polemic. Though *Bagatelles pour un massacre, L'Ecole des cadavres,* and *Les Beaux Draps* were all published before *Guignol's Band,* these several hundred pages of demented ravings and comic diatribes form a contrast with —and a complement to—Céline's first three novels. Moreover, they set the stage for Céline's last works, his semiautobiographical novels or chronicles that are directly rooted in the misfortunes he suffered for having published his polemic. Published after the war and Céline's return from exile, *Féerie pour une autre fois I* and *Normance* relate his tribulations in Occupied Paris and in his Danish prison cell; *D'un château l'autre, Nord,* and *Rigodon* narrate his wanderings in Germany during the last months of the Third Reich. Céline's novelistic journey thus ends with the tale of a journey that his first novel seems to have foreshadowed, a journey through the madness that the march of history unleashed on Europe.

CHAPTER I The Picaro's Flight into Darkness

Voyage au bout de la nuit (*Journey to the End of the Night*) appeared on the literary scene in 1932, in the wake of surrealism's first experimentation and at a moment when the malaise of the troubled postwar years had cast a film of despair over an entire society. Céline's cynicism and denunciations seemed to speak for everyone. To a generation accustomed to the neoclassical language of Gide and Valéry, his popular, obscene language was like a violent gust of fresh air breaking into the literary climate. The Right and the Left, both Daudet and Trotsky, were ready to applaud *Voyage's* scandalized portrayal of a society in dissolution as well as its bewildered outrage at man's innate viciousness. Neither group was entirely wrong in its interpretation, for in *Voyage* Céline had succeeded in writing a work in which a social sense of human exploitation coexisted with a sense of man's incapacity to rise above his dreary propensity for self-destruction. In short, he had composed a radical novel based on reactionary premises.

For the Left, Bardamu, *Voyage*'s traveling hero, could appear to be a representative victim of capitalism. At the beginning of the novel, Bardamu, a young medical student, leaps up in a burst of suicidal patriotic enthusiasm to join a passing regiment. He quickly becomes another bit of cannon fodder as he is caught up in a war he cannot understand — certainly he had nothing against the Germans who insist on shooting at him. After a spell in a psychiatric ward where army doctors try to cure him of fear, the only rational ailment in *Voyage*, Bardamu escapes Europe's mass hysteria by going to Africa. Europe has corrupted the Dark Continent by adding new forms of viciousness to old ones, and Bardamu discovers that colonialism is as barbarous as nationalism. After a futile stay in the jungle as a commercial agent, a very sick Bardamu finds himself sold into slavery on a galley whose captain is enough of an entrepreneur to recognize a bargain when he sees it. Although work as a galley slave is not very demanding and offers a great deal of security, Bardamu escapes from the ship to see what New York has to offer. The capital of capitalism offers hunger, loneliness, and constant frustration. Detroit is hardly better, for a job in a Ford plant is more dehumanizing than rowing a slave galley and the pay is not much better. Having seen the New World, Bardamu goes back to France, though not without having known a few tender moments with a prostitute whose copious earnings allow her to support him. The land of opportunity is not quite what legend would have it to be.

In the second part of *Voyage* the Right could find that Bardamu's satirical denunciations of the modern world went beyond social questions to offer a condemnation of man himself. The novel skips over the time Bardamu spends finishing his medical studies to find him stuck in

the squalid Parisian suburb of "Rancy," where he tries
to live on beans and establish a medical practice. The
journey slows down considerably as Bardamu passes
his days ministering to misery, listening to slander,
observing his neighbors' sadism and bestiality, and
attempting fruitlessly to collect his fees. Succumbing to
his need to eat regularly, he gives up his medical career
to become a walk-on in a cinema-music hall. At the same
time he tries to help his friend Robinson, another nocturnal traveler who has periodically accompanied Bardamu in his journey. The novel's final episodes involving Robinson underscore Céline's belief in man as an
essentially self-destructive animal. Bardamu takes a
quiet job in an insane asylum, where it appears he can
get along with a minimum of risks. Here he must be a
witness to Robinson's refusal of conventional life.
Robinson's refusal is really aimed at life's limits and
results in his being murdered by his angered fiancée.

The final resolution of this nearly allegorical journey
lies in the alternatives of accepting either madness or
death. Since Bardamu does not have enough strength
of mind to consider either possibility, his tale comes to a
halt with his abrupt refusal to speak any more. Robinson
and perhaps Bardamu's inmates have made it to the end
of the night, but for Bardamu the journey can only continue senselessly until death decides to end it for him.

In later Céline criticism there is a tendency to neglect
the novel's indictment of society, perhaps because
Céline's sociology is essentially a schematic vision of
the distant rich who exploit the masses of the poor.
Bardamu is generally classified as a picaresque hero in
this later criticism. R.-M. Albérès, who sees Bardamu as
the ancestor of the legion of post-World War II pica-

resque heroes, offers the following description of the
modern picaro and the world in which he moves: "a
cynical, unstable hero, engaged in adventures that are
constantly renewed, serves as a pretext for a systematic
and juicy satire of society and men. Everything is corrupt, broken down, and working badly; all is denounced
without pity; laughter or ill humor constitutes the book's
moral and aesthetic, often with a stab of defiance. . . ." [1]
Although it is true that in the first part of *Voyage* Bardamu is very much a picaro, this description hardly does
justice to the novel's narrative complexity, nor to what
happens in the second part of *Voyage*. In the first part
there is a large distance between the picaro hero and
the older narrator who is recalling his experience as a
young man. In the second part it becomes evident that
there are two picaros in *Voyage*, since Bardamu's journey is .doubled by that of Robinson, his enigmatic alter
ego who is always a step ahead of him in his travels. The
most immediately obvious structural principle in *Voyage*
is thus found in this double journey into the night. In
the first part of the novel it is Bardamu who is embroiled
in the task of saving his skin in a pointlessly hostile
world. At the same time an older Bardamu, the narrator
for whom the novel is time past, comments on his
travels as a young man and offers a stream of acerbic
reflections that contrast vividly with the young picaro's
tale of fear and flight. In the second part of *Voyage* the
distance between the young protagonist and the older
narrator has lessened considerably. This accounts to
a large extent for the change in narrative tone that many
critics have noticed. As the novel progresses — or fails to
progress — it becomes evident that Bardamu, having
gone as far into the night as he can go, must let Robinson
finish the journey. One might liken the novel to a relay

race in which Bardamu, having run until exhaustion, hands the baton to Robinson, a stronger runner who can finish the last lap and cross the finish line while Bardamu applauds him from the side lines.

It may be useful first to situate the older narrator, the older Bardamu for whom the novel is something of a distasteful confession. Bardamu introduces himself as a young medical student whose head was not too solid at a time when "War was sneaking up." Speaking to a fellow student, he quickly offers his opinions on a number of matters. Love, for instance, is a form of the infinite for poodles, while the French race can be defined as "ce grand ramassis de miteux dans mon genre, chassieux, puceux, transis" ("this big bunch of miserable bums like me, bleary, lousy, frozen") (pp. 11–12). He compares life to a slave galley and then jumps up to join the army, crying that he is going to see if that is the way it is. The mature narrator quickly and ironically detaches himself from his past by commenting that Bardamu was "Un petit malin . . . tout ce qu'il y avait d'avancé dans les opinions" ("A really clever little guy . . . really knew everything when it came to advanced ideas") (p. 12). This sardonic view of what he once was sets the narrative tone for the novel's first part. The older narrator already knows that life is what he imagined it to be, only worse, for he has already done duty on the slave galley.

The picaro's immediate situation is obvious. By the end of the first chapter he is in the army, "trapped like a rat," ready to be sent to the impending carnage. It is not so obvious, however, from what vantage point the older narrator is supposedly remembering and narrating his past. The temporal distance between the narrator and the protagonist is maintained, however tenuously, throughout *Voyage,* and the narrator's disgruntled concluding words, "qu'on n'en parle plus" ("let's not talk about it any more"), give the reader no better clue as to where to look for a narrator than do the opening remarks. It would appear that the older Bardamu is a narrator much like Proust's Marcel, though with an important difference: Céline's Bardamu has set himself not outside the Time he is going to recapture, but outside the Night through which he must journey. Such is the sense of the "Chanson des Gardes Suisses" that Céline uses to preface the novel:

> Notre vie est un voyage
> Dans l'hiver et dans la Nuit
> Nous cherchons notre passage
> Dans le Ciel où rien ne luit.

> (Our life is a voyage
> In winter and in the Night
> We look for our way
> In the Sky where there is no light.)

Anyone lost in the darkness of the journey will have no light by which to see how things are. Moreover, the voyage through darkness means not only not seeing things; it also means being caught up in the madness of this world without light of any kind.

As Céline suggests in *Voyage*'s prologue, to understand a world plunged into darkness and chaos one must get to "the other side of life" and be free from the contagious madness that destroys lucidity and vision. Thus the older narrator often speculates on the necessity of getting outside the journey's time span if one is to understand it:

On découvre dans tout son passé ridicule tellement de ridicule, de tromperie, de crédulité qu'on voudrait peut-être s'arrêter tout net d'être jeune, attendre la jeunesse qu'elle se détache, . . . et puis soi partir . . . repasser tout doucement de l'autre côté du Temps pour regarder vraiment comment qu'ils sont les gens et les choses. (p. 284.)

(You discover in your whole ridiculous past so much stupidity, deceitfulness, and gullibility that you'd like to stop all of a sudden being young, wait for youth to get away . . . and then take off yourself . . . to slip quietly over again to the other side of Time to see really how people and things are.)

Céline has in one sense placed his narrator outside life and time, for it is from this vantage point that he can reveal all the insanity that is inherent in existence. The importance of the distance Céline creates between the young picaro and the older narrator becomes more evident when one examines how the narration is often structured by this polarity. On the one hand the reader sees life as reflected through the eyes of the naïve picaro, who, as a prisoner of the destructive flow of time, rushes through his journey to discover life. Like Lazarillo or Quevedo's Pablo, Bardamu sets out on a journey that is to be an education as well as a series of adventures. He wanders into the insanity of organized war and back into the equally insane civilian life behind the lines. New forms of absurd hostility await him in Africa. In New York he takes a job as a "flea counter" and statistician; in Detroit he must work in a Ford plant that resembles the factory in Chaplin's *Modern Times*. In brief: "A naïve and astonished observer is pointing out the scandalous absurdity of war, of colonialism, of modern industrialism." [2] Of course, this use of a naïve but honest observer is a satirical device that can be found in works as diverse as Lucian's *True History* and *Gulliver's Travels*. As a picaro in flight, Bardamu senses that his ultimate concern is the very rational but elementary question of survival, and his vision thus presents a continually deformed image of the world that contrasts with the reader's received image. Is this not the essence of satire?

The older narrator makes his presence constantly felt with a running commentary that points up the satire while it underscores Céline's vision of men given over to madness and destruction. In the following passage the structure of this narrative overlay shows how important is the polarity between the older narrator and the young hero. Bardamu here finds himself trapped aboard the *Amiral Bragueton* while sailing to Africa. He has become the scapegoat for the depraved instincts of white men turned loose in the tropics. Only by yelling "Vive la France" and by flattering a group of menacing officers has he escaped evisceration:

J'empoignai deux bras au hasard dans le groupe des officiers et invitai tout le monde à venir se régaler au Bar à ma santé et à notre réconciliation. Ces vaillants ne résistèrent qu'une minute et nous bûmes ensuite pendant deux heures. Seulement les femelles du bord nous suivaient des yeux, silencieuses et graduellement déçues. Par les hublots du Bar, j'apercevais entre autres la pianiste institutrice entêtée qui passait et revenait au milieu d'un cercle de passagères, la hyène. Elles soupçonnaient bien ces garces que je m'étais tiré du guet-apens par ruse et se promettaient de me rattraper au détour. . . . Il me fallait cependant encore retrouver de la verve, de la faconde qui puisse plaire à mes nouveaux amis, de la facile. Je ne tarissais pas, peur de me tromper, en admiration patriotique et je demandais et redemandais à ces héros, chacun son tour, des histoires et encore des histoires de bravoure coloniale.

The angle of vision suddenly widens as the older narrator directly intervenes:

C'est comme les cochonneries, les histoires de bravoure,
elles plaisent toujours à tous les militaires de tous les pays.
Ce qu'il faut au fond pour obtenir une espèce de paix avec les
hommes, officiers ou non, armistices fragiles il est vrai, mais
précieux quand même, c'est leur permettre en toutes circonstances, de s'étaler, de se vautrer parmi les vantardises niaises.
Il n'y a pas de vanité intelligente. C'est un instinct. Il n'y a
pas d'homme non plus qui ne soit pas avant tout vaniteux.
(pp. 121–122.)

(I grabbed two arms at random in the group of officers and
invited everyone to come in the Bar and drink to my health
and to our reconciliation. Those valiant warriors resisted but
a minute and then we drank together for two hours. Only the
females on board watched us silently and slowly became dis-
appointed. Through the portholes of the Bar I noticed among
others the stubborn piano-playing schoolteacher who was
coming and going in the middle of a circle of women pas-
sengers, that hyena. Those bitches figured out that I'd got out
of the ambush through cleverness, and they intended to catch
me on the roundabout. . . . I still had to keep coming up with
tricks, good ones that could please my new friends, nice, easy
ones. I didn't dry up, for fear of making an error, in patriotic
admiration, and I kept on asking these heroes one after another for more and more stories of colonial bravery.

War stories are like smutty jokes, military men of every nation-
ality like them. At bottom what you need so as to have a sort
of peace with men—officers or not—fragile armistices, it's
true, but precious just the same—is to let them in all circumstances expand and wallow in their idiotic boasting. Intelli-
gent vanity doesn't exist. It's an instinct. There isn't any man
who isn't above all else vainglorious.)

Bardamu's field of vision is limited to what is hostile in
his immediate surroundings. He must stay alert and at
the same time carry out his strategy for survival. This
means dealing with men thirsty for blood while keeping

an eye on animal-like women who are enraged about losing the pleasures of a good show. Such is his immediate vision of the colonialists who are carrying "civilization" to Africa.

The older narrator has a good deal more to say about this episode as he offers the aphorisms ᵗhat conclude the passage. Disengaged from the world of the novel, he can note that "histoires de bravoure" are much like smutty jokes: military men never tire of them. He then offers aphorisms of a more general nature under which each preceding observation may be classified as a species to a genus. Vanity is another instinct, and every man is driven, homicidally it would appear, by this instinct. The lapidary universality of the older narrator's conclusions shows that they apply not only to the picaro's immediate crisis but to man in general. They represent the wisdom the older narrator has garnered by having a nearly a-temporal perspective on life's dementia, though these aphorisms also set the picaro's situation in full relief. David Hayman, in his essay on Céline, goes so far as to say that Céline's older narrator, "evaluating past misfortune, adds density and depth to the portrait and creates even in the first novel a stereopticon effect." [3]

That *Voyage* has been Céline's most successful novel is undoubtedly due in part to the older narrator's being a *moraliste,* a descendant in that long French tradition of disabused observers of human folly. Milton Hindus, for instance, has compared some of *Voyage*'s aphorisms to those of La Rochefoucauld. [4] Céline, in a letter to Hindus, recommended Chamfort as the "quintessence de l'esprit de finesse" and thus called to mind his own affinities with Pascal. [5] In *Voyage* itself the narrator admits: "De nos jours, faire le 'La Bruyère' c'est pas

commode. Tout l'inconscient se débine devant vous
dès qu'on s'approche." ("In our time it's not so easy to
play 'La Bruyère.' The whole subconscious takes off in
front of you as soon as you get near.") (p. 388.)

A comparison of a few classical maxims with the older
narrator's observations makes clear that he is indeed a
moraliste of an almost traditional sort. Chamfort, for
example, remarked on the beginning of wisdom:

Je ne conçois pas de sagesse sans défiance. L'écriture a dit
que le commencement de la Sagesse était la crainte de Dieu;
moi, je crois que c'est la crainte des hommes.

(I can conceive of no wisdom without distrust. The Scripture
says that the beginning of Wisdom was the fear of God; I
believe it is the fear of men.)

The older Bardamu is entirely in agreement:

C'est des hommes et d'eux seulement qu'il faut avoir peur
toujours. (p. 19.)

(You just have to be always afraid of men and of them alone.)

Pascal is scandalized by man's refusal to confront his
condition:

Les hommes n'ayant pu guérir la mort, la misère, l'ignorance,
ils se sont avisés, pour se rendre heureux, de n'y point penser.

(Since men were not able to cure death, misery, and ignorance,
they decided, in order to be happy, not to think about them.)

Céline's view of man's inconsequence sounds much
like Pascal's:

Nous sommes, par nature, si futiles, que seules les distractions
peuvent nous empêcher vraiment de mourir. (pp. 203–204.)

(We are, by nature, so futile that only distractions can really prevent us from dying.)

Yet death, as La Bruyère said, must be lived at every moment:

La mort n'arrive qu'une fois et se fait sentir à tous les moments de la vie: il est plus dur de l'appréhender que de la souffrir.

(Death happens only once and makes itself felt at every moment in life: it is harder to apprehend it than to suffer it.)

For Céline's narrator there is no other form of true consciousness:

La vérité, c'est une agonie qui n'en finit pas. La vérité de ce monde, c'est la mort. Il faut choisir, mourir ou mentir. Je n'ai jamais pu me tuer moi. (pp. 199–200.)

(The truth is a last gasp that doesn't end. The truth of this world is death. You have to choose, to die or to lie. I was never able to kill myself.)

Pulled from their context, the older narrator's reflections strike with all the vigor, the intuitive persuasiveness, and the a-temporal ring of truth that one finds in the classical *moraliste's* pointed formulations. What is a *moraliste* if not an observer who has withdrawn from the flux of experience in order to attain the proper perspective for discerning the ultimate truths of *l'humaine condition*. Céline's narrator is withdrawn from the chaos that besieges the picaro in order to assess fully the recurrent laws that dictate this pandemonium.

In *Voyage* Céline's narrator often recalls Pascal, for both are separated from the comic gestures of life by a continual sense of scandal. One critic, Alex Jacquemin, sees the following affinities between Céline and Pascal: "at bottom it is *divertissement* in the Pascalian sense that he detests: he wishes to reduce man to his essential reality because, in place of the happiness of those who lose themselves in distractions, he prefers the unhappiness of being lucid." [6] In the case of both writers, scandalized lucidity leads to a piercing irony that seeks to force man to view his misery.

Lucidity is the goal of every Célinian hero, for survival demands total awareness; but lucidity can be defined only in negative terms in Céline's world. It is essentially a refusal to give in to the irrational forces of destruction that blind men as they propel men through life. In this sense the older narrator differs from the traditional *moraliste*, for he is always aware that the violent, unconscious forces of instinct will triumph over the rational calculations of *amour-propre*. The narrator is closer to Nietzsche or Freud when, after a period in the insane asylum, he comes to believe that the ultimate expression of man's inner life is in violence and disease:

je ne peux m'empêcher de mettre en doute qu'il existe d'autres véritables réalisations de nos profonds tempéraments que la guerre et la maladie, ces deux infinis du cauchemar. (p. 407.)

(I cannot stop myself from doubting that there exist any true manifestations of our profound nature other than war and disease, those two infinities of nightmare.)

War, decay, fever, these are all projections of the nightmare that is Céline's metaphor for man's most essential reality. Céline's older narrator is thus a thoroughly modern *moraliste*, for his task is to discern the various projections of the dark forces of madness that lie in every man.

If the older narrator is removed from the world he calls forth, the picaro of his youth is squarely entangled in the waves of hostility that sweep over him (especially in the novel's first part). The picaro's initiation into collective hysteria, in the form of war, occurs with the revelation that fear brings. As Bardamu puts it in his characteristic way:

> On est puceau de l'Horreur comme on l'est de la volupté. . . . J'étais dépucelé. (pp. 17–18.)

> (You're a virgin in Horror as you are in sex. . . . I was de-flowered.)

Fear, like fever and disgust, gives access to privileged modes of perception in Céline's novels. It intensifies Bardamu's vision while limiting its range to all that is insanely hostile in his surroundings, to all that threatens him with absurd destruction. Fear leads to the systematically deformed image that is at the heart of *Voyage*'s satire, but it also produces a visceral reaction that offers new ways of viewing the world. And fear is the painfully rational reaction of a man striving to remain lucid in the face of contagious insanity.

Episodic experience, as seen through the picaro's fear-dilated eyes, is nothing more than a series of projections of the madness within, of the hostile madness from which he must continually try to escape. War, colonialism, capitalism, the modern city, all are seen as delirium manifested in contemporary forms. The limit of Bardamu's vision is imposed by the forms of insanity that give rise in turn to his fear. Nearly every episode

in *Voyage* can be considered a manifestation of madness
and hysteria. The war is fought by "enragés" and
"fous" whose delirium seems to know no bounds (p. 19).
Behind the lines, "délire" has caught up the entire
civilian population in an orgy of official lying (p. 56). In
Africa the very environment breathes madness; the heat
and vegetation are hallucinating (pp. 139, 142). In New
York Bardamu must go to the cinema to inoculate
himself with a little "délire" in images, since a dose of
hallucination in images is an antitoxin for the city's
insanity (p. 201). As a Ford worker, he lives in a state
somewhere between "hébétude" (stupor) and "délire"
(p. 226). And after returning to France Dr. Bardamu finds
delirium everywhere about him in the incredible sadism
and folly that he sees in his daily rounds. It is hardly
surprising that he should finally decide to work in an
insane asylum. Here, at least, the mad are under sur-
veillance.

Critics have given little attention to the long period of
time Bardamu spends working in the insane asylum. Yet,
it is an ironically logical conclusion for the journey.
Moreover, it is here that the aging picaro finally attains
a certain wisdom about madness and sets forth views
that Céline will use as a basis for the narrative structures
of his later novels. Bardamu dare not remain too long in
the company of the mad, for he discovers that delirium
is contagious:

Les routines du traitement nullement pénibles, bien
qu'évidemment, de temps à autre, un petit malaise me prît
quand j'avais par exemple conversé trop longuement avec les
pensionnaires, une sorte de vertige m'entraînait alors comme
s'ils m'avaient emmené loin de mon rivage habituel les pensionnaires, avec eux, sans en avoir l'air, d'une phrase ordinaire
à l'autre, en paroles innocentes, jusqu'au beau milieu de leur

délire. Je me demandais pendant un petit instant comment en sortir, et si par hasard je n'étais pas enfermé une fois pour toutes avec leur folie, sans m'en douter. (p. 417.)

(The routine work of treatment wasn't at all strenuous, although now and then of course a little uneasiness would get hold of me, when, for instance, I had conversed at too great a length with the inmates; a sort of vertigo would carry me off, as if they'd taken me too far from my usual shore, away with them, without seeming to do so, from one ordinary sentence to another, with innocent words, right into the middle of their delirium. I would wonder for a second how to get out of it, and if by chance I weren't locked up once and for all in their madness without suspecting it.)

Madness in *Voyage* usually delimits the exterior horizon of Bardamu's world, but only through constant struggle can he prevent madness from crashing in upon him and destroying his lucidity. Later novels such as *Mort à crédit* and *Guignol's Band* do not let their protagonists escape from delirium so easily, for madness often impinges upon their consciousness and seizes their powers of lucidity. Even in *Voyage* Bardamu can occasionally fall prey to delirium and lose himself in hallucination, that mode of perception that takes place when the world's madness and the picaro's consciousness coincide.

One of the high points in *Voyage*, for instance, is when Bardamu, having fallen ill with fever in the jungle, is sold to a slave galley and transported to America. The galley is a replica of the modern welfare state, for the slaves are allowed to play at voting, have job security, and can eventually retire. This hallucination is, of course, satirical, but it also represents the absolute destruction of Bardamu's consciousness by the forces of disease,

which are another projection of madness. In America
Bardamu asks Robinson about the galley, but Robinson
dismisses the episode as a fantasy born of his fever. The
hallucination is thus integrated into the supposedly
realistic narration while it retains its character of satirical fantasy. Bardamu has nonetheless lived the hallucination, for fever ultimately reveals another valid mode
of perception in a world of contagious delirium. Fever is
another means of getting to the heart of things.

Fever, like fear, leads to another privileged mode of
perception because it directly reveals madness' manifestation in disease and decomposition while it opens up
the vistas of hallucination and delirium. Disease, hallucination, and fever, all projections of the dementia at
the core of existence, are interrelated throughout
Céline's works both as ways of perceiving and as objects of perception. In *Voyage,* but not in the later novels,
the ravages that hallucination works are subordinated to
the hero's vision of disease and decay unfolding in
time, though, as Michel Beaujour has pointed out, Bardamu's constant vision of decomposition also tears
apart his consciousness: "Fascinated by the viscous,
which is essentially a form of consent to the course of
time, he rejects it with all his being. Fascinated by the
action of time within himself, unable to put an end by
suicide to this tearing of his consciousness, he gives in
to a compromise: he continues to live." [7]

Bardamu is thus trapped in an entropic world whose
ontological state is essentially one of disease.[8] Being,
infected from within by madness, cannot resist the
tendency to run down in time, turn into chaos, and fall
into sickening amorphousness that horrifies and disgusts the picaro. He may try to flee, but his flight is
always frustrated because his own fever and disease

continually reveal to him that he, too, is a part of this
decomposing world.

The first revelation of being's instability that Bardamu
receives is essentially a revelation of the nature of flesh.
At the beginning of *Voyage* he sees two soldiers blown
apart and discovers that man's being is nothing more
than an unstable compound of viscera and blood:

Ils s'embrassaient tous les deux pour le moment et pour
toujours, mais le cavalier n'avait plus sa tête, rien qu'une
ouverture au-dessus du cou, avec du sang dedans qui mijotait
en glouglous comme de la confiture dans la marmite. (p. 21.)

(They were embracing each other for the moment and forever, but the cavalryman no longer had his head, just a hole on
top of his neck with blood stewing in gurgles like jam in a pot.)

Bardamu is fascinated by this "jam," by the sight of a
decomposing stickiness that seems to absorb his consciousness. Shortly after seeing "all this meat bleeding
together," he must look at the raw meat at the regiment
mess:

Sur des sacs et des toiles de tentes largement étendues et sur
l'herbe même, il y en avait pour des kilos et des kilos de tripes
étalées, de gras en flocons jaunes et pâles, des moutons
éventrés avec leurs organes en pagaïe, suintant en ruisse-
lets ingénieux dans la verdure d'alentour, un bœuf entier
sectionné en deux, pendu à l'arbre, et sur lequel s'escrimaient
encore en jurant les quatre bouchers du régiment pour lui
tirer des morceaux d'abatis. On s'engueulait ferme entre
escouades à propos de graisses, et de rognons surtout, au
milieu des mouches comme on en voit que dans ces moments-
là, importantes et musicales comme des petits oiseaux. (p. 24.)

(On sacks and on tent canvas broadly spread out on the ground
and on the grass itself, there were pounds and pounds of guts
on display, fat in pale yellow flakes, disemboweled sheep with

their entrails in a mess, oozing in ingenious little streams on the surrounding grass, a beef carcass cut in two, hung on a tree, with which the four regiment butchers, swearing away, were struggling to pull off pieces of flesh. They were giving each other hell among the squads for pieces of fat, and especially for kidneys, right in the midst of flies such as you see only on these occasions, busy and musical as little birds.)

Bardamu's fascinated stare brings home the ontological equivalence of men and beasts—all are unstable, disgusting flesh. The sight of this mountain of viscera forces Bardamu to vomit, for nausea in Céline's works is a visceral reaction, induced by fear and disgust, a revolt against the world's obscene dementia and, at the same time, a form of participation in its decay and decomposition. Nausea, like fever, is both a release and, as Sartre surely recognized, a way of entering into a new mode of perceiving the world.

Bardamu's discovery of being's obscene amorphousness is prolonged throughout the novel by a continual stream of images depicting things that flow and melt, mold and rot, go sour and fall apart. In Africa, for example, Bardamu finds that men are rapidly dissolved in the overwhelming heat and decay:

Quelques officiers promenaient leur famille, attentives aux saluts militaires et civils, l'épouse boudinée dans ses serviettes hygiéniques spéciales, les enfants, sorte pénible de gros asticots européens, se dissolvaient de leur côté par la chaleur, en diarrhée permanente. (p. 144.)

(A few officers would take their families for a walk, always attentive to military salutes and civilian salutations, the wife tightly screwed into her special sanitary napkins, the children, like a painful sort of fat European maggot, kept dissolving in the heat, on their side, in a permanent diarrhea.)

The children, transformed into amorphous worms, decompose in a scatological way, as does Bardamu's jungle shack:

Ce qui était banal dans cette structure pouvait encore s'écrouler mais ne se redresserait plus, le chaume infecté de vermine s'effilochait, on n'aurait décidément pas fait avec ma demeure une pissotière convenable. (p. 171.)

(Whatever was ordinary in this structure could still fall down some more, but would never stand up again; the thatched roof, infested with vermin, was coming apart in pieces, my dwelling really wouldn't have made a decent street urinal.)

In Bardamu's fascinated vision, men and things are bound together in their common inability to resist rotting and decay, or, as the narrator sums it up in a typical aphorism:

A mesure qu'on reste dans un endroit, les choses et les gens se débraillent, pourrissent et se mettent à puer tout exprès pour vous. (p. 272.)

(As you stay in a place, things and people really come apart, grow rotten and start stinking on purpose just for you.)

Aging, decaying, growing purulent, are all part of Céline's ontology, and his vision is not limited to individual men or objects. An entire city may be a giant ulcer. New York is "le chancre du monde, éclatant en réclames prometteuses et pustulentes" ("the ulcer of the world, bursting in promising and purulent ads") (p. 204). "Rancy" is a name suggestive of massive decomposition and disintegration; it is a formless mass in which, as Bardamu describes it, the inhabitants are literally stuck. Even time is infected with putridness, since Bardamu's conception of time is to move along "le fil des jours . . . poisseux" ("the thread of . . . sticky days") (p. 237). Since disease and decay are projections of the dementia that lies at the heart of existence, time is merely the process of revelation in which disease and rottenness are unveiled.

Here and there in the night, however, Bardamu comes across "forms" that seem to offer resistance to the disintegration of the world through time, forms generally exemplified in a good pair of legs. The female body has a dual importance for Bardamu. First, eros, like the cinema, is another counter-form of delirium that permits the picaro to keep dragging forward. It is a useless form of frenzy (p. 72), a delirium whose final result is to propagate more delirium. Yet, Bardamu can never stay away from lust for long, and nearly every step in the journey is marked by Bardamu's erotic encounters. First there is Lola, the young American come to save France during the war. Her legs give Bardamu his first incentive to go to the United States. When he arrives in New York, his main desire is to find more legs like Lola's. In Detroit he finds Molly, the prostitute whose legs make her a member of the "true aristocracy." In France Bardamu leaves Rancy to find ecstasy in the legs of the English dancers at the "Tarapout." And in the insane asylum he is quick to hire Sophie, a Slovak nurse whose qualifications go far beyond her medical abilities. Of all Céline's works *Voyage* is the only one to offer such constant panegyrics in favor of eros. In other works, such as *Mort à crédit*, he often portrays sexuality as part of our "biological ignominy," as a form of physiological degradation of which the result is not far from nausea.

Feminine legs possess a second importance, one that seems to go beyond eros for Bardamu. Muscular legs

appear to incarnate forms that can resist the sticky vis-
cosity of his decaying world. For instance, Sophie, the
last woman encountered in *Voyage*, has a muscle tone
whose resiliency suggests a possible transcendance for
the down and out picaro. She has a "force allègre, précise
et douce à la fois" ("a strength that's brisk, precise, and
soft at the same time"). Endowed with "cette démarche
ailée, souple et précise . . . la démarche des grands
êtres d'avenir que la vie porte ambitieuse et légère
encore vers de nouvelles façons d'aventures" ("a winged
step that's lithe and precise . . . the bearing of the great
creatures of the future that life carries ambitious and
still light toward new kinds of adventures") (p. 463),
her body suggests a sailing ship, a symbol of something
that might pull Bardamu from the "cave of existence"
and transport him toward the "Infinite." The female
body in its perfect form seems to defy, momentarily at
least, life's absurd propensity to rot; for, as Bardamu
says of Sophie, the rhythms of her life are drawn from
other sources than those we know (p. 476).

Erotic forms are only a promise, however, and Bardamu is forever frustrated in his attempt to stop being
human. As when he discovers the beauties of New York:

Les beautés que je découvrais, incessantes, m'eussent avec
un peu de confiance et de confort ravi à ma condition triviale-
ment humaine. Il ne me manquait qu'un sandwich en somme
pour me croire en plein miracle. Mais comme il me manquait
le sandwich! (p. 193.)

(The beauties that I kept discovering, without end, would
have, with a little confidence and comfort, torn me away from
my basely human condition. All I needed was a sandwich to
think that I was in the middle of a miracle. But how I needed
the sandwich!)

Not only is the picaro frustrated by his rank in the social order—beauty is reserved for the rich—but the very nature of feminine beauty is corrupted from within. Bardamu, a less than magnanimous character at best, reveals his fascination with beauty's inevitable decay when he steals in to see Sophie sleeping:

Elle s'acharnait sur le sommeil Sophie dans les profondeurs du corps, elle en ronflait. C'était le seul moment où je la trouvais bien à ma portée. Plus de sorcelleries. Plus de rigolade. Rien que du sérieux. Elle besognait comme à l'envers de l'existence, à lui pomper de la vie encore. . . . Fallait la voir après ces séances de roupillon, toute gonflée encore et sous sa peau rose les organes qui n'en finissaient pas de s'extasier. Elle était drôle alors et ridicule comme tout le monde. (pp. 463–464.)

(She was really working at her sleep, Sophie was, in the depths of her body she snored away. That was the only time I really found her on my level. No more spells. No more jokes. Just serious business. She worked away as though on the other side of existence, sucking in some more life from it. . . . You had to see her after those sessions of sawing logs, all swollen still and under her pink skin the organs that wouldn't stop being ecstatic. She was funny then and ridiculous like everyone else.)

During the time she sleeps, the flesh is relaxed, and Bardamu can find some comfort in seeing that her firmness is only an affair of the moment. Her troubling "force allègre" is no longer to be envied. When Sophie awakens, Bardamu stares at her organs, the formless viscera that hide beneath the hard flesh when she is fully awake. The viscera already displays the softness of decomposition that Sophie seems to defy. She, like everyone else, is nothing but "some rottenness in a suspended state" (p. 416).

Rottenness in a suspended state — "de la pourriture en suspens" — sums up Bardamu's final vision of man's futile project to live, though it is Dr. Baryton, the doctor who often sounds like Céline's mouthpiece, who formulates this point of essential wisdom in the secluded tranquillity of the insane asylum. Having well learned this lesson, Bardamu ends his journey in the quiet despair of living surrounded by the incarcerated mad, assisted by Dr. Parapine, the scientist who refuses to speak. Language, as will be more evident in *Mort à credit*, is useless when dealing with the demented. The narrative movement, ending in Bardamu's resignation and silence, has thus gone from youth to maturity and maturity's helpless acceptance of insanity and decay. Bardamu finds that silence is the only hope. Long before the novel's end, he is well aware,

On a rien à causer, parce qu'au fond il ne vous arrive plus rien, on est trop pauvre, on a peut-être dégoûté l'existence? Ça serait régulier. (p. 294.)

(You don't have anything more to talk about, because nothing ever really happens to you; you're too poor, maybe you've disgusted existence? That'd be normal.)

Yet the narration continues well after this recognition, offering a miscellany of misery, degradation, and mindless suffering that contrasts vividly with the rapid movement of the picaro's earlier travels. Bardamu can go no farther forward in the journey to the end of the night, for, as he expresses it, he has not yet acquired "la force de sagesse qu'il faudrait pour s'arrêter pile sur la route du temps" ("the strength of wisdom you'd need to stop flat on the road of time") (p. 284). Unable to muster the vigor to refuse life and come to the journey's real end, he must content himself with being a passive observer on the periphery of a world in dissolution.

As an observer, he can watch his picaro double, Robinson, who does have the strength to journey to the end. Robinson's presence as an alter ego is perhaps necessitated by the nature of Céline's narrative. Since Bardamu supposedly tells his own story, it is difficult to imagine him going all the way to the end of the night, for, quite simply, he would have to narrate his own demise. *Voyage*'s seminaturalistic conventions would also make it difficult for even an older narrator on the other side of time to tell of his own annihilation.

The second part of the novel's change in narrative focus is largely based on the need to narrate Robinson's journey. In the first half of *Voyage* the emphasis is on the physical journey through different forms of hostility and dementia. In this context Robinson is an enigmatic traveler who is always one step ahead of Bardamu. During the war he is already at Noirceur-sur-la-lys, trying to get himself captured by the Germans, when Bardamu arrives with the same idea vaguely in mind. He is waiting for Bardamu at the African trading post when Bardamu comes there, and then he flees with all he can carry away, a flight that Bardamu later imitates in his bumbling fashion. Robinson gets to America first and becomes a nocturnal worker in the depths of the city. Aside from Robinson's mirror or doubling function in the first part of the novel, his appearances seem rather mechanical. In the second part, however, his true role becomes evident. Just as he always arrives ahead of Bardamu in the physical journey, so will he precede him in the flight to the end.

Robinson is not only a picaro who leads Bardamu in
the journey, he is also Bardamu's double in his moral
(or amoral) development as a picaro who learns quickly
from his experience to expect nothing from life's dementia. At their first encounter, for example, Robinson,
too, has been marked by fear, and his unique concern is
with survival:

"J'pense plus à rien, moi, qu'il a fait. . . . À rien, t'entends!...
J'pense qu'à pas crever... Ça suffit." (p. 49.)

("I don't think about nothing, he said. . . . About nothing,
you hear!... I just think about not getting knocked off... That's
enough.")

Along the way Robinson gains a little wisdom, and, like
Bardamu, he can formulate a few maxims for slipping
through life. This second picaro, for instance, comes to
see that "freedom" can be summarily defined:

"C'est de voir clair d'abord, et puis ensuite d'avoir du pognon
plein les poches, le reste, c'est du mou!..." (p. 383.)

("It's to see clearly first of all, and then to have your pockets
full of jack; the rest is bunk.")

If Robinson lacks Bardamu's educational advantages, he
still echoes the doctor in explaining why he would
liked to have taken up the career of nurse:

"Parce que, tu vois, les hommes quand ils sont bien portants,
y a pas à dire, ils vous font peur... Surtout depuis la guerre...
Moi je sais à quoi ils pensent... Ils s'en rendent pas toujours
compte eux-mêmes... Mais moi, je sais à quoi ils pensent...
Quand ils sont debout, ils pensent à vous tuer... Tandis que
quand ils sont malades, y a pas à dire ils sont moins à craindre...
Faut t'attendre à tout, que je te dis, tant qu'ils tiennent
debout." (p. 303.)

("Because, you see, when men are healthy, you can't deny it, they scare you... Especially since the war... I know what they're thinking about... They don't always know it themselves... But I know what they're thinking about... When they're standing up, they're thinking about killing you... But when they're sick, you can't deny it, you don't have to be so afraid of them... Got to expect anything, I tell you, as long as they can stand up.")

Robinson is another furtive creature of the night, striving to "see clearly," to retain his lucidity as his only defense against the forces of universal hostility. Unlike Bardamu, however, he is willing to follow the logic of his disgust to its most extreme conclusions.

Robinson first differentiates himself from his friend in the second part of *Voyage* by accepting Mme Henrouille's offer to be the paid assassin of her mother-in-law. Robinson's decision represents a further step into the depths of the underworld, though his hope to become rich through blackmail shows how much his decision is in accord with his desperate principles. Robinson has a force of will that Bardamu can only admire. Yet there is an implicit condemnation of Robinson in the very choice of the victim.

The old Henrouille mother-in-law is one of the most sympathetic characters in *Voyage*. Caustic in her language, refusing to bow to intimidation, she is a gay old wench. And after her daughter-in-law has attempted to have her murdered, the old woman has no illusions as to why:

"Parce que je voulais point crever assez vite, dame! Tout simplement! Et nom de Dieu! Bien sûr que non que je veux point mourir!" (p. 316.)

("Because I didn't want to kick off quick enough. What else! As simple as that! And by God! Of course I don't want to die!")

Her revolt is elementary but powerful. She refuses to give in to time and decomposition; she refuses to submit to the maniacal avarice that represents her son and daughter-in-law's dementia. The old woman glories in her revolt, a revolt that is like a sign of some nearly forgotten life force in a decaying world.

Robinson takes a second step into greater darkness when the bomb he is preparing for the old woman blows up in his face. His resulting blindness is a concrete metaphor for his descent into the night and for his loss of lucidity. Blindness means that he is plunged into his own private darkness ("Du noir tout à lui," p. 323), into a night of his own creation; and it also means that the picaro will nearly allow himself to be ensnared in a sentimental trap. In Toulouse, where Robinson has found a way of earning a living with old Mme Henrouille by showing mummies to tourists, Madelon and Robinson decide to become fiancés. Love is a sentimental form of delirium that any lucid picaro would know to avoid. When Robinson recovers his vision, he also recovers his lucidity, the sign of which is his need to move on, to keep traveling, to remain in flight. Able to see clearly again, he knows that a girl's love is another form of madness and, moreover, one in which the disgusted picaro is expected to participate, or as he tells Bardamu:

Quand elle est amoureuse, elle est folle, c'est bien simple! Folle! Et c'est de moi qu'elle est amoureuse et qu'elle est folle!... Tu te rends compte? Tu comprends? Alors tout ce qui est fou ça l'excite! C'est bien simple! Ça l'arrête pas! Au contraire!..." (p. 442.)

("When she's in love, she's crazy, it's simple! Crazy! And she's in love with me and crazy about me!... You see? Do you understand? So everything that's crazy excites her! It's simple! That doesn't stop her! It's just the opposite!...")

Blindness has temporarily brought Robinson to the edge of acquiescence in this kind of folly, but with the return of lucidity, he can only be astonished by the dimensions of amorous insanity. Yet this picaro's hatred of delirium prepares the way for his destruction.

It is Robinson's total rejection of what Bardamu calls Madelon's frenzy that finally brings him to the end of the night. Madelon's rage and her incapacity to understand Robinson's refusal provoke him into giving vent to his feelings of revulsion, feelings that are directed ultimately against everything in life and perhaps against life itself:

"Eh bien, c'est tout, qui me répugne et qui me dégoûte à présent! Pas seulement toi!... Tout!... L'amour surtout!... Le tien aussi bien que celui des autres... Les trucs aux sentiments que tu veux faire, veux-tu que je te dise à quoi ça ressemble moi? Ça ressemble à faire l'amour dans des chiottes! Tu me comprends-t-y à présent? . . . Tu fais la sentimentale pendant que t'es une brute comme pas une... Tu veux en bouffer de la viande pourrie? Avec ta sauce à la tendresse?... Ça passe alors?... Pas à moi!... Si tu sens rien tant mieux pour toi! C'est que t'as le nez bouché! Faut être abrutis comme vous l'êtes tous pour ne pas que ça vous dégoûte... Tu cherches à savoir ce qu'il y a entre toi et moi?... Eh bien entre toi et moi, y a toute la vie..." (p. 483.)

("Well, everything repulses me and disgusts me now! Not just you!... Everything!... Especially love!... Yours as well as everyone else's... This loving stuff you want to do, you want me to tell you how that strikes me? It's like making love in the shit-house! Do you get me now? . . . You play at being sentimental when you're as tough a little bitch as any of them... You like eating rotten meat? With your tenderness sauce?... Does that go down?... Not for me!... If you don't smell anything, so much the better for you! Your nose must be stopped up! Got to be a bunch of dumb asses like you are, all of you, for that not to disgust you... You want to know what's between you and me?... Well, between you and me there's all of life...)

Robinson refuses to blind himself to life's "rotten meat" and the stench of decay that surrounds it. He refuses to stop up his nose as love would have him do and holds tenaciously to his awareness.

His outburst is a form of suicide. Confronted with this long diatribe, Madelon resorts to the only solution she can think of: she shoots Robinson and then disappears into the night. His death seems to be a logical consequence of his total revolt; no longer able to tolerate life's disgusting absurdity, he must go beyond it into death. For death, another typically Célinian paradox, signifies the end of night. Céline's view of death presents a metaphorical reversal in which death is the void beyond the void. Yet, one is uncomfortable with this paradox, because Robinson's revolt against all that is destructive in life has ended in the destruction of life itself.

The picaros' parallel journeys end with Bardamu's lamenting his inability to comfort Robinson as he dies. At the same time, he envies the resolve Robinson has shown in his revolt:

j'avais même pas été aussi loin que Robinson moi dans la vie!... J'avais pas réussi en définitive. J'en avais pas acquis moi une seule idée bien solide comme celle qu'il avait eue pour se faire dérouiller. (p. 489.)

(I hadn't got as far as Robinson in life!... I hadn't succeeded at all. I hadn't picked up a single good, solid idea like the one he'd had to get himself bumped off.)

Bardamu must end his journey in silence, refusing to speak on about a voyage that can progress no further than the recognition of its futility and madness. There is no place to go, while waiting to get to the other side of time; and the final statement of this truth concludes the journey with a desperate irony whose tension seems intolerable. The madhouse and then death, such is the inevitable course that everyone must follow.

Voyage au bout de la nuit has been subject to some rather severe criticism, not to say condemnations, and one must inevitably take note of certain problems that this extraordinary novel has posed for readers. Most general criticism directed against *Voyage* has been primarily aesthetic in nature. Many critics have noted a breakdown in structure in the novel's second half. Céline, the critics charge, has not succeeded in unifying the vast experience that he forces into the novel. In the first part of the novel the main theme often appears to be the voyage used as a vehicle for satire, and the mere chronological sequence of the picaresque narrative form suffices as a structural principle. If satire presented the only thematic interest in the novel's first part, it would be difficult to see any unity in the novel as a whole. However, critics who make this charge fail in general to see the novel's larger workings. *Voyage*'s thematic structure is fairly well unified: the repetitive forms of madness with the concomitant projections of disease, destruction, and decay bind the novel together at least thematically. Satire of social forms is subordinate to these themes and to the dual journeys to the end of the night. Robinson's role in carrying the journey forward to its final destination has not, moreover, been recognized by most adverse critics. Certainly his journey, one complementary to Bardamu's, endows the novel as a whole with a unified structure.

Another problem with the novel's structure turns on
its mode of narration. Though few readers would accept
with Alain that the unity of a novel consists in the
"tableau d'une vie intérieure," Céline seems to have
believed that the constant presence of the older narrator's point of view would suffice to unify all the episodes narrated.[9] In the case of certain episodes—a
randomly selected abortion or a chance death by cancer—it is difficult to regard the incident as any more
than Céline's effort not to let a single horror escape the
reader. These extraneous scenes of misery and degradation generally take place in the novel's second half,
when the distance between the younger picaro and the
older narrator is minimal. Though these scenes are related thematically to the novel as a whole, Céline sometimes seems to lose control of his material as he turns
his protagonist into a *voyeur* who can report all the
grotesqueries that Rancy and Paris offer in abundance.

Another criticism of an aesthetic nature concerns
Céline's language. Some critics feel that, again largely
in the novel's second half, Céline does not maintain the
savage stylistic tempo he sets in the first part of *Voyage*.
There is some truth in this criticism, though it is clear
that the pointed argot the young picaro uses changes as
he matures. His later language is that of disabused cynicism, and this is in keeping with the progress he makes
on the journey. Moreover, most critics have exaggerated
the importance of stylistic innovations in *Voyage* (though
they have generally ignored the innovations in Céline's
later works). As Leo Spitzer showed about *Voyage*,
Céline has an unparalleled ear for the rhythms and syntax of popular speech.[10] His use of argot in *Voyage* is
hardly revolutionary, however. Zola, assiduously study-
ing his *Dictionnaire de la langue verte,* developed a

richer vocabulary of argot than Céline. As Céline himself pointed out on a number of occasions, the essence
of his style is not in his use of argot. As far as *Voyage* is
concerned, the energy of his style is generated by the
imagery of disgust, decay, and madness. Argot con-
tributes to this imagery as a kind of seasoning, but it is
not the heart of it. Another stylistic problem in *Voyage*'s
second part is that, since the protagonist and the older
narrator have virtually merged, there are fewer of the
pointed aphorisms that illuminate the first part with
fulgurant revelations. In this sense, the narration becomes more traditional, more one-dimensional. There
are in the second part, however, many extraordinary
passages written in a bombastic form of rhetoric, a
rhetoric whose amplification shows that delirium is
ready to invade language and carry it away to new heights
of madness, such as Céline's rhetoric reaches in the
later novels. In fact, *Voyage*'s style in many respects
merely foreshadows the language of delirium Céline
develops in *Mort à crédit* and *Guignol's Band*.

The second kind of criticism that critics have used to
attack *Voyage* is of an ethical nature, which is somewhat
unexpected in contemporary letters. Yet, it is obvious
that Céline has cut some readers to the quick. Eliseo
Vivas, for instance, gives an interpretation and condemnation in unhesitating terms: "the novel (*Voyage*)
presents us with a thoroughly evil fictional world. . . ."

". . . The work is open to criticism not only in the obvious sense that we must consider the practical effects
it has on us, but also in the sense that we must criticize
the presuppositions that make it possible in moral and
cognitive terms. The criticism to which *Journey* is open
. . . is that the presuppositions that control it are per-
verse and have produced a work which, while perhaps

not open to serious criticism from a purely esthetic standpoint, is open to condemnation because the subject matter it has organized into its informed substance has been selected by a perverted mind and is valid only for that type of mind." [11]

Nor is he alone in attacking Céline for what he considers his perversity. Another American critic, Wayne Booth, condemns *Voyage* on much the same grounds: "If Bardamu's attacks on civilization's values are not attacks, and seen as such, they are nothing.

". . . we cannot excuse him for writing a book which, if taken seriously by the reader, must corrupt him." [12]

These criticisms seem more than a little extravagant and indicate that there is some confusion here about the nature of literature and ethics. But they do underline the difficulty in coming to grips with Céline's purposes as conveyed through his novel, and they raise important questions about the relation between fundamental values and their expression in *Voyage*.

It should be evident that to the extent Céline is a satirist, he is not attacking civilization's values. The very nature of satire is such that it must make an appeal to a few basic and commonly shared values. Take, for example, the following passage in which Bardamu describes Americans entering their banks:

Quand les fidèles entrent dans leur Banque, faut pas croire qu'ils peuvent se servir comme ça selon leur caprice. Pas du tout. Ils parlent à Dollar en lui murmurant des choses à travers un petit grillage, ils se confessent quoi. Pas beaucoup de bruit, des lampes bien douces, un tout minuscule guichet entre de hautes arches, c'est tout. Ils n'avalent pas l'Hostie. Ils se la mettent sur le cœur. (p. 192.)

(When the faithful go into their Bank, don't think they can use it anyway they want to, capriciously. Not at all. They speak to Dollar by whispering things to him through a little grill, they make their confession, just like that. Not much noise, dim lights, a tiny grilled cage set between high columns, that's all. They don't swallow the Host. They stick it on their heart.)

An ordinary banking scene is described here through religious imagery. The reader, however, possesses another image of the same scene, the normal image associated with banking. The normal image is distorted and destroyed by juxtaposition with the image seen through Bardamu's eyes. In effect, Céline is destroying the reader's acceptance of the current image and what it represents. He is suggesting that something is wrong with the reader's unthinking acceptance of what it represents. Quite concretely, he is attempting to convey an image in which men do not debase themselves by worshiping material wealth. Satire is a negative appeal to commonly shared values, or at least a negation that calls for the creation of values.

Satire is a subordinate aspect of *Voyage,* and the hostile critic might retort that it is the narrator's immoral cynicism that is corrupting if taken seriously. Yet, the narrator's cynicism also depends for its existence on commonly shared values. To discern a world of total corruption is to offer by contrast a view of a world of non-corruption, though it must be stressed that this is a vision offered only by implication. In this regard consider the narrator's observation after Bardamu has extorted a thousand francs from the Henrouille couple:

Trahir, qu'on dit, c'est vite dit. Faut encore saisir l'occasion. C'est comme d'ouvrir une fenêtre dans une prison, trahir. Tout le monde en a envie, mais c'est rare qu'on puisse. (p. 338.)

(Betraying, you say, that's quickly said. You've still got to seize the opportunity. Betraying, that's like opening a window in a prison. Everyone wants to, but it's rare that you can.)

It would be naïve to suppose that Céline is proposing extortion as an ideal, however much he may think that everyone would leap at the opportunity. Rather this observation should be considered in two ways. First, it is an ironic stab at man's ignoble instincts. Bardamu, usually a victim, is quick to seize the opportunity to become a persecutor in his turn. He is no exception to man's savagery, nor is he exempted from the older narrator's denunciation. Second, the observation is a comic foil to Bardamu's extorting. It points up Bardamu's mechanically comic reaction to the opportunity to "open a window in a prison." The older narrator's musings are often comic foils that he interposes between himself and the frenzied world of the novel. The foils are means by which he obliquely condemns and revolts against his past and, in this sense, are a form of self-protection. Comedy, as is apparent in the later novels, is a means of defense, a psychological wall that isolates the narrator from the delirium that animates the novels.

Beyond the satire and the narrator's cynicism lies the world of madness and its manifestations in decay, disease, and violence, Céline's world of darkness and negation, his world of fear, nausea, and disgust. For a Christian such as Bernanos, Céline's world is ours, the world of fallen man.[13] For a critic such as Debrie-Panel, Céline's negation of the world shows him to be a dark angel seeking redemption through destruction.[14] For others Céline is the archetypal rebel, revolting against the oppression that destroys him. Certainly his scatological language, his images of decay and putrescence, and his ribald cynicism point to a symbolic enactment of a revolt against the world this language and imagery portray. It is this revolt against absurdity and delirium that seems to have escaped those critics who condemn Céline in the name of their ethical standards.

Céline's revolt against the world he has chosen to depict prevents any reader from supposing he should imitate it. *Voyage* represents a negation of this world. In terms of revolt it is the equivalent of the saying "no" that Camus puts forth in *L'Homme révolté* as the first step in rebellion. Yet, one can make no affirmative statement about the revolt conveyed in *Voyage,* for Céline does not follow his negation with a "yes," with the affirmation that, again according to Camus, completes the dialectic of a successful revolt. When the reader considers Céline's anti-Semitic polemic, he can easily see what a disaster was Céline's attempt to find a ground of affirmation for his revolt. *Voyage*'s revolt is limited to a total refusal of the destructive powers in life. Céline is a nihilist by default—his refusal proclaims a thirst for affirmation and perhaps for transcendance—and Robinson's revolt against "everything that's going on" illustrates the intolerable paradox that Céline's refusal ends in. For it is precisely against all that limits life, against the all-embracing forces of madness, those forces that continually work destruction on life, that Céline's revolt is directed. Acquiescence to death is a form of capitulation that undermines Céline's revolt in its very foundations. Céline's later change in his approach to fiction seems to indicate he was aware of this contradiction. And perhaps Bardamu is, in spite of himself, the stronger of the two picaros, or at least the more logical. He continues to live, which is undoubtedly a lesser form of contradiction.

Voyage itself is ultimately beyond good and evil. It is a symbolic enactment of Céline's revolt, but it is also an antidote for the evil and destruction against which it screams its refusal. The very existence of the novel seems to represent a purging of the past's delirium. The narrator in *Voyage* is explicit:

Il n'y a de terrible en nous et sur la terre et dans le ciel peut-être que ce qui n'a pas encore été dit. On ne sera tranquille que lorsque tout aura été dit, une bonne fois pour toutes, alors enfin on fera silence et on aura plus peur de se taire. Ça y sera. (p. 323.)

(There's nothing dreadful in us and on the earth and perhaps in the heavens above except what hasn't been said yet. We won't be at peace until everything has been said, once and for all, then finally we'll be silent, and we won't be afraid to remain quiet. That'll be it.)

Céline's narrator has attempted to say "everything," and thus, after Robinson's death, becomes silent and refuses to continue his tale. Yet Céline did not consider that *Voyage* had sufficiently exorcized the horror "in us and on the earth," perhaps in part because of the intolerable paradox that ends the novel. So, having finished this journey, he immediately set out to tell it all again, to get it all out, to vomit forth his rage and anger in another novel. The task of exorcism is endless.

CHAPTER II The Delirium of Childhood

After four more years of laboring with the intolerable paradox of his negative revolt, Céline published *Mort à crédit* (*Death on the Installment Plan*), in 1936. For some critics this is the last major novel Céline wrote, but it has received only a fraction of the critical attention given to *Voyage*. *Mort à crédit*, a novel almost as long as Joyce's *Ulysses* and seemingly as perplexing, has often been ignored, if not condemned as incoherent.

The language Céline adopted is perhaps the most troubling aspect of this massive novel. *Voyage*, once hailed for its revolutionary style, now appears to be written in a fairly conventional language. In contrast, the language in *Mort à crédit* still roars across the page like an "emotive subway," as Céline often called it.[1] The argot and slang in the novel are much richer than in *Voyage*, more explosive and more savagely blended with Céline's neologisms and obscenities. The sentences are often short, violent bursts of verbal energy, punctuated with exclamation marks and points of suspension. It is

not surprising that *Mort à crédit* retains its iconoclastic
vigor. Whereas the stylistic innovations Céline introduced in *Voyage* could be and were easily imitated by
writers of as varying talents as Sartre and Queneau,
Roger Nimier and Albert Paraz, in *Mort à crédit* Céline
found his own style, one that only a genius in vituperation such as he could successfully handle.

The style Céline created is only one aspect of the
difficulty the reader encounters in *Mort à crédit.* In
Voyage he finds a novel that can be placed within an
established frame of reference, for in terms of style,
form, and aesthetic intent it seems to have many affinities with the naturalistic novel. These affinities give an
approach to the novel, even if the dissimilarities between *Voyage* and the naturalistic novel outweigh the
similarities. In 1933 Céline, in his *Hommage à Zola,*
make clear that he shared few of the preoccupations of
Zola's naturalism:

Aujourd'hui, le naturalisme de Zola, avec les moyens que
nous possédons pour nous renseigner, devient presque impossible. On ne sortirait pas de prison si on racontait la vie
telle qu'on la sait, à commencer par la sienne. . . . La réalité
d'aujourd'hui ne serait permise à personne.[2]

(Today, with the means we have for gathering information,
Zola's naturalism has become almost impossible. You would
never get out of prison if you were to tell of life as you know it
to be, starting with your own. . . . Today's reality would not
be allowed to anyone.)

After rejecting even the possibility of presenting the
truth directly, Céline went on to say that the writer must
content himself with dreams and symbols while waiting
for another outburst of collective frenzy which, like the

last war, will give vent to man's death instinct. The *Hommage à Zola* leaves no doubt that Céline continued to see reality as a continual process of delirium, one hardly amenable to naturalistic methods of inquiry, and thus it points to his rejection of the naturalistic cataloguing of misery and horror he sometimes practiced in *Voyage*. The final result of this rejection of most naturalistic conventions was a novel whose fundamentally comic vision of delirium is unlike that of any other contemporary novel.

Mort à crédit is linked to *Voyage*, however, in a rather curious way, for it supposedly tells the story of Dr. Ferdinand Bardamu's childhood. The Dr. Ferdinand who presents himself at the beginning of *Mort à crédit* bears a marked resemblance to the Dr. Bardamu at the end of *Voyage:* both have fallen into a state of resignation and stagnation in which their only concern is with death. In the first pages of *Mort à crédit* the elderly doctor describes his miserable situation, though the narrative present tense is only a vaguely defined temporal position. The doctor's first rambling comments serve in effect as a narrator's prelude or overture to the rest of the novel. It is only after he has thoroughly acquainted the reader with his sickness and hallucinations that he can begin to recall the scattered childhood memories that gradually coalesce and lead to the narrative development *per se*. The novel's movement thus leads from a static, disintegrating present back in time to the doctor's earliest memories.

Ferdinand's earliest memories are of his mother, a naïve and partially crippled woman who is a perpetual martyr to the small curio shop she struggles to keep going. His father, possessing a diploma that is not worth a cent for earning a living, worries endlessly about los-

ing a minor position with an insurance company. Unable
to affirm himself in his work, he vents his frustration in
violent, mindless rages against his wife and son. Ferdinand's parents are a paradigm of the *petit bourgeois*
couple: their endless work can offer them only a wretched
life in a cheap Paris neighborhood that smells constantly
of urine.

After Ferdinand finishes elementary school, his search
for a job is the story of his childhood. He spends days
dragging about the streets, often accompanied by his
hobbling mother, fruitlessly knocking on potential em-
ployers' doors. At home he has to listen to his father's
enraged verdicts on his son's general depravity and "bad
instincts." Ferdinand finds one job, is quickly fired,
finds another with a jeweler, and, after being seduced
by the boss's wife, is fired again—for having lost a val-
uable gold pin that the wife stole during the orgy. Upon
a generous uncle's intervention, Ferdinand's parents
send him to England so that he can learn a modern language, that indispensable prerequisite for modern commerce. Upon arriving at "Meanwell College," he firmly
resolves not to speak a word, of either French or English, since words are the source of all his troubles. He
is thus a silent witness to the school's financial collapse,
the schoolmaster's moral disintegration, and the suicide
of the master's wife. Economic law is as ruthless on one
side of the Channel as on the other.

Ferdinand returns to Paris and his former miserable
lot, though he is sufficiently mature now to give in to his
famous "bad instincts" and nearly strangle his father.
Ferdinand finally leaves his family to live and work with
Courtial des Pereires. Des Pereires, one of Céline's
great comic characters, incarnates all the vices and
virtues of that newly mechanized era, *la belle époque*.

He is an inventor, a designer, a publisher of a scientific journal, a pamphleteer on all subjects, a pioneer in balloon aviation, and, by his own admission, a man totally dedicated to *l'esprit.* He is also a charlatan, a fake, a manic gambler, perhaps a sexual deviant, a great bluffer, and quite mad. In the des Pereires episodes Ferdinand must play the role of a Sancho Panza who narrates the adventures of a *belle époque* Don Quijote, though des Pereires's jousts are with the enraged victims of his fraudulent schemes and his delirium comes to an end in suicide.

In *Voyage* Céline made use of an older narrator to supplement Bardamu's frequently deficient vision. In *Mort à crédit* he has reduced the older narrator's presence to the novel's first thirty pages. *Voyage's* narrator is withdrawn from the world of the novel. In *Mort à crédit* Céline, by placing his narrator in an undefined present, gives him no definite temporal location, but he does place his narrator in a definite spot, so definite that he seems to be parodying the supposedly reclining position of the Proustian narrator: as Dr. Ferdinand recollects his childhood memories, he lies sick in bed, periodically vomiting. Like Bardamu, Ferdinand is very near the end of the night:

Nous voici encore seuls. Tout cela est si lent, si lourd, si triste... Bientôt je serai vieux. Et ce sera fini. Il est venu tant de monde dans ma chambre. Ils ont dit des choses. Ils ne m'ont pas dit grand'chose. Ils sont partis. Ils sont devenus vieux, misérables et lents chacun dans un coin du monde. (p. 501.)

(Here we are, alone again. It's all so slow, so heavy, so sad... I'll be old soon. Then at last it will be over. So many

people have come into my room. They've talked. They haven't
said much. They've gone away. They've grown old, wretched,
sluggish, each in some corner of the world.)

These opening lines, much like those of one of Beckett's
disintegrating heroes, mirror Ferdinand's state of decay
as he prepares for a death that is just out of reach. He is
racked with fever, a sign of his body's decomposition
and of the onset of hallucination. His frequent retching
seems to be his body's last, convulsive efforts at self-
annihilation, but it is also a physical analogue to his
efforts to vomit forth within the novel his bitter childhood memories. Nausea, like fever, leads to the past.

Ferdinand possesses enough strength, however, to
tell a few anecdotes drawn from his life as a doctor,
anecdotes that recall the scenes of misery Bardamu described in *Voyage*. Ferdinand graphically depicts the
brutal and sadistic world of his Parisian neighborhood;
and his tales seem to justify his desire to be done with
it all. He includes stories about Gustin, an alcoholic
doctor whose daily encounters with human degradation
reflect his own. Gustin, Ferdinand's double in this
respect, has found that his medical career has given him
a few inside views about what man is:

"Ah! s'amuser avec sa mort tout pendant qu'il la fabrique,
ça c'est l'Homme, Ferdinand!" (pp. 510–511.)

("Ah! getting a kick out of one's death while manufacturing it,
that's Man, Ferdinand!")

Ferdinand is also willing to share his wisdom with
Gustin. He minutely describes, for example, a slow,
screaming death by angina pectoris and comments:

C'est malheureux qu'on revienne jamais de l'angine de poi-
trine. Y aurait de la sagesse et du génie pour tout le monde.
(p. 515.)

(It's too bad nobody ever comes back from angina pectoris.
There'd be wisdom and genius to go around for everyone.)

Ferdinand and Gustin's reflections have more than
intrinsic interest, for these sardonic, often Pascalian
jabs at man's misery establish Ferdinand as a lucid observer who has no sentimental prejudices that would
blind him to life's fundamental physical reality. Moreover, the world of childhood is set against the elderly
narrator's world. The old doctor's world, one defined in
terms of fever, disease, and death, becomes a kind of
norm by which the reader can evaluate the child's
world, one populated by lunatics who are deliriously
blind to their human condition. As Ferdinand says of his
old, part-time prostitute secretary, "Elle jugeait bas, elle
jugeait juste" ("She took the lowest view, she took the
true view"), so the overture functions to force the reader
to lower his sights and judge men from the viewpoint of
the pathologist's inevitable postmortem.

In the overture Céline makes use of a kind of narration
that is not found in *Voyage,* though it is much like the
ballet scenarios Céline later wrote. Dr. Ferdinand as-
serts that he once wrote a "Légende du Roi Krogold."
Unfortunately his secretary either lost it or maliciously
destroyed it, though he does manage to recover its beginning, which he reads to Gustin. Critics have had
difficulty knowing what to make of this "Légende," a
ludicrous, quasi-medieval romance that is doubly ridiculous in the novel's context. The "Légende" was more
than a momentary concern, for Céline later mentions

it in *Féerie pour une autre fois* and in the manuscript
of *D'un château l'autre*.[3] Perhaps it, like some of the
ballet scenarios, represents a joyful kind of hallucination, a fantasy that contrasts vividly with the destructive
delirium that always obsessed him. In *Mort à crédit*
Ferdinand appears to use the "Légende" to defend by
contrast the dismal vision found in his writings, which
supposedly include *Voyage* as well as the yet to be re-
called memories of his childhood. Playing the role of
a hostile critic, Gustin has already reprimanded Ferdinand for his pessimism:

  "Tu pourrais . . . raconter des choses agréables... de temps
en temps... C'est pas toujours sale dans la vie..." (p. 505.)

  ("You could . . . tell something pleasant... now and then...
Life isn't always filthy...")

Ferdinand ironically agrees:

Dans un sens c'est assez exact. Y a de la manie dans mon cas,
de la partialité. (p. 505.)

(In a way that's pretty true. It's a mania in my case, a bias.)

So Ferdinand decides to give Gustin a little poetry by
reading aloud to him the adventures of "Gwendor le
Magnifique" and "le Roi Krogold." Unfortunately,
Gustin, whose daily routine is dealing with "Eczéma-
teux, albumineux, sucrés, fétides, trembloteurs . . .
("eczema patients, the albuminous, the diabetic, the
fetid, the palsied . . .") (p. 518), cannot lend himself to
poetic reverie and falls asleep. His falling asleep is
essentially a sign of his — and Céline's — rejection of the
possibility of heroic fantasy. Ferdinand's narration of
this story within a story is satirical, for Céline first es-

tablishes an image of a decaying, nonheroic world in which Ferdinand is firmly stuck. He then takes advantage of Ferdinand to project a contrasting heroical image of a fantasy world, an image which is destroyed by its juxtaposition with Ferdinand's world. The same refusal of heroic poetry is conveyed later when the child Ferdinand attempts to regain the confidence of a friend who thinks Ferdinand is trying to get his job. As a gesture of friendship, Ferdinand tells him the "Légende," fruitlessly of course. This double satirical overlap of the child's useless poetical efforts with the narrator's shows that no one at any age is very much interested in heroic poetry.

The "Légende" is a poetic form of hallucination or distorted vision and in this respect anticipates the older narrator's feverish delirium. In *Voyage* Bardamu usually managed to avoid falling into hallucination, though on several occasions, such as in the slave galley episode, Céline takes advantage of his picaro's sick condition to narrate fantasies that, because they are presumedly hallucinations produced by an abnormal physiological state, seem to have a naturalistic explanation. These fantasies, in *Voyage* and especially in the later novels, have comic and poetic meanings that go beyond the pathology of delirium. Perhaps, in keeping with the Renaissance as well as the modern meaning of the word, they should be called *délire*, both distorted vision and poetic fury. In *Voyage*, *délire* was usually manifested in the hostile environment that formed the horizon of the picaro's world. In *Mort à crédit*, *délire* erupts much more frequently, bursting into Ferdinand's consciousness as it destroys his lucidity and distorts his vision. The naturalistic conventions in *Voyage* did not allow Céline to incorporate fully his vision of madness into the fabric of the novel's

narration. By dropping most of these conventions in
Mort à crédit and the later works he is able to give full expression to this vision by transforming language into
délire.

In the overture *délire* immediately disrupts the narration both as a kind of vision and as the logical consequence of Ferdinand's bodily decomposition. He begins
an anecdote in the past tense, telling of a day when he
was walking with his secretary's niece, Mireille. He was
angry with her for spreading vicious rumors about him.
Suddenly the tense changes, and the narration explodes
into the present:

Alors la colère me suffoque... Penser qu'encore une fois je
suis fleur! Je lui refile une mornifle tassée... Elle ricane. Elle
me défie.
    Des taillis, des petits bosquets, de partout les gens sur-
gissent pour nous admirer, par deux, par quatre, en vraies
cohortes. Ils tiennent tous leur panais en mains, les dames
retroussées derrière et devant. (pp. 523–524.)

(I flew into a rage... To think that she'd taken me for a ride
again. I give her a good smack. She grins. She's defying me.
    From the thickets and copses, from all sides, people rush
out to admire us, by two and fours, in droves. They all have
their cocks in their hands, the ladies have their skirts up front
and back.)

Ferdinand as a lucid, self-conscious narrator disappears,
and the vision expands to epic proportions:

Arrivée à l'Arc de Triomphe, toute la foule s'est mise en
manège. Toute la horde poursuivait Mireille. Y avait déjà
plein de morts partout. Les autres s'arrachaient les organes. . . .
    La flamme sous l'Arc monte, monte encore, se coupe, tra-
verse les étoiles, s'éparpille au ciel...
    Ça sent partout le jambon fumé. . . .

25.000 agents ont déblayé la Concorde. On y tenait plus
les uns dans les autres. C'était trop brûlant. Ça fumait. C'était
l'enfer. (pp. 524–525.)

(When we got to the Arc de Triomphe, the whole crowd
began to whirl like a merry-go-round. The whole mob was
chasing Mireille. There were already corpses everywhere.
The others were tearing off their organs. . . .
The flame under the Arc de Triomphe rises, rises higher,
breaks, sweeps through the stars, becomes flinders in the
sky... The whole place smells of smoked ham. . . .
Twenty-five thousand policemen cleared the Place de la
Concorde. We couldn't hold out there, with all of us inside
one another. It was too hot. There was smoke. It was hell.)

In context the hallucination is perhaps justified by
Ferdinand's fever and mental disintegration, but it is
also obvious that fever is an analogue for the flames of
délire that are within man and the world. Before the attack of *délire* the narrator has a lucid center of consciousness, and he autonomously looks out upon the world.
As a clear-sighted observer, Ferdinand views a world
sharply if narrowly delimited in terms of his concern
with disease and death. When he is a victim of hallucination, this outer world impinges on his consciousness and
destroys his awareness. The hallucination brings with
it all the violence and dementia from which the Célinian
hero must constantly try to escape.
Insofar as it demolishes self-awareness, *délire* has
another significance, one the narrator made quite explicit in *Voyage:*

Comme la vie n'est qu'un délire tout bouffi de mensonges,
plus qu'on est loin et plus qu'on peut en mettre dedans des
mensonges et plus alors qu'on est content, c'est naturel et
c'est régulier. La vérité c'est pas mangeable. (p. 358.)

(Since life is just one attack of delirium stuffed with lies, the farther along you get, the more lies you can stick in it and the happier you are, that's natural and normal. The truth's not edible.)

Life is lived as a prolonged *délire,* and men hold to it and its lies as a way of destroying their self-awareness and blinding themselves to the truth. In Céline's novels *délire* is both the detested madness that destroys and a temptation that offers escape from the truth — the excruciatingly physical truth of death that Ferdinand sets forth in the novel's overture. Ferdinand can thus ironically note how often he has come close to madness:

Elle a couru derrière moi, la folie . . . mais j'ai déliré plus vite qu'elle. . . . (p. 525.)

(Madness has been hot on my tail . . . but I've raved faster than it has. . . .)

To remain always aware of the world's horrible absurdity is another form of madness. The paradox of lucidity and *délire* is more than verbal, for it is a paradox that Céline lived to its absurd conclusions. As his anti-Semitic polemic makes clear, Céline saw the antidote for madness as more madness. In *Mort à crédit* the narrator can claim to have the organ of the Universe in his head, for the coexistence of awareness and madness produces a cosmic *délire* that resounds throughout the novel.

Just as Proust used the privileged recall afforded by sensory experience to recover the past, so Céline uses fever-inspired hallucination to go back to time past. After his bout with *délire* the bedridden Ferdinand comes back to the undefined present. He is more feverish, more uncertain of his perceptions. Lying in bed, nauseous, he hears or believes he hears his mother speaking to his secretary, Mme Vitruve:

Quand la fièvre s'étale, la vie devient molle comme un bide de bistrot... On s'enfonce dans un remous de tripes. Ma mère je l'entends qui insiste... Elle raconte son existence à Madame Vitruve... Elle recommence pour qu'elle comprenne combien j'ai été difficile!... Dépensier!... Insoucieux!... Paresseux!... (p. 529.)

(When fever spreads through you, life gets as flabby as a bar-keeper's belly... You sink into a swell of guts. I can hear my mother rubbing it in... She's telling Mme Vitruve the story of her life... She starts all over again so she'll be sure to under-stand how difficult I was!... Extravagant!... Irresponsible!... Lazy!...)

His entrails and their decay tie him to the present, but his mind is free to wander and to recapture the language that recalls his past. As the narration increases its frantic tempo it becomes a verbal *délire* that carries him back in time. Memories and the present are mixed as all the sickening misery of his youth wells up in him. Hallu-cinating in the presence of his mother, he seems to guide a boat into the Parisian night, a boat that is a projection of the evasion death offers. Suddenly, like a nauseous upheaval, the past erupts in all its clarity:

Le siècle dernier je peux en parler, je l'ai vu finir... Il est parti sur la route après Orly... (p. 533.)

(The last century, I can talk about it, I saw it end... It took off on the road after Orly...)

Délire has given way, temporarily at least, to Ferdinand's need to purge himself of time past and all the indigest-ible experience accumulated there.

Time past is the story of Ferdinand's childhood. The
main body of the novel is supposedly narrated by the
older doctor, although the reader views the childhood
experience directly through the child's eyes. The overture, however, establishes the narrator as a lucid observer, and the child Ferdinand is endowed with the
same acrid sense of lucidity. As a child, he is forced to
resist the *délire* that assails him from every quarter,
much as it does the older narrator. In sharp contrast to
Ferdinand stand the other characters, who make no
effort to maintain a critical perspective on life. *Délire*
is usually manifested in the obsessions they attempt to
interpose between themselves and reality. In this sense
délire is often a comic form of blindness, but one that is
nonetheless a constant threat to Ferdinand. Ferdinand
is thus obliged to maintain his lucidity, and, in turn, it
is largely because he is a clear center of consciousness
that the world of the novel stands out as a hyperbolically
prolonged *délire*. In *Mort à crédit* it is essential to see
how clearly Ferdinand is differentiated from the din of
roaring voices that assaults his ears. Pol Vandromme, for
instance, declares that it is a novel "with a single character, with a single voice that always swells up with the
same obsessions, that continually repeats the same
cries." [4] Yet Ferdinand is often a quiet listener who
tries to resist the contagious obsessions that animate the
other characters' ravings. In fact, he is often a *raisonneur*,
a foil Céline uses to put the other characters' dementia
in relief.

For all his efforts to resist, Ferdinand is never totally
immune to the contagion of *délire* that besieges him. As
an infant, he learns that his lucidity is precariously
fragile. One of his earliest memories is of an attack of
hallucination such as strikes the narrator in the overture.

While lying sick in bed, the child is overcome by a vision of the "grande cliente." This fearful customer seems to rush through his mother's shop stealing all she can carry off. She goes into the street and changes into a giant, surrounded by a throng of the living and the dead. This prolonged hysteria culminates in a massacre as an abyss opens and swallows thousands, as thousands more are crushed in the streets. The vision ends in fire:

Il ne reste rien au monde, que le feu de nous... Un rouge terrible qui vient me gronder à travers les tempes avec une barre qui remue tout... déchire l'angoisse... Elle me bouffe le fond de la tétère comme une panade tout en feu... avec la barre comme cuiller... Elle me quittera plus jamais... (p. 581.)

(Nothing is left in the world but our fire... A terrible redness rumbles through my brain with a crowbar that stirs up everything... tears up the terror... It gobbles up the inside of my head like fiery soup... using the bar for a spoon... It will never leave me...)

Fire is again an analogue for the flames of *délire* as well as of fever. The delirious seizure can be attributed not only to the child's disease but also to the effect of his fear and anguish. His childhood anguish, the result of the world's constant hostility, leaves him helpless; it is as though all the fear generated by his daily misery were crashing in upon his consciousness. The fear assumes the same dimensions as the giant customer. Childhood anguish has left permanent traces of *délire* in Ferdinand's head. It is not only the external world that menaces his lucidity. At an older age he discovers that his awareness can be destroyed by the irrational, unconscious forces that lie within him. When he attempts to kill his father, Ferdinand is surprised to discover *délire* within himself:

C'est la surprise... C'est comme un monde tout caché qui
vient saccader dans les mains... C'est la vie!... (p. 807.)

(It's amazing... It's like a hidden world that jerks in your
hands... It's life!...)

Ferdinand is "caught in the dance," an image of frenzy
Céline uses repeatedly throughout his works. Here the
dance is that of homicidal madness that wells up in-
stinctively. Ferdinand's consciousness is suddenly
limited to a world of rage and violent *délire*. The inner
world, like the outer world, is a threat to the self in quest
of autonomy.

This series of violent illuminations by which Ferdinand comes to grips with his own nature and with the
destructive forces of madness that surround him are
markers that measure his progress in gaining the disabused wisdom that the older narrator demonstrates in
the overture. In one sense Céline is writing a portrait
of the young man as he acquires the vision of the artist
(rather than the portrait of the artist as a young man).
Céline has reversed the presentation of perspectives
one finds in Joyce. Joyce opens his novel from the
child's viewpoint and then traces his organic development as he becomes the artist. In reading *Mort à crédit*
the reader views each step in the child's development
as an almost necessary increment in his maturity. Moreover, this reversal makes Ferdinand seem to be a pre-
cocious child. It is certainly an advanced boy who says:

Je trouvais plus ça possible l'école... Tout ce qu'ils fabriquent,
tout ce qu'ils récitent... c'est pas écoutable en somme... à
côté de ce qui nous attend... de la manière qu'on vous arrange
après qu'on en est sorti... (p. 713.)

(I couldn't stand school anymore... All they cook up there, the
junk they recite... you can't listen to it really... compared to

what's waiting for us... the way they'll fix you once you're out
of the place...)

The child's introspective musings are often comparable
to the narrator's aphorisms in *Voyage*. Especially as he
gains in wisdom and withdraws from the world do his
comments take on a pointedness that make him appear
to be a young *moraliste*. His aphoristic wisdom is not,
however, a form of denunciation; rather it is a sign of his
progress toward acquiring the older doctor's acid-like
lucidity.

At a very young age Ferdinand adopts an almost stoical form of disengagement from the world:

Moi, je voulais plus rien du tout, je voulais surtout plus parler. (p. 675.)

(I didn't want anything anymore, above all, I certainly didn't
want to talk.)

He rejects language, for words are a physical expression
of hostility that shatter the self like a stream of bullets.
Language is *délire:* his mother's constant martyrdom, his
father's maniacal rages, the customers' impossible demands, des Pereires's mad obsessions, all exist as verbal
projections of *délire*. Ferdinand's dogged mutism in
England is a protective stance by which he, at least,
withdraws from the volleys of words that fill the air with
dementia.

At the same time Ferdinand's withdrawal allows him
to narrate the novel's episodic experience with a detachment that makes the catastrophes stand out as even
more monstrous examples of folly. This type of observation is especially evident in the two main sequences that
define "death on the installment plan," Ferdinand's stay
at Meanwell College and his adventures with Courtial

des Pereires, for each episode ends in a suicidal financial collapse. The pattern of each episode is basically the
same, though Céline depicts des Pereires's battle for
survival on an epic scale, whereas the Meanwell College sequence is more of an interlude in Ferdinand's
search for a job. In each of these sequences Ferdinand
is a peripheral participant who attempts to keep as much
distance as possible between himself and the characters' penchant for self-destruction. In each case he is an
observer who makes a series of discoveries and gives the
reader a series of revelations that disclose the illusions
the characters have about themselves. The revelation of
illusion is, in turn, accompanied by a destructive fall.

On his arrival at Meanwell College, Ferdinand meets
the master and describes him in terms that do not suggest an impending collapse:

Il s'était mis dans les frais!... Complètement lavé, rasé, fringué
d'importance... et du style alors!... Un genre avocat... une cape
noire flottante... depuis les épaules... des plis... des accor-
déons... et sur la pointe du cassis une jolie calotte avec un
gros gland... (p. 706.)

(He'd really decked himself out!... Completely washed,
shaved, dressed fit to kill... and some style!... like a lawyer...
a flowing black cape... hanging from his shoulders... accordion
pleats... and on top of his dome a fine skullcap with a big
tassel...)

Ferdinand's first description of the master conveys a
false impression, but it has situated the master on a high
plateau that subsequently emphasizes his fall. After this
initial encounter Ferdinand undergoes a series of revelations, and each revelation brings the master and his
wife closer to disaster. Even while maintaining his protective withdrawal, Ferdinand can be a fairly active par-

ticipant in this series of discoveries. At times, he is a direct observer, as when he reports that a competitive school is being built nearby. He is, at other times, something of a sleuth who correctly surmises that the façade is giving way. When necessary, he can be a *voyeur*. He sees the master's breakdown by peeking through a door transom: the master is in a befuddled, alcoholic stupor. One sees that death, in this case his wife's suicide, cannot be far away.

The sequence centering on des Pereires is also a process of revelation. Caught up in enthusiasm — a mistake for any Célinian hero — Ferdinand seems to describe accurately his imposing new employer:

Il commandait, aiguillait, décuplait les innovations nationales, européennes, universelles, toute la grande fermentation des petits inventeurs "agrégés"!... (p. 820.)

(He directed, oriented, and multiplied the inventive effort of the nation, of Europe, of the world, the whole vast ferment of the petty "certified" inventors!...)

He then begins to penetrate the façade, to find the delirious delusion beneath it, and to reveal the real des Pereires, or at least another des Pereires. The disclosure of the mad genius' vices, obsessions, and delusions is paralleled by his increasingly desperate financial crisis and his insanely fraudulent schemes for garnering a little money. At first Ferdinand is forced to surmise and suggest that des Pereires is not quite the genius he appears to be, as when, for instance, des Pereires reads to him a ludicrous piece of fan mail:

Moi, je crois, que les favorables, il se les écrivait à lui-même... il les montrait aux visiteurs... Il me l'a jamais très positivement avoué... Y avait des sourires quelquefois... (p. 847.)

(I think he wrote the favorable ones himself... he showed them
to visitors... He never actually admitted it to me... there were
certain smiles...)

This indirect revelation gives way to more direct accusations as Ferdinand has plain proof of what a scoundrel
des Pereires is. No guesses are needed when Ferdinand
learns that his boss is going to make inventors pay a fee
to enter an impossible contest for a perpetual motion
machine. The coming fall seems readily apparent. Yet,
so hyperbolic are des Pereires's grandiose manias that
after Ferdinand has revealed as much as he can about
this Faustian con man, Céline supplements his narration
by introducing des Pereires's wife. She can go even further in laying bare how mad des Pereires really is:

"Ah! je le connais moi le bonhomme! . . . Ah! c'est un joli
cadeau! depuis vingt-huit ans que je l'endure! . . . Il va nous
vendre!... Il nous solde! Positivement!... Il vendrait sa chemise! Il vendrait la vôtre, Ferdinand! Il vend tout!... Quand
la folie le prend de changer!... c'est plus un homme, c'est un
vrai tambour de sottises! C'est les foires qui l'ont perdu! Plus
il vieillit, plus il se dérange! Plus il se fêle!... Moi je m'en
aperçois! Je suis pas dupe! C'est un Infernal!" (p. 955.)

("Oh! I know my little man! . . . Oh! what a life! for twenty-
eight years I've been putting up with him! . . . He's going to
sell us out!... He's putting us on sale! Absolutely!... He'd sell
the shirt on his back! He'd sell yours, Ferdinand! He sells
everything!... When he gets the bug to change!... He's not a
man anymore, he's a loose screw! It's the fairs that ruined him.
The older he gets, the screwier he gets! Even more cracked!...
I can see it, I'm nobody's fool! He's Diabolical!")

The wife's accusations are the prelude to des Pereires's
long, final descent. The parallel structure is maintained

as he attempts a series of harebrained schemes, each of which is another economic setback. When the end comes, when his obsessions leave him and he is trapped by reality, he can find only one escape. He blows out his brains, revealing the sticky gray matter that was the source of his *délire*. Des Pereires's disintegrated head is the final image of the destructive powers of the *délire* Ferdinand has sought to flee throughout the novel.

Much like Bardamu at the end of *Voyage*, Ferdinand in each episode is a captive witness, observing and learning from the final catastrophe. Perhaps more interesting than the predictable catastrophes, however, are the characters themselves. As Michel Beaujour has observed, in *Mort à crédit* Céline has succeeded in giving birth "to a universe entirely populated by delirium." [5] Each character, his voice ranting in emulation of *délire*, is the victim of an extraordinary obsession. But beneath the bombastic ravings the attentive reader notes that Céline has utilized conventional comic types: the avaricious bourgeois, the deluded pedant, the obsessive father, the mad inventor. For Ferdinand, of course, these conventional comic types are another aspect of universal *délire*. His relation to them is dialectical, for it oscillates between lucidity and *délire*, between accurate appraisal and mad mimicry of their obsessions. Madness is as contagious in *Mort à crédit* as in *Voyage*. When Ferdinand can keep his critical distance from these characters, he is often endowed with good sense, like one of Molière's young heroes, and thus plays the role of a comic foil to their grandiose manias. He sometimes fails to maintain his critical perspective, however, and then is submerged in the waves of *délire* that emanate from the other characters. He becomes a voice for their obsessions. It is through this dialectic of lucidity and contagion that Céline presents a comic vision of men blindly struggling in a world given over to rampant destruction.

In the first part of *Mort à crédit* Ferdinand maintains a bitterly ironic perspective on his parents. Take, for example, the manner in which he presents one of the many condemnations he receives from his father:

> Lui, il savait tout. Je comprenais au fond qu'une chose, c'est que j'étais plus approchable, plus à prendre avec des pincettes. J'étais méprisé de partout, même par la morale des Romains, par Cicéron, par tout l'Empire et les Anciens... Il savait tout ça mon papa... Il avait plus un seul doute... Il en hurlait comme un putois... (p. 677.)

> (He knew everything. All I really understood was just one thing, that I was untouchable, not fit to be touched with a ten-foot pole. I was scorned on all sides, even by Roman ethics, by Cicero, by the whole Empire and all the Ancients... He knew all that, my daddy did... He didn't have a single doubt... He howled it like a polecat...)

The reader obliquely sees through Ferdinand's eyes the father as he pronounces the elevated rhetoric conveying his verdict on Ferdinand. His obsessions stand out in his claim to superior judgment on the basis of his superior knowledge, knowledge that is as futile as it is ridiculous. Ferdinand's role as a foil is clear from the first line's irony. By playing the ignoramus the son is disengaged from his father's tirade, and the distance he keeps is the distance necessary to make his father's pretentions stand out. Ferdinand's final caustic remark produces the final comic destruction of his father's pretentions by reducing his father from a Roman rhetorician to a screaming animal. The final deflation is comic, but the berserk animal is still a source of danger for the child.

In the second part of *Mort à crédit,* especially in the des Pereires episode, Ferdinand's critical perspective serves to create a more traditionally comic narrative. When des Pereires, for example, holds his contest for a perpetual motion machine, Ferdinand presents the scheme to the reader by prefacing it with a modicum of common sense:

> S'il existe un truc au monde, dont on ne doit jamais s'occuper qu'avec une extrême méfiance, c'est bien du mouvement perpétuel!... On est sûr d'y laisser des plumes... (p. 871.)

> (If there's one gimmick in the world that you should never mess with except with real caution, it's perpetual motion!... You're sure to lose some feathers with it...)

The realism of Ferdinand's popular language sets forth the norm by which to measure comic deviation. It accurately predicts that des Pereires's conduct will, in a comically mechanical manner, result in trouble, for he does lose a few feathers and nearly goes to jail. Yet, des Pereires's madness is such that it can unleash savage but hilarious cataclysms that Ferdinand's common sense cannot possibly encompass. When des Pereires undertakes a diving bell contest, financed by a mad priest, Ferdinand must confront a potential massacre as an angry horde of frustrated inventors descends upon him:

> Un défilé d'hurluberlus exorbités jusqu'aux sourcils, qui se dépoitraillaient devant la porte, gonflés, soufflés de certitudes, de solutions implacables... C'était pas marrant à regarder... Il en surgissait toujours d'autres!... Ils bouchaient la circulation... Une sarabande de possédés!... (p. 936.)

> (A procession of crackpots with their eyes popping out right to their eyebrows, who were ripping their shirts off in front of

the door, swollen up, bloated with certitudes, with implacable
solutions... It wasn't fun to watch... And more kept showing
up!... They blocked the traffic... A saraband of the possessed!...)

Ferdinand manages to keep his lucidity, but this dance
of the possessed threatens such calamities that he is left
aghast. The mob's *délire,* set loose by Courtial des Pereires's dementia, goes beyond any destructive possibilities Ferdinand has ever known. He must undo their
delirious incantation with the jab of obscenity:

Ils faisaient la revolution pour le plaisir d'être emmerdants.
(p. 936.)

(They were making revolution for the fun of being shitheads.)

The stab of comic defiance that obscenity offers is often
the only means available to the Célinian hero who tries
to resist the contagion of *délire.* Popular language is both
a norm representing common sense and a shield the
beleaguered hero uses to defend himself.

Ferdinand does not always succeed in resisting the
other characters' obsessions, for the magnetism of their
madness can draw him into their orbit of spiraling *délire.*
When his failure to resist removes any mediation between the reader and the novel's extravagant vision, the
reader is immersed directly in a fantastic flow of language that would be inaccessible madness were it not
for the critical perspective offered during Ferdinand's
moments of lucidity. Ferdinand's language is the key to
this mimicry of *délire,* for when he is overwhelmed by
the characters' madness, his words mirror their obsessions. Even after Ferdinand has spent a good deal of
time with des Pereires, for example, des Pereires's

schemes can still cast a spell over him, such as when he describes his employer's plan to establish the "Familistère Rénové de la Race Nouvelle," a school that is to attract children to des Pereires's farm—so that they can do the manual labor:

Les enfants de la "Race Nouvelle" tout en s'amusant, s'instruisant de droite à gauche, se fortifiant les poumons, nous fourniraient avec joie une main-d'œuvre toute spontanée!... rapidement instruite et stable, entièrement gratuite!... mettant ainsi sans contrainte leur juvénile application au service de l'agriculture... La "Néo-Pluri-Rayonnante"... Cette grande réforme venait du fond, de la sève même des compagnes! Elle fleurissait en pleine nature! Nous en serions tous embaumés! Courtial s'en reniflait d'avance!... On comptait sur les pupilles, sur leur zèle et leur entrain, tout à fait particulièrement, pour arracher les mauvaises herbes! extirper! défricher encore!... Vrai passe-temps pour des bambins!... Torture infecte pour des adultes!... (p. 990.)

(Playing all the while, learning on every hand, building up their lungs, the children of the "New Race" would at the same time joyfully provide a spontaneous labor force!... quickly trained and stable, absolutely free of charge!... Without constraint harnessing their youthful vigor to the needs of "Neo-Pluri-Radiant" agriculture... This great reform was rooted in the depths, in the very sap of the countryside! It was flourishing in the heart of nature! We'd all bask in its perfume! Courtial was sniffing in advance!... We were especially counting on our charges, on their zeal and enthusiasm, to pull up the weeds! to uproot them! to clear more ground!... A real pastime for kids!... Rotten torture for adults!...)

Infected by des Pereires's mad enthusiasm for this pedagogical swindle, Ferdinand no longer speaks the pointed argot and obscenities he uses to defend himself against delirious pretentions. His speech is a ridiculous improvisation modeled on the absurdly elevated language that des Pereires speaks, a language whose pseudo-elegance blinds one to the reality that argot discloses.

The characters' *délire* can be so all-pervasive that it infects things and objects, which in turn can entrance Ferdinand by the cosmic proportions of the madness they represent. Struck with horror by the jeweler Gorloge's artistic efforts, Ferdinand views the jewelry he must try to sell as "L'insomnie d'un monde entier... Toute la furie d'un asile en colifichets..." ("The insomnia of the whole world... all the rage of a madhouse in trinkets...") (p. 648). Descriptions of the mountains of junk in his mother's shop are comparable in the cosmic dimensions of *délire* they can reflect when Ferdinand's father begins to demolish the store. Perhaps the most extraordinary instance of this type of madness occurs when des Pereires, having attempted to grow giant vegetables by charging the ground with radio waves, produces an indestructible species of worm. Ferdinand's astounded imagination runs amok in the presence of these voracious larvae, for they eat everything in their path. His mind leaps into a catastrophic future and foresees a disaster beginning in their village Blême-le-Petit and covering the continent:

Ça pouvait très bien se propager à toutes les racines de la France... Bouffer complètement la campagne!... Qu'il reste plus rien que des cailloux sur tout le territoire!... Que nos asticots rendent l'Europe absolument incultivable... Plus qu'un désert de pourriture!... Alors du coup, c'est le cas de le dire, on parlerait de notre grand fléau de Blême-le-Petit... très loin à travers les âges... comme on parle de ceux de la Bible encore aujourd'hui... (pp. 1009–1010.)

(It might perfectly well spread to all the roots in France... Eat the whole countryside!... Until there was nothing but stones on the land of the whole country!... That our maggots might make Europe absolutely untillable... Nothing but a desert of rot!... Well, if that happened, you can be certain, they'd talk about the Great Plague of Blême-le-Petit down through the ages... the way we still talk about the ones in the Bible today...)

Ferdinand's imaginative flight is a negative version of Picrochole's mock epic conquests in *Gargantua*. Courtial des Pereires's *délire* has cut Ferdinand's mind free from reality, and, like Picrochole, his mind unfettered, he pursues a vision of global conquest, an inverted conquest, to be sure. Ferdinand's raptures recall the bewilderment of a Biblical prophet who is astonished by the wonders that divine retribution holds in store, though it is des Pereires's mania for experimentation, not divine powers, that has released the forces of the apocalypse. Ferdinand, like a prophet through whom God's voice speaks, gives voice to des Pereires's *délire* and the marvels of dementia of the cosmos.

The relationship between lucidity and *délire* can also be formulated as a question of language. Céline's imagery is still close to that he used in *Voyage*, but in *Mort à crédit* he has used the polarities of disgust and bombastic rhetoric in a hyperbolic manner that is not often found in *Voyage*. Lucidity, to take one pole, must be equated with popular language, with images of disgust and revulsion, with scatological language expressing cynicism and defiance. The child, for example, views his glass-roofed street, "between the Bourse and the Boulevards," with complete awareness of its misery:

Les chiens urinaient partout. . . . On avait beau répandre du soufre, c'était quand même un genre d'égout le Passage des

Bérésinas. La pisse ça amène du monde. Pissait qui voulait sur nous, même les grandes personnes; surtout dès qu'il pleuvait dans la rue. On entrait pour ça. Le petit conduit adventice l'allée Primorgueil on y faisait caca couramment. On aurait eu tort de nous plaindre. Souvent ça devenait des clients, les pisseurs, avec ou sans chien. (p. 561.)

(Dogs urinated all over the place. . . . It was no use sprinkling sulphur, the fact is that the Passage des Bérésinas was a kind of sewer. Piss attracts people. Anyone who wanted to pissed on us, even grown-ups; especially as soon as it started to rain in the street. They'd come into the Passage just for that. People used to shit in the little side alley, the Allée Primorgueil. How could we complain. Often they'd become customers, the pissers would, with or without a dog.)

The scatological language conveys his revulsion from the literally closed world of petit bourgeois shopkeepers. The image associating men and dogs relates them in the mutual degradation they inflict on the Passage, Ferdinand's stinking home. The silly optimism he hears around him is repeated when he refers to the Passage's relative advantages—men defecate in an adjoining alley—so they have not yet reached the ultimate degradation, which is his family's only solace in life. The last sentence, doubtless a homily his mother often repeats, makes clear that the shopkeepers' misery is a part of their economic lot; they must try to please even those who piss on them. And the popular syntax underlines the absurdity of having to tolerate the meanness of this stench-filled misery.

Délire finds its expression in the hyperbolic accumulation of images and actions, often describing bodily functions such as sex and vomiting in forms of cosmic exaggeration, and in the bombastic rhetoric of obsession, a sign of extraordinary comic blindness. The preceding

passages in which Ferdinand mimics *délire* provide excellent examples of delirious language, as do Courtial
des Pereires's interminable monologues. Consider the
long oration he makes on the wisdom of his decision to
leave Paris after a mob of inventors has ravaged his office:

Ah! ma décision vient de loin... et sagement, nom de Dieu,
mûrie... Des exemples? Des Emules? Nous en avons, Madame,
combien? Mais des bottes! Et des plus illustres! Marc-Aurèle?
Parfaitement! Que faisait-il, lui, ce dabe? En des conjonctures
fort semblables? Harassé! honni! traqué! Succombant presque
sous le fatras des complots... les plus abjects... Les perfidies...
les pires assassines!... Que faisait-il dans ces cas-là?... Il se
retirait, Ferdinand!... Il abandonnait aux chacals les marches
du Forum! Oui! C'est à la solitude! à l'exil! qu'il allait de-
mander son baume! La nouvelle vaillance!... Oui!... Il s'in-
terrogeait lui seul!... Nul autre!... Il ne recherchait point les
suffrages des chiens enragés!... Non! Pffou!... Ah! l'effarante
palinodie!... (p. 951.)

(Ah! my decision wasn't made yesterday... but wisely, by God,
a mature one... Examples? Epigones? We've got them, Madame, how many? Why gobs of them! Illustrious ones! Marcus
Aurelius? That's right! What did he do, that old bugger? In
very comparable circumstances? Harassed! maligned! pursued! On the brink of succumbing under the welter of abject
plots... the worst perfidies... the most murderous!... What did
he do in such cases?... He withdrew, Ferdinand!... He abandoned the steps of the Forum to the jackals! Yes! In solitude!
In exile! That's where he sought his balm! New courage!...
Yes!... He took counsel of himself!... And no other!... He didn't
ask mad dogs for their opinion!... No! Pnnuts!... Ah! the fright-
ening palinode!...)

Des Pereires, often a self-proclaimed combination of
Vigny, Christ, and Marcus Aurelius, seeks to hide his

misfortunes under a veil of language. The first lines' exaggeration marks the dimensions of his delusion, while
the contrast of literary and popular language points to
the dichotomy between his pretentions to dignity and
the ignoble reasons for his flight from Paris. The accumulation of adjectives is a grandiloquent sign of his
mania, especially marked by his use of the literary term
assassine. The prolonged analogy des Pereires makes
between himself and Marcus Aurelius underlines his
comic blindness; the final pedantic word *palinodie* underscores his mania of grandeur. This bombastic language, punctuated comically with argot, incorrect usage,
and oaths, might well be called the rhetoric of *délire*.

In terms of the narrative structure *Mort à crédit* is
undoubtedly Céline's best novel. The work is virtually
seamless. Céline is in complete control of his narrative
material, never losing sight of its development nor yielding to the urge to incorporate extraneous horrors. *Mort
à crédit* is longer than *Voyage*, but the reader follows its
organic unfolding with no sense of formless wandering.
The mad rush of events often possesses a forceful if
demented logic that carries the reader along at a rapid
pace. To a large degree Céline's control of his temporal
perspectives in the key to his structural success. He first
posits a narrator in an undefined present and then
changes the narrative point of view to an earlier point
in time. The illusion of two temporal perspectives adds
another dimension to the work as it moves chronologi-
cally from the earlier time toward the narrator's present.
Time lost is recovered — or at least purged — by the structural movement.

The structure of *Mort à crédit* gives the impression of
an author not only firmly in control of his artistic vision

but, in one sense, even disengaged from it. This disengagement is a corollary of Céline's choice to present his fictional world in an essentially comic manner; for to see a world as comic is, necessarily, to see it from a vantage point of emotional and intellectual distance. Bergson stated this necessary condition for comedy in these terms: "It seems that the comic can produce its perturbation only on the condition that it falls on a calm and unruffled mind. Indifference is its natural milieu. Laughter has no greater enemy than emotion." [6] For both the reader and the author the aesthetics of comedy are founded on disengagement.

To say that *Mort à crédit* is a comic novel is to say that all elements in the novel are subordinate to its comic vision. Thus one of the main differences between *Mort à crédit* and *Voyage* is the difference between the satirical and the comic, though this is not to say that elements of mordant satire are not found in *Mort à crédit* and that comic devices are not used in *Voyage*. As Northrop Frye has noted in making his schematization of genres, "comedy blends insensibly into satire at one extreme." [7] And *Voyage* shows that satire can blend into the formless scream of revolt at another extreme. In general, however, the satiric author is concerned with values, often concerned to the point of writing a negative form of didacticism or even shouting his denunciation at the world. In contrast with the comic author, he is engaged in a world of values that transcends the immediate vision of his literary work. George Meredith caustically observed, in pointing out the satirist's lack of disengagement: "The Satirist is a moral agent, often a social scavenger, working on a storage of bile." [8] The comic author is also concerned with values, but their immediate reference is not to a world that transcends his work but to the world of the work itself. He must establish a foil that allows the reader to view the work's world as comic precisely because it deviates from the standard embodied in the foil and, hence, in the work itself. Comic deviation means, moreover, that the comic world is a world awry, often savagely awry. Author and reader need to be at some distance from it, or it will cease to be comic. One may think of *Le Misanthrope* or *The Merchant of Venice* to see how the comic, with a slight loss of aesthetic distance, can quickly become the tragic and dangerously involve the reader. If we reverse these terms, we can see that comedy is a means of placing distance between the world and the observer, that it can be a means of defense against the world.

Mort à crédit presents a vision of a world in which delirious, comic automatons blindly act out their obsessions with predictably cataclysmic results. For the reader to view these figures as comic, however, and not as merely pompously insane, Céline carefully establishes several foils. In the overture, the narrator elaborates the futility and misery of human existence, thus setting off vividly the characters' grandiose pretentions. The development of the central theme, that of the inevitable destruction to which *délire* leads, also provides a foil to the characters' obsessions. Thematic development also resolves the problem of comic deviation — through death in Céline's universe. The child Ferdinand also plays the role of a foil. Yet, the distance between the child hero and the author is often great, for example when Ferdinand loses his critical lucidity. In those moments Céline is reducing his protagonist to a comic figure. The distance between Céline and his child hero is part of the total distance the author must keep between himself and his novelistic world.

From *Voyage au bout de la nuit* to *Mort à crédit* Céline considerably changed his approach to the novel. There remains, however, in the second novel the constant substratum of revolt and negation that marks the two novels' common authorship. Though Ferdinand's sardonic sense of realism, which could quickly lead to the cry of revolt, is conditioned by his larger role as an unwilling observer of a world in *délire*, it is obvious that the deliriously hostile world of *Mort à crédit* is akin to *Voyage*'s disintegrating world. Common to both novels is Céline's view of life's destructiveness as a projection of the insanity that lies at the core of existence. Understanding Céline's approach to the novel is thus fundamental to understanding the differences between the two works. Rather than trying to combat this madness through a total revolt doomed to failure by its very contradictions, he has chosen to exorcize it through comic reduction. Céline's refusal of his world through comic negation is still a form of protest, but the mechanisms of comedy he so brilliantly uses also show that Céline has accepted madness insofar as it can be transformed into laughter. In this sense, the violence of total rejection has become the hyperbole of extravagant comedy.

CHAPTER III   *Délire* as Ritual Farce

Céline published the first part of *Guignol's Band* in 1944 during the chaotic last months of the Occupation and immediately before his compromising flight to Germany. By this time he had published his anti-Semitic polemic and knew that the Resistance had marked him for reprisals. Perhaps this explains why he rushed to publish only a part of the novel. When Céline returned to France in 1951, the second and concluding part of *Guignol's Band* had disappeared, perhaps with some other manuscripts. Thus it seemed that only a truncated version of the novel would be available to testify to Céline's creativeness during the Occupation. This truncated version has generally mystified critics.[1] With a relish for his role as an *enfant terrible,* Céline had used the novel's prologue to address a warning to future critics:

Lecteurs amis, moins amis, ennemis, Critiques! me voilà encore des histoires avec ce *Guignol's* livre I. Ne me jugez point de sitôt! Attendez un peu la suite! le livre II! le livre III! tout s'éclaire! se développe, s'arrange! Il vous manque tel quel les ¾! Est-ce une façon? Il a fallu imprimer vite because les circonstances si graves qu'on ne sait ni qui vit qui meurt!... (*G.*, p. 7.)[2]

(Reader-friends, less than friends, enemies, Critics! here I've got some stories again with this *Guignol's* book I! Don't judge me right away! Wait a little bit for the rest! everything is cleared up! developed, arranged! As it is you're missing ¾! Is that any way? We had to print quickly what with circumstances so serious you don't know who's living who's dying!...)

In 1944 Céline could hardly have suspected that eighteen years later his secretary would find the balance of his manuscript,[3] or that it would be published in 1964 under the title *Le Pont de Londres.* This title is not Céline's, and one can only regret that the publisher, perhaps feeling the need to offer the public a new "Céline," invented a title that does not encourage reexamination of *Guignol's Band* in its entirety. With the publication of *Le Pont de Londres* it is now evident that *Guignol's Band* is of the same stature and importance as *Voyage au bout de la nuit* and *Mort à crédit.* Reflecting little of the hysteria to which Céline gave vent in the pamphlets that appeared between 1936 and 1941, and none of their anti-Semitism, *Guignol's Band* is in many respects the summit of Céline's creativity and should command the same critical attention the earlier novels have recently received.

The first part of *Guignol's Band* does seem to be a disparate collection of scenes. The prologue turns into a dialogue between Céline and an imaginary, hostile reader, which permits Céline to defend his theory of emotivity as the basis for aesthetics. The opening chap-

ter projects the reader into a delirious vision of the
exodus of refugees fleeing the German invasion. This
chapter presumedly situates the narrator, but the narrator can only be Céline himself. The next three chapters are a sometimes incoherent collection of ravings
that recall both the incriminations of the earlier polemic
and the indictments in *Voyage au bout de la nuit*.
Céline then suddenly stops his bickering and begins
the narration much in the fashion of the traditional
teller of tales:

> Moi, j'ai connu un vrai archange au déclin de son aventure,
> encore tout de même assez fringant, même resplendissant
> dans un sens. (*G.*, p. 32.)

> (I once knew a real archangel, on the downgrade, though
> still rather frisky, even resplendent in a way.)

The narrator introduces one of the members of the
"band," Boro, a Bulgarian anarchist who plays the piano
in London pubs and has a penchant for throwing bombs.
This sudden immersion into the story creates a cinematic effect: the narrator must make a flashback and,
playing the role of guide, lead the reader through the
London of World War I in order to present him to the
band.

The story is then narrated by Ferdinand, supposedly
the same Ferdinand as in *Mort à crédit*. He tells of his
adventures in London, in which he has been wandering
after having been severely wounded in action on the
Western front. He is given shelter by Cascade, a very
successful pimp whose "band" consists of his girls,
various refugees, and other minor pimps — nearly all
Frenchmen. After spending a few months in London,
Ferdinand finds that he is wanted by Scotland Yard

because of his falsified papers and his accidental
presence at a bombing Boro set off to stop a pub brawl.
Ferdinand leaves the band, wanders through London,
and joins Boro in the shop of Titus Van Claben, a grotesque, avaricious pawnbroker who dresses in Oriental
clothes.

Ferdinand arrives to find Boro thoroughly drunk. After more drinking, they send Delphine, a maid with
pretentions of being a lady, to get some medicine for
Van Claben's asthma. She returns instead with some
cigarettes given to her, she claims, by a physician from
the sky. After the four of them have finished with the
cigarettes, a delirious brawl ensues during which Van
Claben is forced to swallow his money. Boro and Ferdinand accidentally kill him as they bounce him on his
head in a benevolent effort to retrieve the lost gold
pieces.

Ferdinand must again flee, but is spotted by Mille-
Pattes, a midget cook and gambler who works for Cascade. Ferdinand has no desire to return to the band and,
in a state of nervous exhaustion, appears to throw Mille-
Pattes beneath an Underground train. He then goes to
the French consulate, determined to reenlist rather than
continue his disastrous wanderings through London. He
is promptly thrown out of the consulate, but he does
meet Sosthène, a Frenchman who dresses like a Chinaman. Sosthène, a self-made magus versed in various
sorts of secret lore, is seeking a means — mainly money —
to go to Tibet and find the "fleur des Mages" (flower of
the Magi), also known as the "Tara-Tohé," a flower that
permits one to enter the fourth dimension. He knights
Ferdinand and makes him his squire and keeper of the
horses, though this Oriental Don Quijote, unlike his
Spanish predecessor, does not even have a broken-down

nag to carry him in quest of adventure. The first volume ends as abruptly as it began; Sosthène and Ferdinand are going to visit Colonel J. F. C. O'Collogham and offer their services as engineering assistants to bolster the Colonel's effort to win a lucrative prize in a gas mask contest.

The second volume, *Le Pont de Londres*, opens with Ferdinand's falling in love at first sight with the Colonel's daughter, Virginia. Sosthène bluffs the Colonel into accepting his services, though the reader quickly learns that the Colonel is as insane as Sosthène. Ferdinand does small tasks to aid these two in their explosive attempts to construct a foolproof gas mask. One day, while doing errands with Virginia, Ferdinand runs into Mille-Pattes, or at least a glimmering, stinking version of him that seems to symbolize Death itself. Ferdinand and Virginia go with "Lord Mille-Pattes" to the "Touit-Touit Club," where, in a fantastic, orgiastic *délire*, Ferdinand makes Virginia pregnant, almost without being aware of what he is doing.

Ferdinand's *délire* and constant fear of arrest are doubled by Sosthène's obsessions. As the day of the gas mask trials draws nearer, Sosthène grows increasingly afraid—the officials will be using real gas. To ward off any catastrophe, Sosthène dances to invoke spirits and devils who can protect him. Céline creates some scenes of extraordinary comedy when Sosthène tries to prove to a skeptical Ferdinand that this magus has captured and now incarnates the spirit "Gôa." Sosthène defies the powers that be by dancing in Piccadilly Circus, an act of defiance that does stop traffic, if not the universe, but results in Sosthène's being severely beaten by several bobbies.

A few days before the trials, the Colonel suddenly disappears. Sosthène and Virginia receive a mysterious

summons to appear at Scotland Yard, and Ferdinand
decides that it is certainly time that they leave England.
Willing to abandon his friends, he finds a place for himself on a boat sailing for South America just as the band
mysteriously shows up. In an almost Kafka-like fashion,
Ferdinand learns that it is the day of his *fête*, Saint Ferdinand's Day. The band will not let him consider leaving. As he wonders whether to attribute the band's appearance to his nervous condition, another comically
delirious orgy takes place, this one accompanied by the
roar of the Zeppelins that are bombing London. While
the band is celebrating Ferdinand's *fête*, Boro and Doctor Clodo, a refugee doctor from London Hospital, bring
in Van Claben's body—now four months old—and dis-
pose of it in the river. Ferdinand sneaks away from the
party with Sosthène and Virginia, and, seemingly free
from his past, he crosses London Bridge.

The first thirty pages of *Guignol's Band* appear at first
to have little intrinsic rapport with the some seven hundred pages that follow. Their immediate interest would
seem to lie in their direct expression of the vituperation
and rage about the French defeat that Céline had vom-
ited forth in earlier polemical works. The first chapter
also foreshadows the apocalyptic vision that dominates
Féerie pour une autre fois. In this chapter Céline screams
out against the "débâcle des esprits," against the collapse of men into total madness. He plunges the reader
directly into the mass panic that Céline lived through
as an ambulance driver during the German invasion.
Men and machines are caught up in an inferno of agony
as they try to cross a bridge under attack:

Les personnes fondent, tassent les crevasses!... dégringolent
sous les vapeurs âcres... dans un ouragan de poussière! . . .

Y a d'autres vivants qui se rattrapent aux parois du gouffre, ils sont en loques par l'explosion, ils font des efforts intenses, ils retombent, ils dégueulent, ils sont cuits... Ils ont été brûlés de partout. Surgit un bébé tout nu sur l'avant d'un camion en flammes. Il est rôti, tout cuit à point... "Bon Dieu!... Bon Dieu!... Merde! C'est pas juste!..." C'est le père en sueur qu'est à côté... Il dit ça... (*G.*, p. 17.)

(People melt, huddle down in the cracks!... topple over under acrid steam... in a hurricane of dust! . . . Some of the living hang on to the walls of the abyss, they're reduced to rags by the explosion, they make an immense effort, they fall back down, they throw up, they're cooked... They've been burned all over. Up pops a baby, all naked on the front of a truck in flames. He's roasted, cooked to a turn... "Good God!... Good God!... Shit! It isn't right!..." That's the father soaked in sweat who's over on the side... He's saying that...)

Céline is dramatizing his wrath of *Les Beaux Draps* in 1941. In that polemical pamphlet he had written:

Moi j'ai fait la retraite comme bien d'autres, j'ai pourchassé l'Armée Française à Bezons jusqu'à La Rochelle, j'ai jamais pu la rattraper. . . . J'ai vu des tanks de 40 tonnes bousculer nos orphelins, nous bazarder dans les colzas pour foncer plus vite au couvert, la foire au cul, orageante ferraille à panique. (pp. 11–12.)

(I made the retreat like a lot of others, I chased after the French Army from Bezons right to La Rochelle, I never could catch up with it. . . . I saw forty-ton tanks knock over our orphans, run us off into the colza fields, so they could take off faster for cover, the hot runnies coming out their ass, a bunch of storming, panicky scrap metal.)

Céline's anger about the French defeat is understandable, but his nearly hallucinated vision of the cata-

clysm, of men and machines caught in a riot of mutual
destruction is perplexing. The reader wonders where
Céline is headed after beginning his novel with such an
awesome, climactic storm of fire. Yet, as the novel makes
clear, the images of the bridge and the burning child are
not fortuitous: both find their counterparts in the novel
itself.

The next chapter is nearly incomprehensible. Céline
gives a verse-like list of the disasters of our time and
then seems to lose control of his fury:

> Une fois que vous êtes initiés vous ne restez pas là dandi-
> nants dessus les abîmes... Pour vous faire sublimer tout vifs,
> vaporisés, jouets frêles au vent! Pardi! Pardi! Foin des timides!
> Mort aux berlues! C'est le moment des preux exploits! Des
> sublimes âpres trafagueries! La foi vous sauve! Nul à faillir ne
> concède qui ne se trouve sitôt meurtri! Haché! Saigné! tout
> blanc de honte! (*G.*, p. 25.)

> (Once you're initiated you don't stay there waddling around
> above the abysses... To get yourself sublimated alive, atom-
> ized, like weak little toys in the wind! By God! By God! To
> Hell with the timid! Death to illusions! It's the moment for
> stout deeds! For sublime, bitter Trafalgars! The faith saves!
> Anyone giving in is murdered on the spot! Hashed! Bled! all
> white with shame!)

This delirious scream, both a protest against the insane
torture of war and a cry of self-defense, represents
Céline's first step in using the novel as a form of direct
expression. He is shouting forth his personal anguish,
much as he did in his polemic, no longer transposing
his nightmares into a self-contained aesthetic whole. It
is a step in what Northrop Frye calls the "existential
fallacy," or the identification of the writer with his
creation.[4] Other critics have described this process in

Céline. Pol Vandromme contends, for example, that
Céline gradually came to identify with the fictional
protagonist he created from his personal experience:
"Céline finally came to identify with the character that
he manufactured from himself. His life, his sensibility,
and his personal world were eventually annexed by that
which, in his work, corresponded the least in the beginning to his deepest self." [5] This interpretation does
much justice to the change that occurs in Céline's work
from *Guignol's Band* to *Féerie pour une autre fois*,
though one might also suggest that the pressure of
historical events that led to Céline's exile and imprisonment was such that he decided to use the novel as a
means of self-defense. Suddenly discovering that his
real world was as delirious as his fictional one, he decided that transposing his biography into fiction was
superfluous. After *Guignol's Band* Céline came to see
that his biography and the world's *délire* coincided for
his literary purposes. In *Guignol's Band* this direct
expression of his anguish and hatred of *délire* is limited
to the first few pages of the novel. After the opening
outburst, Céline effaces himself and allows his narrator
to lead the reader into the world of the novel.

After the abrupt transition from Céline's tirades to the
story proper, the narrator, as in *Voyage* and *Mort à
crédit*, quickly establishes a distance between himself
and the younger protagonist. As he introduces Boro the
older narrator declares that he has no illusions about
what he once was:

Tout d'abord il me faisait sourire, je me croyais ficelle à
l'époque, plus tard, je me suis rendu compte du poids de
l'homme, de sa valeur, sous des dehors incongrus, de ma
propre connerie. (*G.*, p. 32.)

(At first he made me smile, I thought I was a smart guy at the time; later I recognized what the man's stature was, what his value was, under his bizarre appearance, and what a dumb ass I was.)

Just how far Ferdinand was from being the clever fellow he imagined, the narrator will show in the rest of the novel. The older narrator does not, however, want the reader to be too distant from Ferdinand, so he assumes the role of guide — one would hesitate to say tourist guide — and offers a few rules for getting along in the London underworld, more especially for avoiding the police. After he introduces Boro, he takes the reader by the hand and obligingly leads him to the band:

> Mettons que vous venez de Piccadilly... Vous descendez à Wapping... Il faut que je vous guide... Vous trouveriez pas... (*G.,* p. 38.)

> (Let's say you're coming from Piccadilly... You get off at Wapping... I'll have to guide you... You wouldn't find it...)

The direct form of address makes the reader something of an accomplice and brings him unwittingly but sympathetically into a milieu he would scarcely want to frequent. This effort to elicit the reader's sympathy at the beginning of the novel marks a further difference between *Guignol's Band* and the preceding novels. The older narrator desires neither to snarl at the reader nor to utter vehement curses on his youth. He seems almost anxious to return to time past.

There is enchantment to be found in the past. The narrator nimbly leads the reader along the docks, pointing out children playing, rows of boats, and mountains of materials:

les Entrepôts, les géants remparts tout de briques... Falaises
à trésors!... magasins monstres!... greniers fantasmagoriques,
citadelles de marchandises, peaux de bouc quarries par
montagnes, à puer jusqu'au Kamtchatka!... Forêts d'acajou en
mille piles, liées telles asperges, en pyramides, des kilomètres
de matériaux!... des tapis à recouvrir la Lune, le monde
entier... tous les planchers de l'Univers!... Eponges à sécher
la Tamise! de telles quantités!... Des laines à étouffer l'Europe
sous monceaux de chaleur chatoyante... Des harengs à
combler les mers! Des Himalayas de sucre en poudre... Des
allumettes à frire les pôles!... Du poivre par énormes avalanches à faire éternuer Sept Déluges!... (*G.*, p. 44.)

(the Warehouses, giant ramparts all in brick... Cliffs made of
treasures!... monstrous stores!... phantasmagorical granaries,
citadels of wares, goatskins squared off in mountains, enough
to smell right to Kamtchatka!... Forests of mahogany in a thousand piles, tied up like asparagus, in pyramids, kilometers of
materials!... rugs enough to cover the moon, the entire world!
... all the floors of the Universe!... sponges enough to dry up
the Thames! huge amounts!... Woolens enough to smother
Europe under heaps of pampering heat... Herrings to fill up
the seas! Himalayas of powdered sugar... Matches to fry the
Poles!... Pepper in enormous avalanches to make Seven Del-
uges sneeze!...)

In *Mort à crédit* Céline's cosmic imagination often gave
rise to this kind of delirious enumeration, but never did
it so exult in things. Anger and revolt often appear to
have been transmuted into a *délire* of wonderment and
poetic enchantment in *Guignol's Band*. Ferdinand is a
guide, then, not only to London, but to the "féerie de
Mille et une Nuits" ("the fairyland of a Thousand and
One Nights") (p. 45). Taking us by the hand, the narrator leads us away from the horrors of a war where
children are roasted in holocausts of flame and bombs;

he leads us to a guignol, to a riotous Punch and Judy show where children can laugh as wonderfully grotesque marionettes batter each other with the timeless humor of their comic art. The universe is set dancing in a joyful *délire* as Céline reveals "des joies pour l'enfance éternelle promises au fond des Ecritures" ("joys for eternal childhood promised in the depths of the Scriptures") (p. 45).

The older narrator cannot give in to his memories without a feeling of diffidence, even of shame. He often feels the need to apologize for the amazement he felt when he was young:

Je vous raconte tous ces détails parce que discrets au souvenir ils pèsent rien sur les années... Ils enchantent doucement à la mort, c'est leur avantage. (*G.*, p. 44.)

(I'm telling you all these details because, subdued in memory, they lie lightly on the years... they gently enchant you at death, that's their advantage.)

Céline thus maintains the dichotomy between his young hero's vision, set in a world of comic lyricism and *délire,* and that of his older narrator, whose concern, as always, is with death. The distinction between the narrator and the younger protagonist is perhaps less important in *Guignol's Band,* for the older narrator cannot stop himself from yielding to the exultation of the past. It is with reluctance that he turns to purge himself of this past and judge it from the perspective that death provides him. In no other of Céline's novels does the past act like a magnetic force, compelling the narrator to return in spite of himself to a delirious wonderland.

After taking the reader to the brothel where Cascade is holding court, the narrator disappears for the moment,

leaving the reader with a front row seat at the guignol
in progress. Cascade introduces the band and tells, in
long, ranting monologues, the difficulties involved in
pimping—or in being master of the show. As he and the
prostitutes shout and fight with one another, they
provide a splendid show which dramatizes Cascade's
plight. The reader's perspective on the guignol is
doubled by the watchful presence of another observer
within the scene. Inspector Matthew of Scotland Yard
silently observes the performance. He is an outsider
whose sinister presence sets off the guignol in all its
comic, detached fantasy. This way of putting the clown-
ish fantasy in relief is rather cinematic. Inspector
Matthew is much like the silent, foot-thumping cop who,
within the same frame in which a silent comedy hero
goes through his antics, points to the disparity between
reality and comic illusion. Matthew's perspective on the
guignol not only doubles the reader's but assures the
reader that he will not lose his front row seat by losing
the disengagement he must have in his role as spectator
before a Punch and Judy show.

Cascade's speeches also serve as an overture to what
is coming. He complains of continually having to pay
off Matthew, while having to take care of the numerous
prostitutes whose pimps, caught up in suicidal patriotic
enthusiasm, are rushing off to enlist. Cascade cannot
understand their abandoning the enormous profits to
be earned during the war:

Les offensives!... La viande!... La viande!... Il en faut!...
Renvoyez les os! le bavage! la gueule! c'est pour rien!...
Y a pas besoin d'écrire pour ça!... Moi je vois qu'une chose
dans la guerre!... Ça fait de la grive et du pognon! Y a qu'à
se coucher pour en prendre!... C'est le travail des dames!...

Je suis pas Victoire! Je suis pas Défaite! Je débarque pas!...
Je suis pas offensive!... Je suis pas recul!... Je me régale
voilà!... (G., p. 73.)

(Offensives!... Meat for the cannon!... Meat!... They need it!...
Send back the bones! the goo! the kisser! all for nothing!...
What's there to write about!... I see just one thing in war!...
It means raising hell and making dough! Just have to lie down
to get it!... It's women's work!... I'm not talking about Victory!
I'm not talking about Defeat! I don't make landings!... I'm
not for offensives!... I'm not for retreats!... I'm just treating
myself, that's all!...)

Cascade's speeches, whose popular language reflects
his underground lucidity while it creates an ironic
picture of war profiteering, set forth the two constants
of this unstable world: the police and war. Ferdinand
can always count on finding the *flics* on one side of
the channel and carnage on the other. The war, in which
he has suffered physical and emotional damage, is the
immediate source of his *délire* and hallucinations. The
police are a constant presence representing the un-
relenting hostility that tracks the underground hero.
And amidst this insanity the whorehouse represents a
moment of peace in Ferdinand's wanderings; it is a
place of relative sanity, a short-term paradise of which
he is quickly dispossessed, though the movement of
the novel is to reintegrate him into this burlesque family
home. But before Ferdinand can rejoin the band, he
must undergo a good many trials.

As in the preceding novels, it is the younger protagonist who narrates most of his own tale, with only occasional interventions on the part of the older narrator.
Ferdinand does not begin his tale until he sets out on

his "down and out" wanderings in London. He has introduced himself, however, during a pause in one of Cascade's monologues:

ça faisait quatre mois que j'étais à Londres... quatre mois déjà! C'était pas tous les jours commode à cause des curieux! Ça valait tout de même mieux qu'en face!... beaucoup mieux qu'à faire le guignol au "16ᵉ monté"... à crever mouillé tous les jours d'Artois en Quercy. . . . Ça c'était terminé trop mal avec l'entreprise Viviani! Salut Déroulède!... Je ramenais les os et l'hypothèque! des trous partout!... le bras tordu! Juste encore un peu de lard après... assez peut-être pour qu'ils me repiquent! . . . L'oreille aussi vachement baisée... un bourdon dedans!... du sifflet!... (*G.*, p. 80.)

(I'd been in London for four months... four months already! It wasn't always comfortable because of the busybodies! Just the same it was better than on the other side... much better than playing the clown with the 16th cavalry... getting bumped off soaking wet every day from Artois to Quercy. . . . That Viviani business has turned out pretty badly! Here's to you Déroulède!... I brought back my bones and the mortgage! holes everywhere!... my arm twisted! Just a little flesh left... enough maybe for them to yank me in again! . . . My ear really fucked up too... A buzzing inside!... whistling!...)

Ferdinand has fled the bloody guignol on the French side of the channel to join a more comic one on the English side. Like Robinson and the Doctor Ferdinand of *Mort à crédit*, he carries a noise in his head, the result of a wound in this case, but also a signal for the delirious fantasies that beset him. He is in a nearly cadaverous state, and it is no surprise that images of death haunt his world. Ferdinand, unlike his Ferdinand predecessors, is thus an almost entirely unreliable narrator.[6] His consciousness is always ready to give into hallucination, and lucidity can only be momentary at best.

Ferdinand also differs from other Célinian heroes in that he is young and susceptible to romantic flights of the imagination. Such flights quickly become parodies of themselves. His lyric raptures are a new form of *délire* in Céline's work, but *délire* nonetheless. The moment he sees Virginia, for instance, he is struck, like a twentieth-century Petrarch, by "a bolt from the blue":

une jeune fille est survenue, jolie alors, une blondinette, une charmeresse... Ah! ravissante!... ah! je l'aime tout de suite!... Ah! la foudre!... Ah! les beaux yeux bleus!... le sourire!... la poupée, je l'adore!... (*L.*, p. 8.)

(a girl came along, a really pretty one, a little blond, a real little charmer... Oh! ravishing!... Oh! I love her right away!... Oh! the bolt from the blue!... Oh! her beautiful blue eyes!... her smile!... the little doll, I adore her!...)

Ferdinand becomes, for the moment, a delirious version of Bernardin de Saint-Pierre's Paul, lost in communion with some superior force. Céline seems to take great pleasure in pushing his picaro through all the ridiculous gestures of youth. Ferdinand, the "smart guy," falls prey to love's madness and mimics all the traditional motions of the lover. He feels unworthy in the presence of the beloved, for his brute, physical nature makes him feel ashamed. He is so ashamed that, even though he is nearly starving to death, he hesitates in Virginia's presence to satisfy his gross physical needs, such as for food. The ridiculous can quickly become a grotesque parody as Ferdinand's sentimental expansions border insanity:

"Moi *dog! dog!* j'aboie!... j'aboie!... Je lui montre que je l'aime... que je l'adore!... elle me trouve tout de même exu-

bérant. Je gesticule... j'aboie... tellement que je me fais
bourdonner la tête... et puis des sifflets... je suis en carillon...
en chaudière... je palpite... je fulmine... je roule à plat ventre!...
je gémis... je tortille sur les coussins!... comme je suis indigne
encore..." (*L.*, pp. 31–32.)

("Me a dog! a dog! I'm barking... I'm barking... I show her
that I love her... that I adore her!... she finds me exuberant
just the same. I gesticulate... I'm barking... so much so that I
make my head ring... and then whistling... I'm right in the
chimes... in a boiler... I'm palpitating... I'm fulminating... I
roll flat on my stomach!... I moan... I writhe on the cushions!...
how unworthy I still am...")

The disarticulated language mimics madness, as do the
images describing the cacophony in Ferdinand's head,
but the progression from the sentimentally ridiculous
to absurd parody recalls the narrative technique Rabelais
used for similar effect in, say, Panurge's courting of a
fine lady. The comic reversal leads from sentiment to
the grotesque in a narrative dialectic of opposites. In the
above passage Ferdinand has become the animal that
is the opposite of the sublime lover — the lascivious dog.
In another instance Ferdinand proclaims his fidelity in
a manner Panurge would have heartily approved:

Je ne banderai que pour Virginia... C'est juré la main dans
mon sang!... (*L.*, p. 161.)

(I'll never get a hard on except for Virginia... That's an oath,
sworn with my hand in my blood!...)

The form of the oath mimics the traditional form of the
pledge of faith, but the substance is a purely Célinian
reversal of motifs that underscores Ferdinand's confusion of picaro realism and the realm of high sentiment.

For the picaro, love can only be a form of comic obsession that blinds him to reality. Ferdinand goes so far, for example, as to exult in his new-found sense of duty that his role as lover has conferred upon him. Sought by the police and the band, fearing that the brutal Colonel will turn him over to the authorities, Ferdinand valiantly decides to remain with Virginia, even when she announces that she is pregnant. The disabused lucidity of the preceding Célinian heroes has disappeared when Ferdinand engages in his Rolandesque affirmations:

C'est pas ma nature de lâcher... d'abandonner les coups durs!... Ça me coupe bras et jambes. Je suis pas traître! Il faut que j'étale ou que je crève! (*L.*, p. 243.)

(It's not my nature to give up... to run away from hard blows!... That really knocks me down. I'm no traitor! I've got to show myself or croak!)

His magnanimous resolutions are as ludicrous as they are without basis. Completely lacking in means to provide for himself, Ferdinand can only indulge himself in fantasy. His good intentions toward Virginia are another verbal manifestation of his romantic *délire*, a blindness that is as comic as was des Pereires's.

Ferdinand's romantic *délire* provides Céline with the opportunity to aim his parody at some rather specific targets, in fact, at nearly the entire gamut of French literature. The absurd desire of Ferdinand, the *preux chevalier,* to lock his beloved in a tower is medieval and recalls such a work as Chrétien de Troyes's *Cligès.* His sense of duty belongs to a hero of a *chanson de geste.* The language describing Ferdinand's "blondinette" seems to be a satire of Ronsard, and Virginia's name is intended to recall *Paul et Virginie.* This sentimental novel seems to have held much interest for Céline; he had already written a satiric sequel to it in a ballet scenario called *Voyou Paul, Brave Virginie*, a ballet in which Céline's Paul exhibits decidedly more lecherous tendencies than Bernardin de Saint-Pierre's original. Thus Ferdinand dreams of escaping with Virginia to some tropical island where, free from Scotland Yard, the consulate, and the war, he can enjoy "the enchanted life" (*L.*, p. 128). Proust, too, seems to be a target of parody, or at least the Proustian style of jealousy. Ferdinand watches his beloved manhandled by Bigoudi, the Lesbian prostitute, and then has an absurd fit of jealousy and doubt:

je voulais savoir!... pour Bigoudi!... pour tout ça... qu'elle m'avoue un peu... Ah! je l'aimais!... encore bien plus, c'était une torture dix fois pire depuis Bigoudi!... (*L.*, p. 122.)

(I wanted to know!... about Bigoudi!... about all that stuff... for her to admit a little to me... Ah! I loved her!... even more, the torture was ten times worse since Bigoudi!...)

Marcel's endless speculations about Albertine caused no greater tortures.

Céline takes advantage of Ferdinand to present his vision of lyrical *délire*. We have already seen how enchanted the older narrator is as he leads the reader through London and the busy vitality of every street and dock. London is, for the wanderer, a living organism that mirrors Ferdinand's own élan, it is a city of dancing youth and winged ships that promise the impossible happiness he dreams of in his moments of delirious infatuation. One Englishman, V. S. Pritchett, has rather sarcastically evaluated Céline's London: "To Céline, the London dockland of 1914 is a branch of the picturesque London of Doré engravings, which continental writers have always enjoyed the idea of—a place of fog, rain, tobacco smoke, oversweetened by gin." [7] Yet Céline's pulsating vision of London is certainly a delirious projection of Ferdinand's youthful enthusiasm. It is also the decor for a gigantic guignol and the stage on which men dance an uproariously comic ballet.

Céline's lyricism in *Guignol's Band* is expressed through Ferdinand's vision of the continual dance that unfolds in London's streets, pubs, and squares, and it is this vision of life as a delirious, joyful dance that is unique in Céline's works. For example, *Guignol's Band* opens with a merry dance of drinkers who flatten the hated cop Matthew:

Tout le bazar secoue, vogue, sursaute tellement la foule en houle barde, brame, agite, conspue le Matthew!... Serré de près Matthew prend peur, je raconte les choses, il sort son sifflet de sa petite poche... Ah! ça déchaîne tout!... C'est la ruée!... Ah! faut pas qu'il siffle!... Pas de renforts!... Mort à la Police! Basculé, raplati par terre, Matthew se trouve recouvert d'ivrognes, braillants, joyeux, trépignants dessus en monticule jusqu'au lustre... caracolant d'aise et victoire! La ronde aux godets passe dessus... A sa santé!... *For he is a jolly good fellow!*... (*G.*, p. 36.)

(In a big swell the crowd was raging, bellowing, swarming, booing old Matthew so that the whole place was shaking, swaying, jumping!... Hemmed in close Matthew got scared, I'm telling what happened, he takes his whistle out of his small pocket... Ah! that sets everything off!... It's a rush!... Ah! He'd better not whistle!... No reenforcements!... Down with the Police! Knocked down and flattened on the ground, Matthew finds himself covered with drunks, yelling, joyous, stamping on him, a mountain of them as high as the ceiling... cutting a caper for joy and victory! A round of beer mugs over his head... To his health!... *For he's a jolly good fellow!*...)

The crowd is as violent perhaps as those in *Mort à crédit*,
but here they dance, sing, and act out their *délire* in
comic good spirits. The dance, another form of *délire*, is
another antitoxin for existence' sickness. And so Ferdinand, in the midst of his most trying moments, can be
enraptured by the jostle of the London street:

ça vous fonce dans toutes les jambes, remue-ménage, bricoles,
cerceaux, casseroles, tintamarre, faufile partout, piaille à
cloche-pied, nique cabriole, boum! saute-mouton! filles,
garçons culbutés pflouf! au ruisseau! ça vous emporte de
brusquerie! vous éclabousse de joie si vive! le soleil vous
attrape partout, vous brûle le cœur de plaisir, des murs
gluants, des ruelles magiques, filles retroussées, blondinettes
fauves, butors d'étoupe! ce grand ramponneau de jeunesse
délire! délire! gambade pour l'éternité... Mourir ainsi tout
emporté de jeunesse de joie de marmaille! (*L.*, p. 302.)

(It rushes into your legs, hullabaloo, all sorts of things, hoops,
stewpans, racket, runs off everywhere, squealing on one foot,
caper with a thumb on the nose, boom! leap-frog! girls, boys,
knocked over, bam! in the gutter! it carries you away with a
rush! splatters you with such lively joy! the sun catches you
everywhere, burns your heart with pleasure, sticky walls,
magic little streets, girls with skirts in the air, wild little
blonds, tow-headed louts! this great rush of youth in delirium!
in delirium! gambol for eternity... To die like this carried
away by youth by joy by kids!)

What a farandole of youth's *délire!* Meaningless when
judged from the viewpoint of death, this hyperbolic
élan is nonetheless a riotous dance that generates great
joy. As we know from Céline's frequent references to
the dance as the summit of aesthetic perfection, such an
image of youth's dance represents perhaps the only form
of joy he can imagine. The perfect coordination of body,

music, and poetry is perhaps man's only hope of assuaging, momentarily at least, his constant degradation in a world given over to disease and decay. In *Guignol's Band* the dance has become the vibrating image of delirious lyricism, a joyous counterpart to both Ferdinand's romantic *délire* and the antics of the guignol.

The puppets who throw themselves into these dances, especially at the beginning of the novel, represent in general the scum of society. In this respect they call to mind the astute comments Fielding made in *Tom Jones* in order to defend his portrayal of ignoble characters:

I will venture to say the highest life is much the dullest, and affords little humour or entertainment. The various callings in the lower spheres produce the great variety of humourous characters. . . . (XIV, i.)

Fielding is reminding us that comic characters in literature are largely a product of convention: traditionally, kings are not comic, servants are. Céline's band of lesser characters, as in the traditional *roman comique,* do represent the lower spheres. There could hardly be anything lower than his array of pimps, prostitutes, refugees, and their assorted cronies. They are characters of farce, and their antics, like those of puppets, are immediately accessible to the reader. This is not to say that the comedy itself is conventional. The comic stab of this motley band into the conventional social order is all the more pointed because it comes from below. As might be expected from Céline, they are underground puppets whose slapstick parallels in many ways the mad acts of those who rule society.

After Ferdinand leaves the band, the comic tone

changes. In the characterization of Sosthène and, to a
lesser extent, the Colonel, Céline reverts to the high
comedy he created in depicting des Pereires. The narrative modulations are also comparable to those in *Mort
à crédit,* for Ferdinand is alternately a foil to and obsessed by the characters' *délire.* When Ferdinand is not
lost in his own romantic madness or haunted by morbid
hallucinations, he struggles to judge these berserk
characters as he attempts to stay free of their destructive
manias. He is by no means always successful. In the
Colonel, Ferdinand must confront an obsessed, Vic-
torian imperialist dedicated to inventing a gas mask
that will enable England to "rule the gases" as well as
the Empire. Ferdinand's role with regard to the Colonel
is usually that of a *raisonneur* or foil. He translates the
Colonel's verbal extravaganzas into earthy terms that,
by contrast or outright rejection, plainly point out the
Colonel's *délire.* The Colonel, for example, shows
Ferdinand and Sosthène his workshop:

"La! je travaille, *gentlemen!... Work! Work! I and my enge-
neers!* Moi et mes ingénieurs..."

A cynical Ferdinand is quick to react:

Il nous annonce ça solennel. Ingénieurs la peau!... personne
dans le local... (*L.,* p. 15.)

(He announces that, solemn-like. Engineers, my foot!...
no one around here.)

The mixture of French and English, the latter seemingly
often misspelled on purpose, underscores the nature of
the bilingual cacophony that surrounds Ferdinand.
Little wonder that he is more unstable than the Ferdi-

nand of *Mort à crédit*. His tattered consciousness must withstand the blasts of twice as many words.

As in *Mort à crédit*, Ferdinand's consciousness is also filled with the absurd objects and gadgets that reflect the other characters' madness. The Colonel's gas masks, for example, are as ineptly ludicrous as their inventor. Ferdinand is a very sardonic foil as he explains that the Colonel insists on decorating these masks with all manner of ornaments:

Il trouvait très indispensable les enjolivements, les plumes d'autruche, les forts panaches qui retombaient sur les visières à la bersaglière. Tout pour les embellissements! la mécanique élégante!... c'était son slogan. (*L.*, p. 95.)

(He found the embellishments to be indispensable, the ostrich feathers, the big plumes that hung over the visor as on a bersagliere soldier's hat. Everything for ornamentation! elegant mechanics!... that was his slogan.)

But Ferdinand's common sense is no more effective against disasters than are the absurd masks. In this example Ferdinand must run for his life when Sosthène and the Colonel test the masks with a homicidal gas called "Ferocious." The two inventors' illusions are shattered—though only temporarily—for the masks turn out to be good only to keep them from beating each other to death after the gas incites them to a murderous rage. The cosmic *délire* that objects reflected in *Mort à crédit* is not often present in *Guignol's Band*. Objects are more like props for the Punch and Judy show. And the explosive fight between Sosthène and the Colonel is a nearly perfect enactment of the guignol spirit. Their obsessions release a rage that reduces them to marionettes who batter each other while the puppet-narrator stands by aghast.

Sosthène is the dominating character in *Guignol's Band*. His pretentions to cosmic power rival des Pereires's search for universal knowledge, at least as a form of blinding *délire*. Ferdinand's perspective on this self-proclaimed seer varies more than is the case with Ferdinand and des Pereires. Ferdinand's first meeting with Sosthène produces a collision of two obsessions. He tries to interest this strange "false Chinaman" in his story of crime and mutilation, but Sosthène is not at all interested in Ferdinand's obsession with his mundane horrors, and an astonished Ferdinand has great difficulty in concentrating on his woes as the "initiated one" counters with his "Cult of the Dead." Pressed into service on a fantasy trip to Tibet in search of the magic flower, Ferdinand, a victim of his own hallucination, wants to believe in this magus–knight-errant. He willingly allows his imagination to espouse the most absurd manias that Sosthène proposes and thus steps into a minor role as the lead puppet's accomplice.

Ferdinand's relation to Sosthène affords Céline many opportunities for comic juxtaposition of opposing obsessions. At the outset of their venture, for example, we see a clash of obsessions set in the magic decor afforded by the Colonel's extraordinary wealth. The Colonel's table offers a variety of enchantments, as did the docks of London:

Les laquais apportent des plateaux, toute une table servie... couverte de raviers, de victuailles!... quel déploiement de merveilles!... ah! quelles succulences!... Ah! la bave me coule! Je bulle!... Ah! le vertige me saisit!... Rillettes! Anchoix! Jambons variés! beefs! gorgonzolas! à gogo!... Ah! quel choix féerique!... (*L.*, p. 11.)

(The servants bring in the trays, a whole table set... covered with hors-d'œuvres dishes, with victuals!... what a spread of marvels!... ah! what delicacies!... Ah! I'm flowing with slobber! I'm frothing!... Ah! I'm hit with vertigo!... Rillettes! Anchovies! Different kinds of ham! beef dishes! Gorgonzolas! all you want!... What a fairy-like choice!...)

These delights set off the mechanisms of *délire,* for Ferdinand suddenly finds that he "can't see straight." Sosthène, on the other hand, views this gastronomic *délire* as something other than poetry. He throws himself upon the mountains of food like a glutton, a physical gesture that deflates his pretentions to being totally dedicated to the "Faith":

Sosthène devant moi vacille, se hausse, se dresse un moment sur la pointe des pieds en suspens!... et pflof s'abat en plein sur un plateau!... d'un seul coup à quatre pattes! à plat ventre! baffre! mastique, engloutit tout!... un chien!... c'est horrible à voir... Je ne sais plus où me mettre!... (*L.*, p. 11.)

(Sosthène wavers before me, rises up, gets up for a second, suspended on the tip of his toes!... and plop falls down in the middle of the platter!... all at once on all fours! flat on his stomach! gobbles! chews, swallows everything!... what a dog!... it's horrible to see... I don't know where to hide!...)

Sosthène has transformed himself into a dog, an animal metaphor that in Céline's works is always the sign of delirious grotesqueries. The reader, however, views this assault on the table through Ferdinand's eyes and must be aware that the young man's vision has been distorted by vertigo as well as romantic *délire.* Ferdinand has become an embarrassed romantic hero who strives to maintain an aura of spirituality in the presence of his beloved Virginia. Within the scene the reader cannot be certain to what extent Sosthène is displaying his bestiality and to what extent Ferdinand's amorous obsession has puffed it up to scandalous proportions. The narrative perspective is remarkable, for it succeeds in putting both the would-be epic hero, Sosthène, and the romantic hero, Ferdinand, in a comic light.

Ferdinand's adoption of Sosthène's obsessions can also produce comic aberrations. Mimicry is again the source of comedy, for Ferdinand, in good puppet fashion, then mechanically acts out the *délire* that emanates from his master. In the following episode, for instance, Ferdinand describes Sosthène's admirable efforts to invoke the powers of the universe. Ferdinand beats out the arcane rhythms indicated in the *Véga des Charmes* while Sosthène executes a cryptic dance:

Il levait un pied et puis l'autre... top! top! tac! tac!... Il retournait son bras ainsi top! top! tac! tac!... il faisait la gueule épouvantée et puis les yeux de poisson sorti tag! tag! pif!... je faisais moi pif! (*L.*, p. 100.)

(He raised one foot and then the other... click! click! clack! clack!... He twisted his arm around like this click! click! clack! clack!... he screwed up his face in an awful mask and then did some fish eyes clap! clap! bop!... I did the bop!)

The rhythms of the dance are waves of *délire* to which Ferdinand vibrates, and he becomes an enchanted though rather unbalanced mime as he gives in to the pulsating beat:

je devenais aussi dingue que mon maître!... (*L.*, p. 102.)

(I was getting as nuts as my master!...)

And he excitedly initiates the reader into the mechanics of trapping devils:

L'astuce d'après la *Véga*, c'était d'amuser les démons, de les éblouir, de les étourdir, de les posséder par plaisanterie, et puis quand ils étaient en joie, tout secoués par la rigolade, de leur passer par-derrière, de les sonner l'un après l'autre, à grands coups de bambou! toc! sur le crâne!... Là j'avais mon rôle dans l'affaire!... (*L.,* p. 103.)

(The trick according to the *Vega* was to amuse the demons, to dazzle them, stun them, possess them through joking, and then when they were having a good time, all shaken with laughter, to slip around behind them, to knock them out with whacks of bamboo! bam! on the head!... There's where I had my job in the thing!...)

To pursue the analogy with *Don Quijote,* this narration is something like what might have resulted had Cervantes allowed Sancho Panza to describe his master's glorious projects after a cursory reading of *Amadís de Gaula.* The squire has enthusiastically embraced the master's view of the world, and, in his less elevated manner, he explains what he has discovered from his new perspective. The language reflects the not very certain understanding of the squire who must put his master's projects—killing giants or catching spirits— into action. The inelegant realism of the squire's language spells out the failure of the master's mad schemes even before the pair come up against reality. Language again is used to measure comic deviation, for one will never catch a giggling demon.

Sosthène does come up against reality, much in the manner of a Don Quijote charging windmills. Characteristically, his most extravagant combat takes the form

of a dance to the accompaniment of an incantation
directed against the cosmos. The magus leads Ferdinand
to Piccadilly Circus, where he announces to his un-
suspecting squire that he is about to witness "le grand
défi" — the great challenge against the powers that be
(*L.*, pp. 251–253). Ferdinand must participate in this
insanity, for it is his task to beat out the proper rhythm
as his master throws himself into the traffic:

> Lui alors en grand rigodon magique à plus savoir qui
> comme, enlevé de terre avec sa robe, emporté, tourbillonné,
> elfe en essor, grâce et miracle, espiègle entre les bus, effacé,
> reparaissant, mutin, cache-cache, sourire encore, les figures
> de l'Incantation, le 96 des *Végas*, plus là le flic en transe, au
> cul, écumant de rage, galopant. (*L.*, pp. 252–253.)

> (He then in a great magic rigadoon where you don't know
> which end is up, raised from the earth with his robe, carried
> away, whirled about, an elf in flight, grace and miracle, mis-
> chievous among the buses, out of sight, reappearing, roguish,
> hide-and-seek, still a smile, the figures of the Incantation,
> number 96 of the *Vegas*, plus the cop in a trance there, on his
> ass, frothing with rage, galloping.)

He dances the rigadoon, a dance that, as the title of
Céline's last work shows, Céline especially associated
with the rhythms of madness. In this scene, Ferdinand,
like the crowd that gathers, is astonished by the sight of
délire transposed in physical motion. His raptures convey a sense of poetic admiration, though this moment of
poetry cannot long endure — a policeman unpoetically
gives chase. Ferdinand's enchantment is such that he
forgets to beat the rhythm. He becomes a spectator
watching a marvelous ballet and intervenes only when,
as a good squire, he must reenter the guignol to save

his master from the policemen who are ritually beating him senseless.

When Ferdinand's obsessions clash with those of the other characters and when he mimics their *délire,* the guignol is an interiorized play of verbal obsessions. Ferdinand's shattered consciousness is a delirious vortex around which the dancing puppets spin as they rant and declaim their manias. Ferdinand himself is but another puppet, however, and does not control the manipulating strings. The key to his modulations of consciousness is again language, and much of what has been said about *Mort à crèdit,* especially with regard to the rhetoric of *délire,* holds true for *Guignol's Band.* In *Guignol's Band* it often appears, moreover, that Céline has attempted to capture the vibrancy of the dance through linguistic mimesis. His broken syntax and language fragments, guided by his rhythmic punctuation, capture the tempo and rhythms that convey the emotional resonances of the dance's frenzy.

The argot and obscenity that Céline pours forth in *Guignol's Band* do not usually represent the language of hatred and disgust. Whereas lurid obscenity animates many scenes of *délire* in *Mort à crédit,* it rarely attains the hilarious pitch, the Rabelaisian tone, that one finds in *Guignol's Band.* The joyfully abusive exuberance that abounds in this novel's dialogues is often the verbal equivalent of the well-aimed blow in the Punch and Judy show. Obscenity in *Guignol's Band* can often be likened to the puppets' traditional clubs that they never hesitate to use on their indestructible opponents. In Céline's hyperbolic world the vituperative volleys become extravaganzas that are harmless by their very dimensions. By the same token, they are examples of verbal comedy that has rarely been attained before.

Ferdinand's unreliability as a narrator in *Guignol's Band* is produced by a reversal of the dialectic that characterizes Ferdinand's modulations of conscious-ness in *Mort à crédit.* In the earlier novel Ferdinand possesses a clear center of consciousness, and *délire* is an exceptional state. In *Guignol's Band, délire,* both as hallucination and mimicry, is relieved only periodically by moments of lucidity. It is Ferdinand's hallucinated state that informs the unfolding of episodic experience, for Céline uses his hero's nearly permanent state of *délire* as the basis for a narrative structure that sets forth a fantasy that ultimately destroys the line of demarcation between life and death, between reality and madness. Hallucinated narration begins almost as soon as Ferdi-nand is responsible for telling his own story. The entire episode in which Ferdinand and Boro accidentally kill Van Claben has a dreamlike, delirious quality. Fer-dinand, for example, takes hold of a rifle which, in a Salvador Dali fashion, becomes elongated and melts in his hands. Céline offers a humoristic causal antecedent for the hallucination, since the distorted vision is pre-sumedly caused by the strange cigarettes that Delphine says were a gift from the "doctor in the sky." After Ferdinand believes that he is no longer under the effect of the cigarettes, the narration would appear to be re-liable: Van Claben's body seems to be lying in plain sight. Yet, the distortion is prolonged. After the all-night, murderous orgy is finished, an apparently sober Ferdinand watches the maid Delphine lament over the body and play the role of Mary Stuart:

> *"Why murderers! don't you know me!... You don't know whom I am?...* Vous ne savez pas qui je suis?... *Finish your job!...* Assassins!... Achevez votre tâche!..." (*G.*, p. 204.)

This lament prolongs the vision's fantastic dimension, for one cannot decide if Delphine is drugged or merely mad, or perhaps both. Her tragic soliloquy, punctuated by bombs dropping on the wharves in the distance, sets the stage for Ferdinand's flight from the band. His flight is also a futile effort to escape from *délire*.

The destruction of the line of demarcation between reality and *délire* is carried one step further in the episode that begins with the meeting of Ferdinand and Mille-Pattes, who is now supposedly dead, and culminates in the delirious orgy at the Touit-Touit Club. Céline prepares the reader for the forthcoming hallucination; immediately before meeting the ghostly version of Mille-Pattes, Ferdinand complains that his nervous condition has disordered his perceptions: "J'ai des visions diaboliques!..." ("I've got some diabolical visions!...") (*L.*, p. 132). Believing he has murdered Mille-Pattes, Ferdinand is quite shaken when he encounters his cadaverous figure on a busy London street. He resolves to act as though nothing were amiss. Indeed, Virginia seems to find nothing unusual in Mille-Pattes's appearance, which casts doubt on the validity of Ferdinand's vision. Virginia is delighted with "Lord Mille-Pattes," though, after the three have begun dining together, even she notes a peculiar odor in the air. She does not, however, seem to be aware that her noble host also glimmers. The reader can only wonder if Ferdinand's perceptions are the ones in which he should have confidence. Mille-Pattes, a glimmering ghost who stinks, is a fantastic yet concrete image of death. He seems to be a product of Ferdinand's hallucinating imagination, but for Ferdinand the stench of his presence is as real as death itself.

Reality yields even more to macabre fantasy when

Mille-Pattes takes Ferdinand and Virginia to the Touit-Touit Club. Here Ferdinand is separated from Virginia. Céline, in effect, removes the foil, the outside standard of reference by which the reader might verify Ferdinand's perceptions. The use of Virginia as a foil has rooted Ferdinand's vision in an exterior reality, and her disappearance serves to augment the uncertainty that pervades the next vision. For after entering the club, Mille-Pattes — or "Lord Asticot" (Lord Maggot) as Ferdinand calls him — throws himself into a dance of death:

Il plane... il oscille encore... Il s'en paie là-haut... Il se gêne plus!... Il vogue... il louvoie!... il frôle le piano. . . . Il jette des lueurs de ses membres... de sa tête... de ses orbites... le vert, le bleu, le jaune... il est enveloppé dans les lueurs!... Ça c'est un effet!... Maintenant il cavale... il sursaute dans les arpèges... décharné, cabriolant... (*L.*, p. 159.)

(He soars... he sways back and forth some more... He's giving it hell up there... He doesn't hold back!... He sails... he tacks!... he skims the piano. . . . He's throwing off glimmers from his limbs... from his head... from his sockets... green, blue, yellow... he's enveloped in flashes!... That's really something!... Now he takes off... he's hopping in an arpeggio... cutting a fleshless caper...)

This comic dance of Thanatos presents Céline's equivalent of a "dancing god," though it is also a projection of Ferdinand's shattered psyche. Death and eroticism are intermingled in a technicolor bacchanalia as Ferdinand succumbs to his *délire*. Even after Milles-Pattes has been taken back to his cemetery, the orgy continues with unabated furor. It ends only when Ferdinand can find Virginia, though his orgiastic *délire* seems to continue when they are alone in the street.

One might think that the Touit-Touit Club episode was completely hallucinatory, but the following day Virginia testifies that Ferdinand went crazy in the afternoon and forced her to enter a club. Céline again uses her as a foil to tie, ambiguously, Ferdinand's delirious vision into the presumably reliable narration that preceded and followed it. Virginia's pregnancy later proves, too, that the orgy was something more than hallucination. The fantasy, rooted in the supposedly objective narration, creates an ambiguous dimension that neither *Voyage* nor *Mort à crédit* possesses. The seemingly objective testimony of the other characters throws in doubt the reliability of Ferdinand's narration. Yet the reader has no access to the world of the novel except through narration from Ferdinand's point of view. The reader must accept Ferdinand's word for what the other characters say. In the final episode of the novel Céline takes advantage of Ferdinand's closed world to obliterate the distinction between reality and fantasy.

In a general sense Céline has prepared the reader throughout the novel for the final, delirious celebration of Ferdinand's *fête*. Ferdinand has continually complained about his mental state, for the war has permanently marked him:

"Céphalorée, troubles de mémoire, hébéphérie [*sic*] comitiale, séquelles de choc et trauma..." Ça voulait dire que pour des riens je foutais le camp, je battais la campagne sur une petite contrariété. (*L.*, p. 270.)

("Cephalic disorder, memory lapses, comitial 'hebepherie,' sequelae of shock and trauma..." That meant that for damn near nothing I was gone, my screws would come loose at the least annoyance.)

This general preparation is more suggestive than explanatory, and Céline gives up any attempt at a causal explanation of Ferdinand's *délire* when the band mysteriously appears to celebrate Saint Ferdinand's Day and to prevent Ferdinand from sailing. The band begins an orgy in honor of Ferdinand while Zeppelins provide suitable background music as they bomb London.

Ferdinand muses on this absurd celebration — he had never heard of Saint Ferdinand's Day — when Van Claben's stinking corpse is brought on the scene almost like a stage prop from the wings. The strange image of Delphine, Van Claben's maid, wailing over her master's corpse, is picked up again in the final episode and casts added doubt on the reality of the earlier episode where she lamented and played Mary Stuart. A fascinated Ferdinand stares at the body, while Delphine, whose presence is as unexplained as that of the band, plays the role this time of Lady Macbeth, proclaiming, "A smell of blood! A smell of blood!" (*L.*, p. 372). Ferdinand, a comic realist of the most meticulous sort, tries to assure himself of the validity of his perceptions by noting that a four-month-old body decidedly does not smell of blood. Sancho-like realism and epic destruction blend in a typically Célinian medley the ludicrous and the sinister. This narrative blend is another way of blurring the distinction between hallucination and reality, in this instance the reality of death. By setting the minutely realistic detail within a framework of extravagant absurdity, Céline creates a plastic fantasy that recalls Kafka's humorous nightmares.

As the band's appearance completes the circle of events that leads Ferdinand and the reader back to the beginning of the novel it completes the destruction of our sense of reality. The lack of explanation for the final vision endows the whole novel with an added dimension of ambiguity. If one accepts Ferdinand's final vision as authentic, then one must view all the preceding episodes as an extended crisis of *délire*. If one views the final episode as another instance of *délire*, then the vision takes on a magic quality that undermines our acceptance of the preceding episodes. In this hall of distorting mirrors, the final orgiastic episode acts as a rock that breaks the only true mirror and leaves the reader with no source of confirmation for Ferdinand's perceptions. Only the continuing war, represented by the interminable bombardment of London, seems to have any claim to ultimate reality, and war in the Célinian universe is a projection of life's *délire* at its most feverish pitch.

Guignol's Band is Céline's most comic novel, and yet the presence of death is more pervasive in it than in either *Voyage* or *Mort à crédit,* novels which in terms of theme deal explicitly with death. At the very beginning of the novel Céline plunges the reader into an intolerable scene that makes clear that he is both fascinated and horrified by the mass murder in war of civilian populations. The sight of burning men forces him to turn away, to look back in time, and to seek refuge in the wonderland of romance. In one respect *Guignol's Band* is a comic romance. It is a romance enacted on the stage of a guignol, but nonetheless a fantastic flight of the comic imagination. It seems paradoxical that Céline could combine the comic romance and his obsession with death. His autocriticism offers an insight into this paradox. Céline was perhaps thinking of his lost manuscript when he told Robert Poulet:

Voilà ce qu'il ne faut pas oublier: que ma danse macabre m'amuse, comme une immense farce. Chaque fois que l'image

du fatal trépas s'impose dans mes livres, on y entend des gens
qui s'esclaffent. Ma camarde, c'est un effet comique. Et aussi
la réalité d'où elle sort, qu'elle éclaire!... Une réalité cocasse-
ment agencée, avec mille détails encore plus burlesques que
sinistres, et à la surface de laquelle s'agitent quelques mil-
liards de nœuds d'atomes, qui à peine serrés commencent à
se dénouer, après avoir crié vaniteusement leur nom d'hommes: y a-t-il rien de plus bouffon?[8]

(Here's what you must not forget: that my *danse macabre*
amuses me, as an immense farce. Every time the image of
"fatal death" comes forward in my books, you hear people
who burst out laughing. Kicking off in my novels has a comic
effect. And also the reality from which it springs, that it illu-
minates!... A laughably arranged reality, with a thousand details that are more burlesque than sinister, and on the surface
of which squirm a few billion knots of atoms that, scarcely
having been tied together and having conceitedly cried out
their name of man, start to come apart: is there anything that's
more farcical?)

It would appear, however, that the Céline who looks at
the exploding bridge at the beginning of *Guignol's Band*
does not see a "laughably arranged reality." Rather, he
takes his terrible vision of life's *danse macabre* and,
transposing it, places it on the stage of the guignol. By
frenetically pulling the strings, he then forces his puppets to enact the "immense farce," to enact a parody of
death, set in the decor of the comic romance.

Céline's initial intervention, in spite of its incoher-
ences, is thus a forceful prelude to the puppet romance.
By its graphic repulsiveness it forces the reader to follow
the narrator into the fantastic world of comedy and poetry. Only in this world can the spell that death works on
the author's mind be exorcised through the magic of the
comedian's art. In *Mort à crédit* Céline used comic re-

duction to exorcise the atrocious absurdity of life. In *Guignol's Band* he turns against the horror of death by reducing it to a frantic puppet dance, a burlesque *danse macabre*, set in the wonderland of romance.

The counter-spell, against death, is first cast, however, when the narrator guides us through an enchanted London. This transition from the author's prelude to the guignol itself is more than a guided tour; it is the beginning of the enchantment that will lead us from the first chapter's bomber-assaulted bridge to London Bridge, the bridge Ferdinand can cross only after the comic dance of death has been brought to its conclusion. After allowing his narrator to entrance the reader with his *Arabian Nights* wonders, Céline becomes the master puppeteer who introduces, with Cascade's assistance, his rollicking marionettes. The reader's perspective is now that of the spectator who sees the puppets' strings and yet is willing to be delighted. This perspective removes the reader, and perhaps the author, from the most macabre scenes in *Guignol's Band*, for these scenes involve mere puppets who fly through the motions of the ritual dance of death. Death itself is only another puppet, "Lord Mille-Pattes," whose soaring dance epitomizes the frenzy of death.

Ferdinand, whose youth casts him in the lead role opposite the villain, Death, is, as Céline suggests in the opening pages, the "paillasse de l'Univers" ("clown of the Universe," *G.*, p. 28). He is the clown who is both Pierrot and the victorious hero of the romance. It is his role to act out the traditional part of the hero in romance, to overcome the obstacles that lie between him and the realization of his love. In the Célinian universe, his task is to overcome death. His task is fulfilled, however, only by the quasi-magical appearance of the band at the end of the novel. On one level, it is Céline, the puppeteer, who again intervenes after having subjected his hero to many burlesque tests. Céline assures the proper ending to his romance when the villain Death, now represented by Van Claben's body, is overcome. On another level, it is Céline, the conjurer, who intervenes, putting his puppet dancers through the final ritual dance that completes the exorcism. *Guignol's Band* is another form of exorcism, much like *Voyage* and *Mort à crédit*, and the mechanisms of comedy testify that Céline has not really attenuated his revolt of negation and refusal.

Another curious aspect of *Guignol's Band* is that Céline as a magician draws heavily on the *roman populaire*. Beneath the surface of this popular genre, in which a remarkable hero vanquishes insurmountable difficulties, lies a magic resolution of all conflicts. Yet the magical conclusion of strife is never definitive. Jean Tortel describes the world of the *roman populaire* in these terms: "if the representation of the social universe that the *roman populaire* offers is without real depth, it is nonetheless mythical. For this universe, the only one that is proposed in the absence of any interior world, is considered uniquely as that of the eternal combat of good and evil. Eternal, because in reality, in the *roman populaire* there is no final victory: neither for good nor for evil. The good often wins in the last chapter, of course. . . . But . . . and this is most important, when the ending is happy, the novel leaves its characters, once they have undergone their ordeal, in the same state in which it found them. . . ." [9]

Céline has adopted the boisterous mechanism of the *roman populaire* to resolve Ferdinand's conflict, and, accordingly, Ferdinand's liberation does no more than bring him back to his original situation. He can cross

London Bridge and be reintegrated into the band, but only, we feel, to face new conflict, only to find death and *délire* waiting for him again. It is as though the reader had just witnessed one long episode in a serial adventure epic—or mock epic. The hero must be prepared to face and defeat an infinite number of overwhelmingly powerful enemies. In the Célinian universe this enemy will always be death and madness.

Moreover, Céline's choice of a magical resolution of strife is very revealing of his approach to his hatred of *délire* and its accompanying destruction. Céline's choice of an irrational solution to the problem of irrational violence, fighting *délire* with magic, is found throughout his anti-Semitic polemic.

Finally, *Guignol's Band* presents an image of a writer who hates death, but it is an image that is balanced by the impression of a man who loves the rare moments of joy in life. The fantasy that the romance generates often becomes a poetic moment in itself. The hyperbolic expressions of joy detach themselves from the guignol to remain a unique expression of an exuberant sensibility. The author of *Guignol's Band* is wary of such effusions. Neither his sense of humor nor his sense of uneasiness, we feel, will permit him to indulge his great élan, and his unrestrained rhapsodies are quickly transformed into the antics of the guignol players.

CHAPTER IV   Political Delirium

Céline's works fall into sets of three: the three novels written before he fled France in 1944, the three anti-Semitic pamphlets he wrote from 1937 to 1941, and the three postwar "chronicles" that tell of his wanderings in Germany. These trilogies do not seem to be intentional. He also wrote one other novel in the late thirties, *Casse-Pipe;* only a few fragments remain of this tale of Ferdinand's life in a cavalry boot camp. Nor does *Féerie pour une autre fois* have companion volumes. *Voyage au bout de la nuit, Mort à crédit,* and *Guignol's Band* are the most powerful of Céline's works and comprise the trilogy on which his reputation as a writer will rest. In these works he fabricated an epic in madness that encompasses the bitter ordeal of childhood, the romantic *délire* of youth, and, in *Voyage,* both the revolt and resignation of maturity. At the same time, he created new forms of comedy that have not been equaled in contemporary fiction. How, then, did Céline, this genius in vituperation and bombastic rhetoric, come to use his

verbal gifts to write *Bagatelles pour un massacre,*
L'Ecole des cadavres, and *Les Beaux Draps,* three of the
most rabid anti-Semitic tracts that have ever been
printed?

Céline's critics have generally avoided this question
unless they wished to prove that he was a Nazi agent.
Sartre, in his "Portrait de l'antisémite," was perhaps the
first to accuse Céline publicly of taking money from the
Germans, since Sartre did not think that Céline could
really believe in his racism.[1] Céline could only believe,
Sartre felt, in collective suicide as the ultimate solution
to man's misery. Although Céline might have approved
the latter suggestion, there seems to be no basis for the
accusation. In fact, there is no reason to suppose that
Céline was ever a fascist, though he borrowed their ar-
guments in the same way he plagiarized other sources
for his polemical purposes.[2] On the other hand, more
favorable critics have suggested that we must learn how
to read Céline, that we must view, for example, the word
"Jew" in his works as an unfortunate neologism he used
to express his rage against all forms of oppression. There
is some truth in this contention, especially insofar as
Céline employed the word far beyond the limits of even
the most insane anti-Semitism of his time. But he know-
ingly used the word in a specific historical context, and
he intended for the word "Jew" to designate Jews as
well as everything else he detested. There can be no
doubt that Céline was guilty of anti-Semitism, and at the
very moment Hitler was preparing the crematories.

Céline's pamphlets are nonetheless an integral part
of his work, the reverse side of it perhaps, and they
should be read, discussed, and analyzed. Not only do
they display at times the same comic genius that animates his novels but they are an extraordinary testimony

to the limits of an absolute revolt of negation whose
tensions can lead only to madness. Sartre, who bases a
large part of his discussion of anti-Semitism on Céline,
proposes that the anti-Semite seeks a principle of evil
to explain the existence of a Manichaean universe. It
does appear that in his polemic Céline tries to use the
Jew to explain the world's degradation. In attacking the
universal principle of evil, Céline is attempting to overcome the absolute negation that has characterized his
revolt. In one sense, Céline is trying to find the affirmation, the "yes," that must come after the first step of
negation that founds a rebellion. He seeks an affirmation
that can be a principle of light in his darkened universe.
His polemic, then, not only underscores the dangers of
a negative revolt but points out the aberrations that can
spring from the rebel's desperate need for a light in the
darkness.

It is difficult to surmise how Céline could take to heart
anti-Semitism so readily. One cannot say that he always
was an anti-Semite; for in *Mort à crédit* the father's
ravings include a diatribe against the Jews, and the
father is plainly characterized as berserk. Céline's past
undoubtedly familiarized him with the myth of the Jew
as it is propagated in the lower middle and working
classes, and certainly he was familiar with the anti-
Semitism of right-wing intellectuals. A Barrès, for
instance, could claim that the word "Jew" was an adjec-
tive that meant monopolist and usurer.[3] Céline may have
been very susceptible to this kind of argument, for his
simplified sociology, as seen in *Voyage,* inclined him to
view the world in terms of great masses of the exploited
and those few who walk on top of the slave galley, the
Rich.

Very little in his early writings indicates that Céline

had any anti-Semitic inclinations. The French reading
public was taken by surprise by his first outburst in
Bagatelles pour un massacre; Gide even thought that
the pamphlet's anti-Semitism was so exaggerated that
it had to be a parody of anti-Semitism.[4] In retrospect,
however, one can find a few signs of Céline's attitude in
his early works. Céline's first literary work, his play
L'Eglise, portrays in part the machinations that go on in
the League of Nations. Certain unpleasant characters
with obviously Jewish names are responsible, though
the play can hardly be called anti-Semitic. The first real
sign of his anti-Semitism came later, in 1936, the year
he published *Mort à crédit* and also made a trip to the
Soviet Union. The result of this trip was a ferocious little
pamphlet, *Mea Culpa,* in which Céline took Stalin's
Russia to task in his usual vehement manner. A little-
noticed line of *Mea Culpa* seems to indicate that his
anti-Semitism was ready to burst forth:

Se faire voir aux côtés du peuple, par les temps qui courent,
c'est prendre une "assurance nougat." Pourvu qu'on se sente
un peu juif, ça devient une "assurance vie." Tout cela est fort
compréhensible. (p. 10.)

(In the days that are coming, getting yourself seen by the side
of the people, that's taking out an apple pie insurance policy.
Provided you feel a little Jewish, it becomes life insurance.
All that is quite understandable.)

In 1937 Céline decided to make it quite understandable
and published *Bagatelles pour un massacre.*
 A close reading of Céline's polemic shows that it does
not differ greatly from his fictional works insofar as the
narrative structures are concerned. Modulations of
délire characterize Céline's way of viewing the Jews,

just as such modulations are at the heart of his novelistic worlds. Moreover, it is Céline's fear of *délire* that seems to be at the origin of his anti-Semitic crisis, for it was the approach of a second war, of a second outbreak of *délire*, that caused Céline to take up his pen and write feverishly in the hope of avoiding a second massacre on the Western front. Throughout the pamphlets Céline portrays the coming war as an outbreak of dementia that will reach cosmic proportions. *Bagatelles*, for instance, offers a vision of the future *délire* that recalls Bardamu's discovery of flesh at the beginning of *Voyage:*

Les blancs, ils la verront même pas la Paix de la France en morceaux... De l'Ariège à la rue Lappe, de Billancourt à Trégastel on emmènera tout!... Boudins!... Vous passerez tous dans la farce! . . . Dudule et grand Lulu!... et la Gencive! et le Tondu!... Keriben et Vandenput... vous verrez pas ça!... Vous y verrez qu'un nuage de sang et puis vous serez morts!... éclatés!... tout écartelés vivants... le long des trois fronts... Dans un entonnoir vous laissez à tremper vos tripes... dans l'autre vous tournerez la soupe, le grand rata des gadouilles avec vos moignons... vos poumons sortis, travaillés en franges, translucides, feront de la broderie dans les fils de fer... (p. 265.)

(White men won't even see the Peace of France in pieces... From the Ariège to the rue Lappe, from Billancourt to Trégastel they'll take away everything!... Blood pudding!... You'll all get pushed into the farce! . . . Dudule and big Lulu! and La Gencive and le Tondu!... Keriben and Vandenput... you won't see it! You'll just see a cloud of blood and then you'll be dead!... blown apart!... all flayed alive... along three fronts... in one crater you'll leave your guts to soak... in another you'll stir the soup, the big manure stew with your stumps... your torn out lungs, tailored into a fringe, translucent, will look like some embroidery on the barbed wires...)

The war is foreseen as massive evisceration on three fronts, a carnage for which Céline cannot find enough images to describe it. *L'Ecole des cadavres* presents war as another image of *délire* by portraying it as a cannibalistic dance of madness:

L'enfer possède tous les trucs. Ah! que nous sommes, franscailles, désirés dans la danse! c'est plus l'amour! c'est la folie anthropophage! Une délectation farouche anticipée, tous nos cadavres épars sur les champs de la Meuse, par millions et dizaines de millions. (p. 39.)

(Hell has all the gimmicks. Ah! how much we Frenchies are wanted in the dance! it isn't love anymore! it's cannibalistic madness! A wild feast, they're expecting, with all our corpses scattered on the fields by the Meuse, millions and tens of millions of them.)

War is thus a form of madness that can be desired only by those who are suffering from *délire*, such as the Americans who are anti–anti-Semitic:

Voici des payes que je la pratique l'Amérique, dans toutes les pires conditions, et les joyeuses, d'hystérie, d'ivrognerie, de déconnerie alternante, de gangsterie vaniteuse, de déconfiture, de dégonflerie, de braillage moralisateur. Jamais je ne l'avais trouvée aussi obscènement délirante que cet été, ce fanatisme anti-quelque chose. (*L'Ecole,* p. 38.)

(I've known America for a helluva long time, in the worst and most happy conditions of hysteria, drunkenness, alternating stupidity, of conceited gangsterism, ruin, backing down, moralizing bellowing. Never have I found it so obscenely delirious as this summer, with its fanatic anti-something or the other.)

The French, seemingly a nation of victims, will be sacrificed on the altar of the madness that possesses other

nations. The final expression of this madness will be the
utter devastation of France, unless, it would appear,
Céline's lucidity can prevail against the forces of hysteria and dementia that surround him.

Although Céline's fear of war and the madness it represents seems to have provoked his immediate crisis,
it is impossible to say why he decided that the Jews
were ultimately responsible for this *délire*. Perhaps there
is some truth in Céline's later contentions that he saw
the Jews as being too aggressive in their anti-Hitler at-
titudes, that it was his fear of the war he thought they
might cause that led him to attack them so vehemently.
But Céline did more than merely attack the Jews. He
transformed them into the cosmic source of all *délire*
and evil in the universe. Behind every manifestation of
dementia he discerns, Céline always finds, at least in the
first two pamphlets, that it is "les youtres qui dirigent
l'Univers, ils ont toutes les ficelles en mains" ("the
kikes who run the Universe, they've got all the strings
in their hands") (*Bagatelles*, p. 44). Céline can find their
malevolent presence everywhere, as the source of *délire*.
The war, of course, is the Jews' most demented project,
one that will afflict all the Western democracies:

Les Démocraties auront la guerre finalement. Démocraties =
Masses aryennes domestiquées, rançonnées, vinaigrées,
divisées, muflisées, ahuries par les Juifs au saccage, hyp-
notisées, dépersonnalisées, dressées aux haines absurdes,
fratricides. (*L'Ecole*, p. 25.)

(The Democracies will finally have war. Democracies = Aryan
masses who've been domesticated, ransomed, pickled, divided, jerkified, stupefied by the Jews for pillage, hypnotized,
depersonalized, trained for absurd, fratricidal hatreds.)

Céline's hyperbole here shows that *délire* is at work, that the power of madness incarnate in the Jew has erupted into consciousness and made the language explode.

Having found in the Jew the source of cosmic *délire*, Céline can show him to be at work in every form of oppression, sickness, and degradation that comes to his fertile mind. For instance, Soviet communism, that "shitty nightmare" he attacked in *Mea Culpa*, turns out to be a Jewish conspiracy:

En U.R.S.S., il n'est même plus besoin de ces fantoches politiques "libéraux," Staline suffit... Franchement youtre il serait peut-être devenu la cible facile des anti-communistes ou du monde entier, des rebelles à l'impérialisme juif. Avec Staline à leur tête, les Juifs sont parés... Qu'est-ce qui tue toute la Russie?... qui massacre?... qui décime?... Quel est cet abject assassin? ce bourreau superborgiesque? Qui est-ce qui pille?... Mais nom de Dieu! Mais c'est Staline!... C'est lui le bouc pour toute la Russie!... Pour tous les juifs! (*Bagatelles*, p. 43.)

(In the U.S.S.R. there's no longer any need for puppet "liberal" politicians. Stalin suffices... If he were openly a kike, he might have become an easy target for anticommunists or the whole world, for the rebels against Jewish imperialism. With Stalin at their head, the Jews are set... Who's killing all Russia?... who's massacring?... who's decimating?... Who is this abject assassin? this super-Borgiaesque executioner? Who's pillaging?... Why by God! Why it's Stalin!... He's the scapegoat for all Russia!... For all Jews!)

Not only the Soviet Union, but the Catholic church, the Pope, and the Christian God are Jewish. Industrialization is a Jewish plot designed to sap the Aryan of his emotional resources by turning him into an automaton.

Maurras, like Proust, has a "Hebrewesque" style, and
so he is a Jew, another intellectual who undermines the
Aryan's power of creativity. The cinema is controlled
by Jews who use its banality to lull the French into a
stupor. Wine production is encouraged by the Jews,
teetotalers themselves, so that the French will become
a nation of alcoholics — a charge Céline documents with
such anger that he forgets the Jews are responsible for it.

The words "juif" and the derogatory "youtre" are
much like a club that Céline swings in his panic, striking
out at the phantoms that are leading to violence and madness. The words seem to have an almost scatological
value for Céline, as when, for example, he faces the
moneygrubbing French bourgeois:

Je me demande toujours ce qui est le plus dégueulasse, une
merde de juif bien aplatie, ou un bourgeois français tout
debout... lequel qu'est infect davantage? Je peux vraiment
pas décider. (*Bagatelles*, pp. 74–75.)

(I always wonder which is the more disgusting, a really
flattened Jewish turd or a French bourgeois who's standing
up... which one is the more foul? I can't really make up my
mind.)

In the comparison Céline uses the word "juif" to
heighten his expression of revolt. By comparing the
bourgeois to Jewish excrement, an almost redundant
comparison in Céline, he finds the ultimate scatological expression of revolt since it encompasses both the
principle of *délire* and the ultimate image of biological
disgust. Scatological language presents a symbolic
enactment of Céline's revolt against the world's ontological sickness, but it is also used as the language of
Céline's lucidity, much in the way it represented the

language of lucidity for Céline's picaros. The use of the words "juif" and its pejorative synonyms is Céline's way of proclaiming his lucidity in the face of madness, of his picaro realism when all others are blind to the oncoming disasters.

One might very well wonder how the Jews have been so successful in propagating the *délire* that appears to afflict all Western nations, except Germany and Italy. Their success is, in part, a magical one. Their power of *délire* is such that it enchants the poor Aryan:

En avant l'intimidation juive! les conflits hurlés! la politique, les angoisses perpétuelles, décevantes toujours, les extases imposées, les haines entre Aryens sous tous les prétextes, électoraux, religieux, sportifs, etc.... Les catastrophes ranimées à délirantes cadences, rechutes paradoxales, suspens, d'autres crises toujours plus tragiques, l'épilepsie pour tous! Là raison du Goye à ce rythme de cabanon, la vinasse aidante, tôt vacille, trébuche, déraille, foirade, dégouline, renonce. Après quelques années de ce démentiel régime, il n'est plus le Goye, qu'un imbécile écho de toutes les volontés juives, décervelé par le chaos de ces fameuses cacophonies. (*L'Ecole,* p. 26.)

(Forward with the Jewish intimidation! conflicts screamed abroad! politics, perpetual and always deceiving anguishes, the ecstatic crises forced on us, hatreds among Aryans on any pretext, electoral, religious, sportive, etc.... Catastrophes revved up at delirious rhythms, paradoxical relapses, a moment's rest, still other more tragic crises, epilepsy for everyone! With this nuthouse rhythm the Goy's reason, with booze helping, soon vacillates, stumbles, goes off the track, gets the runs, falls down, and gives up. After a few years of this demented regimen the Goy is nothing but the imbecile echo of any Jewish desire, lobotomized by the chaos of these famous cacophonies.)

The Jews emanate waves of *délire* that act through conflicts to assault the Aryan. The vibrations of madness set
up sympathetic vibrations in the Aryan's mind, and he
soon topples into the abyss of dementia. Of course, the
metaphors here only point to the magical solution that
Céline proposes for his problem; yet the powers of
délire in the polemic are much like its powers in
Céline's novels. The Aryan is not even as resistant as
Céline's heroes, for he has been totally seduced by the
cosmos' dementia. The Aryan is essentially a puppet
who dances on the Jews' magical strings.

In explaining the Jews' success, Céline employs another metaphor that he frequently uses in his novels.
The Jews' *délire* is a contagion, and the Jews themselves are likened to germs, cancer, and other agents
of disease. This analogy is not unique with Céline, for
much anti-Semitism has compared the Jews to "foreign
bodies" that must be combated if the "social body"
is to be healthy. What is unique is the way in which the
analogy suits Céline's manner of viewing madness both
as contagious and as a source of disease. Jews, then, are
both a disease and the source of the sickness that afflicts
society. Céline can thus pose as society's doctor, a man
of science who is analyzing a deliriously sick patient:

La judéologie est une science, l'étude de la maladie juive du
monde, du métissage aryano-juif, de la mosaïque mandelienne,
de la cancérisation mandelienne du monde actuel. Décon-
nage? Jeux de mots? Anathèmes délirants? Non. Très authen-
tiquement cancer, néoplasies, créées, provoquées comme
toutes les néoplasies, par hybridations excessives, croisements
forcenés, imbéciles, désastreux, anarchies cellulaires,
déclenchées par fécondations dégradantes, absurdes, mon-
strueuses. (*L'Ecole*, p. 31.)

(Judeology is a science, the study of the world's Jewish disease, of Aryano-Jewish crossbreeding, of the Mandelian mosaic disease, of the Mandelian cancerization of the contemporary world. Bullshit? Play on words? Delirious anathemas? No. Very authentically cancer, neoplasms that have been created and set off like all neoplasms, by excessive hybridization, mad imbecilic, and disastrous crossbreedings, by cellular anarchy that has been released by monstrous, absurd, and degrading fertilizations.)

The biological metaphor shows that the Jew has also injected his *délire* into the Aryan by disorganizing the very cells that make up his body. Attacked from without by the Jews' magical vibrations, attacked from within by the Jews' disruption of his genetics, the Aryan, it would seem, has no hope at all of resisting dementia.

Céline's task is to fight to keep his lucidity while he sounds the alarm for his fellow Frenchmen. In one sense he is playing the role he gives to the protagonists in his novels; they too struggle to keep their lucidity while they denounce the world's *délire*. Moreover, Céline's racism is a self-conscious articulation of the revolt that was implicit in his portrayal of his victimized fictional heroes. The Aryans that Céline describes and wants to save resemble Céline's protagonists in several ways. They are the "clowns of the universe" who are continually on the point of being eviscerated. They row the galley while the Rich enjoy themselves topside, though the Rich, those universal oppressors of the novels, have become the Jews in the pamphlets. Céline's victimized heroes and his Aryans are underground men who never dare step out of line for fear of being destroyed.

Racism, for Céline, represents the pariah's sudden

about-face, his sudden demand to be heard, and Céline
delights in the surprise that his racism has caused:

> Comment? Comment? Insolence! Horreur! L'Aryen, cette
> nature de beurre, si docile, infiniment plastique, toujours en
> tous temps soumis aux volontés juives, que le couteau juif
> tritouille, barbouille, écrabouille, tartine de toute éternité, la
> denrée parfaite du commerce, par excellence, pour tous
> trafics de guerre et de paix, que n'importe quel youtre chas-
> sieux, tranche, débite, spécule, troque, mijote, avilit, merdifie
> tout à loisir, le voilà qui se prend en masse à présent, d'un
> coup! rebiffe! soudain! La rébellion du beurre! L'insurrection
> des éternels écrémés! Cela ne s'était vu! entendu! soupçonné
> possible, jamais! (*L'Ecole*, p. 88.)

> (What's this! What's this! Insolence! Horror! The Aryan, that
> so docile, always bending butter brain, who always on every
> occasion has submitted to Jewish will, whom the Jewish knife
> has ground up, splattered, mashed, spread on bread like butter
> for all eternity, that perfect comestible for commerce, *par
> excellence*, for all war and peacetime trafficking, whom any
> bleary kike can slice up, chop up, speculate on, barter, stew,
> vilify, shit on at leisure, here he is getting together with his
> own now, *en masse*, suddenly standing up! The butter re-
> bellion! The insurrection of the eternally skimmed! That's
> never been seen before! heard of! suspected possible, ever!)

Céline's racism is ultimately a frenetic attempt to find a
positive form of revolt that will enable him to overcome
the darkness of the night where his constant negation of
existence has placed him. In the above passage his
revolt is that of the persecuted turned persecutor, though
Céline wants to see it as a sudden redressing of cosmic
abuses. Here his revolt goes beyond mere refusal to
become a demented cry for justice.

Perhaps because he could not really believe in his

vision of the pariah's revolt, Céline's pamphlets are, like the novels, an effort to exorcise the demons that besiege Céline. They ramble on interminably, as though he felt compelled to repeat unceasingly the counter-spell he works through language in order to undo the vicious incantations that cast madness on the world. As the preceding quotations demonstrate, his language is his usual language of *délire*, an extraordinary accumulation of hyperbole, rhetoric, and epithets that hurl madness at the reader, while the exaggerated dimensions of this demented language attempt to create a comic form of exorcism. When one reads, for example, that the French kings have "very suspicious noses" (*Bagatelles*, p. 265), one must inevitably laugh at this hyperbole, for the mechanism of comic exaggeration and obsession is at work whether Céline is conscious of it or not. And one might well think that he is more than a little aware that his manias are comic, a comic revelation of the disasters he foresees. It is hardly surprising that readers might have thought *Bagatelles pour un massacre* to be a parody of anti-Semitism, or that French fascists quickly learned they could not use Céline.[5]

Céline's last work of polemic, *Les Beaux Draps*, written after the German occupation of France, shows that he had begun to doubt his racism. Perhaps since he saw that the war quickly resolved itself in a defeat that was far less destructive than the victory of 1918, he could begin to question if not overcome his fear of *délire*. *Les Beaux Draps* is still anti-Semitic, but Céline could write in that work:

La question sociale elle demeure, les juifs ont pas tout inventé, ça serait trop beau, l'inégalité des classes, les privilèges des repus, l'injustice en tout et pour tout! Les juifs auraient pas l'occasion de fomenter les révoltes si il y avait pas les motifs. (p. 86.)

(The social problems are still there, the Jews didn't invent everything, that'd be too easy, class inequality, the privileges of the stuffed, injustice in everything and for everything! The Jews wouldn't have the opportunity to stir up revolts if there weren't reasons.)

Les Beaux Draps makes clear that Céline was still searching for some affirmation beyond racism that would allow him to overcome his negative revolt. In *L'Ecole des cadavres* he had proclaimed himself to be a communist—not a Marxist to be sure—but a communist of the "soul." His communism is a poetic faith that will destroy bourgeois materialism in the name of injustice and the suffering of the poor (pp. 100–101). Céline's rather vague communism is another aspect of his search for a mystical principle of light to oppose to the dark. His attacks on the *lycée*, on French intellectuals, on the rationalist bourgeois mentality, and on the classical tradition in general point to his search for emotive forms that can save Western man, desiccated by his rationalism and materialism. In one sense Céline recalls Péguy and his attacks on the "party of the intellectuals," while his search for a purified form of "organic" social units recalls Péguy's defense of the necessary mystical base on which every healthy society is built.

Yet Céline seems to have a great deal of difficulty in believing in his own "mystique," so he proposes in *Les Beaux Draps* a rather mediocre version of his communism as an ideal:

Faut pas du grand communisme, ils comprendraient rien il faut du communisme Labiche, du communisme petit bourgeois, avec le pavillon permis, héréditaire et bien de famille, insaisissable dans tous les cas, et le jardin de cinq cents mètres, et l'assurance contre tout. (p. 137.)

(You don't want total communism, they wouldn't understand anything about it; you've got to have Labiche kind of communism, some petit bourgeois communism, with a hereditary little house permitted, and family wealth that can't be seized in any circumstances, and five hundred yards of ground for the garden, and insurance for everything.)

On the other hand, Céline cannot prevent himself from giving expression to a vision of lyrical perfection in which man would rediscover the emotivity and affective powers from which industrial society has alienated him:

Il faut réapprendre à créer, à deviner humblement, passionnément, aux sources du corps, aux accords plastiques, aux arts éléments, les secrets de danse et musique, la catalyse de toute grâce, de toute joie et la tendresse aux animaux, aux tout petits, aux insectes, à tout ce qui trébuche, vacille, s'affaire, échoue, dégringole, trimbale, rebondi, recommence de touffes en brin d'herbe et de brin d'herbe en azur, tout autour de notre aventure, si précaire, si mal disposée... (*Les Beaux Draps,* p. 175.)

(We must learn again to create, to guess humbly, passionately, in the wellsprings of the body, in the harmonies of the plastic arts, in the elements of art the secrets of dance and music, the catalysis of every grace, of every joy, and tenderness for animals, for the very small, for insects, for everything that totters, wavers, bustles about, runs aground, falls down, trails about, leaps up, begins again going from tufts to leaves of grass, and from leaves of grass to the sky, all around our so precarious and badly arranged adventure...)

Céline's mystical ideal is a communism attuned to the grace and the mystery exteriorized in dance and music.

In the final analysis, however, Céline's vision of tran-
scendence is really a call for the perfection of the physical existence whose degradation he could not bear. It
is again largely a rejection of all that he detested both
in life's suffering and in contemporary society. His social
ideal then is a refusal of what he hated: injustice, alienation, rationalism, the cosmopolitanization of French
society, urban misery. His mystique is another form of
negation that Céline desperately proposes as an antidote
for his intolerable vision of the world. The call for the
perfection of the body, for example, is really another
way of expressing his hatred of the body's decomposition. Céline's mystique was by its very nature destined
to remain an amorphous wish, an impossible desire,
though the pressure of historical events in Céline's life
hardly gave him any time to develop it further.

If Céline's anguish led him to the crime of anti-
Semitism, that same anguish led him to the creation of
three of the most powerful novels of the twentieth century. Our condemnation of the polemic should not lead
us to deny ourselves the insights and vision of the
aesthetic works, nor, for that matter, of the polemic
itself. Céline, as a reactionary writer who could not stand
his era, is hardly a unique case. Peter Viereck, writing
about such reactionaries as Balzac, Melville, and
Dostoyevsky, offers the following insight into the power
of the writer who refuses to be of his time: "What in
politics is the self-destructive vice of the extreme reactionary—his remoteness from the present—sometimes
becomes his virtue in art. The remoteness may give him
the perspective, the detachment that facilitates imaginative flights. Therefore, the most objectionable and big-
oted reactionary may become in his art the most profound psychologist, the most sensitive moralist. . . .

What counts most is not their sometimes embarrassing politics but their insights into the soul and the wounds it suffers from a too-shallow kind of liberal material progress."[6] Céline's insight into his generation's madness allowed him to foresee with accuracy the coming war, but, unfortunately, his remoteness from the present prevented him from guessing the consequences of his form of political engagement. His naïveté with regard to those consequences is, in fact, hardly believable.

To use Péguy's distinction again, it was Céline's departure from his "mystique" and his dirtying his hands in "politics" that really compromised him. Had he limited himself to the expression of a racist mysticism, he might have suffered little more than, say, a Montherlant who indulged himself in fantasies about the meaning of the swastika. But Céline also offered political proposals in his polemic. First, he concretely proposed that the Jews be placed in the front lines so as to let them know that it would be they who would suffer if they kept pushing for an anti-Hitler crusade. Second, and far more seriously, he called for a Franco-German alliance: "L'alliance franco-allemande, c'est la puissance judéo-britannique réduit à zéro. Le fond même du problème atteint, enfin. La Solution." ("The Franco-German alliance will reduce the Judeo-British power to nothing. Will reach the real crux of the problem, finally. The Solution.") (*L'Ecole*, p. 215.) And no war. But not even French fascists could accept this solution when Hitler was preparing to conquer Europe. Céline had assured himself the reputation of collaborator even before France was defeated. His absurd polemic had forced him into the position of being despised in nearly every quarter. Céline suddenly found himself, or so he believed, in a position comparable to that of Bardamu or one of his Ferdinands—isolated in a totally hostile world.

Though Céline seems to have had the beginnings of a persecution complex well before World War II, by the time of France's defeat he had found enough factual evidence to muster a good argument and defend his contention that he was a pariah. In 1942 he wrote a preface for another edition of *L'Ecole des cadavres* (first published in 1938) in which he vaunted his isolation:

> La parution de "L'Ecole" ne fit aucun bruit—silence total, scrupuleux de toute la presse française—y compris la pacifiste, l'antisémite, la franco-allemande, etc. etc., pas un écho, pas une ligne, le frigo intégral, la pétoche totale, le désaveu absolu. Raisons de ce hoquet unanime: "L'Ecole" était le seul texte à l'époque (journal ou livre) *à la fois et en même temps:* antisémite, *raciste,* collaborateur (avant le mot) jusqu'à l'alliance militaire immédiate, anti-anglais, antimaçon et présageant la catastrophe absolue en cas de conflit. (pp. 11–12.)

> (The appearance of *L'Ecole* didn't raise a ripple—total, scrupulous silence on the part of the entire French press— including the pacifist, the anti-Semitic, the Franco-German, etc., etc., not an echo, not a line, just a complete cold shoulder, total fear, absolute disavowal. Reasons for this unanimous belch: *L'Ecole* was the only text at the time (periodical or book) that was *at once and at the same time:* anti-Semitic, *racist,* collaborator (before the word) to the point of wanting an immediate anti-English, anti-freemason military alliance and that foresaw absolute catastrophe in case of conflict.)

And in the last years of his life he was still able to take great pleasure in writing:

> Le petit succès de mon existence c'est d'avoir tout de même réussi ce tour de force qu'ils se trouvent tous d'accord, un

instant, droite, gauche, centre, sacristies, loges, cellules, charniers, le comte de Paris, Joséphine, ma tante Odile, Kroukroubezeff, l'abbé Tirelire, que je suis le plus grand ordure vivant! (*Nord*, pp. 346–347.)

(My life's little success is to have pulled off the extraordinary feat that, for a moment, everyone is in agreement, Right, Left, Center, sacristies, loges, cells, charnel houses, the Count of Paris, Josephine, my Aunt Odile, Krukrubezev, abbé Tirelire, that I'm the greatest scum alive!)

Reality and fiction seem finally to have merged for Céline. Having at last identified with the pariahs of his fictional universe, Céline could dismiss his polemic as a sincere effort to stop the coming of the war and turn his rage against those who, through demented maliciousness, had persecuted him with exile and imprisonment in Denmark. Though some of the reprisals Céline suffered were excessive, such as the pillaging of his Paris apartment and the French government's refusal to take action when he was ill in Denmark, only his growing paranoia can explain his incapacity to understand why he was a victim. But Céline was firmly convinced that he was innocent, and, as his last novels amply demonstrate, his paranoia gave him a new approach to fiction. Fiction, for Céline, had become reality.

CHAPTER V *Délire* as Myth

Céline's flight to Germany and then to Denmark, his imprisonment and exile there, and his court battles in France came to their conclusion in 1951. He was able to return to Paris with amnesty. *Féerie pour une autre fois I,* a novel Céline had written in Denmark, appeared the following year, and a sequel, *Normance* or *Féerie II,* was published in 1954. With the exception of a few expressions of disappointment, neither work received much attention. One might suspect, however, that the critical silence was due as much to a general desire to forget Céline and the humiliations of the German Occupation as to the novels' disconcerting chaos. *Féerie I* and *II* was not a work designed to let the past rest in peace. Céline, having usurped the roles of narrator and protagonist in his work, was bent on recalling the injustice and misery he had suffered. In *Féerie I* he decided to show himself as the most maligned victim of the natural French penchant for bloodletting. In *Normance* he set forth on a cosmic scale the madness that had descended on Europe during the war, a madness of which he alone seemed to be aware. The French, still suffering from the fratricidal hatreds of the Occupation period and the traumas of Liberation, were probably in no mood to listen to Céline's megalomaniacal ravings.

Although Céline had decided to become the center of his own quasi-fictional universe, he did not reject altogether his basic novelistic techniques. In fact, the two-volume *Féerie* marks something of an evolution in the approach to the novel adopted by Céline in *Mort à crédit* and *Guignol's Band*. *Féerie I* and *Normance* also carry Céline's stylistic experimentation to a new extreme. Language is reduced to the scream and the shout, and his sentence structure is often compressed to mere fragments, without a verb, or simply a verb alone. Striving to defend himself, and, at the same time, give proof of his genius, Céline has pushed his verbal power to the limit in these works, and at times he goes beyond his limits into utter confusion.

At first glance it is even difficult to decide whether to consider these two volumes as one novel or two. The narration in *Féerie pour une autre fois I,* the first volume, takes place after the events narrated in *Normance,* the second volume. Nicole Debrie-Panel sees the structure as a typically Célinian "involution," for, if considered as a whole, the work folds back in time upon itself.[1] Yet, the two volumes can almost be read as separate works. Aside from Céline's role in each work, there is only the most tenuous connection between them: the common presence of the character Jules, a legless artist whose comic presence assures some episodic continuity. This common presence and a modicum of autobiographical continuity indicate that *Féerie I* is to be taken as something of a prologue or narrator's prelude to *Normance.*

In the usual Célinian fashion, it is only after the some
three hundred pages of *Féerie I* that the narrator turns
to evoke time past, to recall the *délire* he has known. In
this instance the narrator is Céline, rotting in his Danish
prison cell. The experience he recalls in *Normance*
may be likened to the main body of the Célinian novel,
though the past it narrates is the very recent one of Paris
during the Occupation. It is told by the protagonist,
Ferdinand Céline, though it should be made clear that
the Ferdinands who speak in the two novels are hardly
the same. In *Féerie I* the reader encounters an enraged
narrator through whom Céline seems to speak directly.
In *Normance* the narrating Ferdinand is an entirely
fictional character to whom Céline has lent his name.
Céline's two different uses of himself as a character in
these novels account for a good deal of the confusion
when one tries to see them as a single work. The reader
can quickly recognize the imprisoned Céline, but may
well be at a loss to explain his relation to the mythical
Céline of *Normance.*

Féerie pour une autre fois I, this first part of an ironic
"fairyland," is a portrait of the artist as a clowning pariah.
It is a verbal performance in *délire* given by Céline as
he plays the role he usually gave to his older narrator,
though this narrator's static present is one imposed by
prison walls, and his nearness to death seems to be quite
real.[2] The narrator's *délire* is not only a prelude to the
main body of the novel; it is also a clown show in itself,
in which Céline plays the "clown of the universe." The
clown is angry, however, as he moves to the center of
his dark stage, and the ensuing narration is a series of
gags and shrieks channeled through a rapid-fire monologue. The clown is also a vituperative, constipated
political prisoner suffering from pellagra. He is bewil-

dered, bitter, and ready to berate us one and all for the injustice that has sealed him in his dungeon. As though to add to the chaos, however, Céline opens the novel with a scene set in the "famous traitor's" apartment in Montmartre during World War II. Céline has been marked for assassination by the B.B.C., Radio Brazzaville, and the Resistance; and he wonders why a friend's wife and son have come to visit him — perhaps to kill him and be the first to claim his apartment? Neither the reader nor Céline ever finds out: Montmartre slides into the past and the prisoner comes to the front of his prison cell stage.

With the lights low, he eases into his harsh and strident monologue, alternating mad buffoonery with explosive incriminations. Céline's verbal antics now move with the irregularity of a spotlight that is jerked from side to side to illuminate first one scene and then another. The constant play of chiaroscuro leaves the reader blinking and perturbed. The ironic *féerie* too often dissolves into a mere disordered scramble of roars and shouts. Céline's monologue is a form of *délire* that mixes past, present, and future, though with no degree of consistency. He plunges into the past and offers various perspectives on its joys and, more usually, miseries: Montmartre, the Resistance, his early medical career, and other memories rush into his mind. He shifts from past to present to force us to hear the din that surrounds him and to see his pain and sickness as he speaks from his prison cell. He also projects a view of a hypothetical if improbable future. Céline is playing with the "web of time" (p. 99) to present a *féerie* for some other time:

Je vous l'écris de partout par le fait! de Montmartre chez moi! du fond de ma prison baltave! et en même temps du

bord de la mer, de notre cahute! Confusion des lieux, des
temps! Merde! C'est la féerie vous comprenez... (p. 30.)

(In fact I'm writing it for you from everywhere! from Montmartre at my place! in the bottom of my Baltic prison! and at
the same time at the seashore, from our shack! Confusion of
places, of times! Shit! This is a wonderland, you understand...)

Délire has disordered the flow of time as Céline tries to
stay abreast of the words streaming through his head.
Any attempt to impose a structure on this monologue
would falsely represent the manner in which Céline
follows one idea by association to the next. Yet, even
though his leaping back and forth in time follows no
particular order, his destruction of chronology permits
the reader to see thematic constants that are at the heart
of Céline's desire to portray himself. The disordering
of time is Céline's way of mimicking madness, but it is
also his way of depicting the evil that has crushed him.
    Narration of time past in *Féerie I* springs from Céline's
desire to be a *mémorialiste,* to preserve a record of time
past, and in this respect it foreshadows the "chronicles"
Céline sets forth in all his succeeding works. Here, however, Céline offers no ordered series of memoirs as he
jumps from one incident to another in his past. Taken as
whole, these various episodes have the value of an apol-
ogia, in the most positive sense of the word. Céline looks
back, with angry uncertainty, to see how convergent
series of past events, his well-intentioned polemic, and
the bloodthirsty momentum of the Liberation, have
reached a common point: his prison cell. It is only natural, Céline thinks, that for having attempted to warn
against *délire,* he should now be its victim. His perspective on the past is that of the innocent, the wronged,

and the unaccepting scapegoat. He is the blameless
clown who set out to save the French from themselves,
and now, through some inexorably hostile process, he
finds himself in irons. His explanations for this catastrophe are various. At times he implies that he was destined to be a sacrificial lamb since his youth:

Les gens m'ont traité pas très bien. C'était la curée bordel
sang! Ça a commencé en 14! Tous les prétextes! Au canon
d'abord puis aux ragots, à la police! J'ai voulu leur sauver la
glotte, compatriotes! leurs gueules infectes, leurs cœurs de
merde, leur faire esquiver l'Abattoir... mes livres pour ça.
(p. 25.)

(People haven't treated me very well! It's been a rush to the
slaughter, damn it to hell! It began in '14! Any pretext! With
cannon first, then with vicious gossip, to the Police! I wanted
to save their throats! compatriots! their lousy kissers, their
shitty hearts, make them avoid the slaughterhouse... my books
were for that.)

And so much for his anti-Semitism.[3]
   At other times he sees himself as a victim of the dementia that seized France with the Liberation. Then, it
is true, the Right and the Left frequently found each
other to be fair game. Céline, of course, belongs to the
vanquished:

Folie, cohue, les mêmes en Grève à l'équarrissage national!
à l'arrachage des yeux de vaincu! Les grands orgasmes des
Prudents! l'Armée Sade en piquenic d'Histoire! (p. 53.)

(Madness, mob, the same ones at the Place de la Grève, for
the national quartering! for tearing out the eyes of the defeated! great orgasms for the Prudent! The Sade Army on History's picnic!)

Délire is charged with sexuality, for in Céline's eyes the
vengeance that the French took on collaborators was a
form of rape, an unleashing of the normal hostility and
frustration within, that History suddenly authorized. As
seen by Céline, the Liberation might be likened to the
Amiral Bragueton episode in *Voyage:* History, like the
tropics, has given men the chance to show their innate
love of cruelty and carnage.

In contrast with the recent past's inhumanity, Céline
projects for himself a historical perspective that is meant
to place him in a mythical light. Céline wants to step into
historical myth as another of history's most illustrious
persecuted victims, for the historical process, as seen by
the pariah, is essentially the revelation of demented
forms of sadism as it affects individuals. Céline recalls,
for instance, time spent in Brittany and is led by association to compare himself to Chateaubriand, another
Breton exile. He finds many other predecessors. Much
in the way Philip Augustus returned from the Crusades
weakened by pellagra, Céline will return from his tribulations. Roland, too, was a victim of history's treachery,
among many others:

Vercingétorix! Pétain! Voltaire! Blanqui! Oscar Wilde! Le-
coin! Jaurès! Thorez! M. Braguet! François Ier! Sacco! c'est
des prédécesseurs un peu! et d'autres! (p. 63.)

(. . . Those are a few predecessors for you! and others, too!)

This jumbled list, putting the communist Thorez in company with the collaborator Pétain, underlines how little
Céline is interested in ideology. He is concerned only
with himself as another great figure that history has
added to its list of victims. He seems to believe firmly
that he, too, will soon be a part of historical myth:

L'Histoire, attendez! C'est pas fini! J'en suis de l'Histoire. (p. 83.)

(History, wait! It's not over yet! I'm a part of History.)

Céline thus uses to illuminate his darkness not only the immediate past but also a historical and mythical past rooted in the beginning of French history. Of this historical past he is the latest and perhaps most vociferous victim.

The past, even with its enlarged, mythical dimension, is not enough to do Céline justice, and he takes an almost exhibitionistic delight in forcing the reader to see what injustice has done to him in the present. Unlike Vigny's stoical wolf who "crève sans hurler" ("kicks off without screaming") (p. 43), Céline fully intends to scream until his misery overcomes him. He is not the only prisoner making noise, for his dark cell reverberates to a cacophony of shouts and thuds. Screams and shrieks, coming from no definite source, fill the air. The clamor of bedlam is completed by the prisoner in the neighboring cell who continually slams his head into the wall, perhaps in an effort to release the *délire* within. But Céline refuses to be drowned out by the din of lunatics. He offers snatches of poetry and song—proof that he is still alive—and soars forth to do battle with his enemies.

His monologue is at many points doubled by voices shouting at Céline. In effect, he engages in dialogues with himself in which he mimics his enemies, though it is always to baffle or denounce them. His most persistent adversary, for example, is a nameless speaker who would like to see Céline sent to Siberia:

Je vous voie en Sibérie! médecin! missionnaire! ours! cadavre! (p. 95.)

(I see you in Siberia! doctor! missionary! bear! corpse!)

Céline, thinking of other victims of the Liberation's *épuration*, shows that his heart is overflowing with love of country and sardonically defends himself:

"Ah vous me découvrez l'Idéal! Ah là, qu'on sera heureux ensemble! des milles et des milliers là-bas! ensemble se parlant français! Joye! Joye! Joye! comme on s'embrassera! mon vice là moi, j'avoue, mon seul: le parler français!" (p. 95.)

("Oh you're showing me the Ideal! Ah there we'll be happy together! thousands and thousands there! together speaking French! Joy! Joy! Joy! how we'll hug each other! there's my vice, I admit it, my only one: speaking French!")

Céline's buffoonery and vituperation allow him to baffle his nameless opponent, though the insulting speaker is not the only "character" Céline introduces in order to vanquish him. The French ambassador, the man Céline believes is responsible for much of his misery, claims that he is Louis XV, among others, and demands that Céline adore him. The prisoner haughtily refuses his overtures and makes his tormentor look like a fool. When a reporter comes to interview him, Céline falls into Rabelaisian mimicry and promptly turns his visitor into a babbling idiot:

"Ah mon cher Maître, la France est folle!... Ah! l'infernal quiproquo!... le génie irradiant d'Europe! . . . Ah, bo! bo! bo! bo! cher Maître! Ah, c'est effroyable! tenez que la ba! ba! ba! ve! me sèche! Mi! mi! mina! Bobo! nable!... Ce trou! ce trou! la! vous retrou! trou! ve! vous! vous! . . . Je ne sais plus ce que je dis!" (p. 78.)

("Ah, my dear *Maître*, France is mad!... Oh the infernal mis-understanding!... the radiating genius of Europe! . . . Ah! bo! bo! bo! bo! dear *Maître!* Ah, it's frightful! look my slo! slo!

bber drys up! Mi! mi! mina! Bobo! nable!... This hole! this hole! there! you rehole [refind]! . . . I don't know what I'm saying anymore!")

This madcap dialogue, inserted chaotically into the flow of the monologue, is only one of the narrative tricks Céline uses to joust with his reader while he increases the volume in his mock pandemonium.

Céline forces the reader to follow his monologue in the expectation that he will reverse field at any moment. By undermining every statement he makes, every accusation he has received, he seems to believe that he can emerge triumphant, perhaps purified through excess degradation. At one moment, for example, he joyfully proclaims that he is the worst traitor in History, having sold the Maginot Line for a kiss. At the next moment he exposes himself without shame, forcing the reader to inspect the disastrous results of his constipation and pellagra. And the entire narrative is undercut when he admits that: "je déconne, c'est naturel... après les tourments que j'ai subis!" ("I'm running off at the mouth, it's natural... after the pains I've endured!") (p. 174).

Perhaps the crowning image of this delirious series of associations comes when Céline imagines that his enemies, many from the Académie Française, are taking him out of his cell in a wheelbarrow, only to dump him in a manure pile. The humiliation is complete when Sartre (or Tartre), shouting that Céline was paid for his anti-Semitism, urinates on him. Humiliation seems to be synonymous with justification in Céline's mind. The prison cell, then, is only a common locus around which the insane narrative swings in a chaotic fashion. There is no progression, no development, only the incessant harangue of the pariah who lays bare his sickness while he seeks vengeance by groveling in the excrement his enemies pile upon him.

Céline's burlesque has the least bite when he projects his narrative into the future, usually to imagine the huge benefits that will accrue to him and to the reader from *Féerie I*. Like *Gargantua*, *Féerie I* will give the reader who is fortunate enough to purchase it great medicinal aid; and if it will not cure him of an exemplary case of rectal cancer, it will at least enable him to have a happy death. On the other hand, Céline sees himself leaving prison with all the honor he deserves — especially if we buy a copy of *Féerie I*, or even three copies. He will have a bicycle, a villa or two, a place reserved in the Panthéon, and if the future treats him well, his own city, Célinegrad.

There is a measure of despair in this buffoonery. The sick clown looks to a future that will redeem the past, but he also looks for an escape from the present. The darkness, with its increasing pandemonium, is intolerable. Céline finds himself trapped in a situation that concretely reproduces the image of life that he had previously formed in more metaphorical terms: a place without light inhabited by madness. Thus he must seek a form of comic redemption that, set apart from the horrors of Occupied France and the pain of his dungeon, can only be found in the future. The redemption can be found only in a *féerie* and at some other time. Hence the inscription that serves as a prologue to *Féerie pour une autre fois I:*

L'horreur des réalités!
Tous les lieux, noms, personnages, situations, présentés dans ce roman, sont imaginaires! Absolument imaginaires!

Aucun rapport avec aucune réalité! Ce n'est là qu'une
"Féerie"... et encore!... pour une autre fois!

(Horror of realities!

All the places, names, characters, and situations presented
in this novel are imaginary! Absolutely imaginary! No relationship with any reality! This is only a fairyland... and even
more!... for some other time!)

Céline's reality and his imaginary world have coincided,
and his reaction is to reverse the terms by screaming his
refusal of reality. He must, however, find some perspective that will offer a view of a future that is not so "imaginary," and that future can only be a fantasy.

Thanks to Céline's marvelous future, he can leave
prison, at least for the moment. He imagines the bicycle
that his *Féerie* will enable him to buy. He then gets on it
and pedals back in time to the Montmartre of the Occupation period. Céline juggles his temporal perspectives to allow himself to participate in what is presumedly one of his memoirs while seeming to narrate
it as a prisoner. The forward-backward movement of
the narration spins the reader around so that Céline may
step into a farce in which he is both the narrator and the
cuckolded victim. His future bicycle carries him back
in time to the studio of Jules, the *cul-de-jatte* artist.
Future time becomes time past as Céline disapprovingly
describes the antics of Jules, "the clown in a box," the
legless artist who wheels about in a wagon.

Jules becomes for the moment the focal point of
Céline's vision, much as he is in *Normance*. Céline
seems entranced by this impish cripple, an evil clown,
who pinches the buttocks of the girls who love to model
for him. The narrator-clown is indignant as he watches
Jules throw missiles at unwanted visitors while he in-

discriminately gulps down Champagne, paints, and gasoline. Much like Harpo Marx, he is living anarchy, but with a more malicious turn. Jules has Lili, Céline's wife, pose nude beneath a lewd green light and then — the final insult to the reproving narrator — seduces her, as best he can. Céline, a cuckolded Pierrot, is fascinated by these outrages, but is unable to react. This comic evil force seems to hypnotize him. Even when Jules takes advantage of his legless condition to call Ferdinand a "Boche" in front of a hostile crowd, Céline can only sputter in anger as he finds himself about to be massacred as well as cuckolded:

Il savait parfaitement, Tronc de Fiel! tronc scélérat hypocrite! Il savait ce qu'il avait dit! qu'il m'avait désigné traître! traité! les crocs que je voyais! les crocs de personnes! leurs babines relevées! ils me déchiraient un mot de plus!... (p. 282.)

(That bilious Trunk knew perfectly well! hypocritical scoundrel Trunk! He knew what he'd said! that he'd pointed me out as a traitor! dealt with! the fangs I saw! people's fangs! their fat lips rolled back! another word and they'd tear me apart!...)

Céline, the buffoon who baffles all opposition in his monologue, now finds himself to be the clown who is about to be clubbed. Humiliation is perhaps again a form of justification; the hapless clown in any case can hardly be blamed for the evil that surrounds him.

Céline has turned his narrator into a marionette who participates in another savage but hilarious guignol. Of course, the puppet is supposedly Céline himself, the well-intentioned pariah who steps inadvertently into every trap that is laid in his path. Within the context of

Féerie I this guignol episode appears to be presented much for its own sake as a form of much-needed relief from the monologue's incessant jousting. But this comic interlude also ties *Féerie I* to *Normance*, where Ferdinand, the delirious marionette, is jostled about while he tries to cope with his "fairyland" vision and, at the same time, avoid destruction. Jules also has his role as a malicious artist in *Normance*, though on a cosmic scale. The farcical episode with Jules comes to an end when Ferdinand undergoes an attack of nauseous vertigo, the certain prelude to *délire* in Céline's works. This vertigo also ties *Féerie I* to *Normance* and foreshadows the attack of nausea that opens *Normance*'s series of hallucinations. Nausea again is a prelude to the recapitulation and purgation of time past.

Céline breaks off this episode with Jules and returns to his monologue, though he continues to refer to the incident with the crippled imp as though it were a factual memory. The episode, set within the stream of memories that flows through Céline's mind, gains a semblance of authenticity that roots it in Céline's life as a point of departure for *Normance*. The monologue progresses no more after this episode than it did before. It turns in circles as Céline alternately clowns and rages. In one sense his monologue represents the extreme development of the maniacal monologues he created in *Mort à crédit* and *Guignol's Band*. In *Féerie I* the monologue of comic obsession is no longer transposed and presented obliquely through the protagonist's consciousness. Rather, it is hurled directly at the reader with a frenetic intensity rarely encountered in the earlier works. Céline has attempted to transmute his wrath into the delirious language of the earlier novels, but *Féerie I* lacks the narrative structure that made this *délire* immediately accessible to the reader in those works. As a result, the reader's first impression is that in *Féerie I* he confronts a work of utter madness and confusion. Yet, Céline's nameless opponent in *Féerie I* charges that this *délire* is only simulated. In accusing himself Céline, who never claimed in later years to be more than a stylist, reveals that he is undertaking a feverish narrative experiment. Though the experiment may be judged a failure, it is an amazing demonstration of Céline's effort to jolt the reader with the most immediate forms of emotive communication.

Taken as a whole, then, Céline's disordered monologue seems to defy description. His soliloquy is a burlesque *de profundis* that bursts with self-confidence. It is a candid self-portrayal that takes a hilarious turn when it seems ready to bog down in self-pity. It is a caustic indictment of the Liberation's excesses and a series of comic demonstrations of Céline's intellectual and human limitations. The monologue, aimed like a gun at Céline's enemies, radically narrows Céline's scope while it intensifies the heat of the attack to the point of incomprehensibility. Sheer verbal abuse, however intensive, is not enough to depict the catastrophes that have befallen Céline. Thus, after having portrayed his present misery, he has written a sequel, *Normance,* in an attempt to raise the past to the level of myth. His present plight is so terrible that it can be adequately explained only as the result of cosmic forces of madness, those forces against which Céline has always been in revolt and which have finally, in some magical way, contrived to bring about his downfall.

Normance carries a dedication to Pliny the Elder and to Gaston Gallimard. In light of Céline's later vitupera-

tion against his publisher, one might well think the latter
dedication to be more than a little ironic. But Pliny the
Elder, the Roman natural historian who perished while
observing one of Vesuvius' eruptions, is close to Céline's heart. In *Normance* Céline dons the mask of natural
historian or chronicler, and his task, he claims, is to
observe a Vesuvius-like eruption. The exploding vol-
cano is another of Céline's metaphors for history, and
he, like another Pliny, is a dedicated scientific observer
who carefully notes each variation in the historical
cataclysm that manifests itself in the form of an aerial
bombardment of Paris. This cataclysm is only a vague
historical event, for it is, in essence, an hallucinated
projection of the dementia that nausea reveals. At the
beginning of the novel, Ferdinand reports that he has
just fallen down an elevator shaft in his apartment building; this gives rise to another attack of nauseous vertigo.
His head battered, he is carried to his apartment, and
then begins the vision of the colossal bombardment that
occupies nearly the entire novel. Céline's Vesuvius is
created by the coincidence of the madness within and
history's *délire*.

The Ferdinand of *Normance*, like the narrator in *Féerie
I,* is again on a darkened stage from which he directs the
reader's attention to illuminating flashes. These flashes
are now those of exploding bombs. His stage is the Montmartre apartment building where, first from his apartment, and then from the lobby, he describes the unending rain of destruction that seems to engulf all of Paris.
At the same time Ferdinand frantically points out Jules,
who, in some unknown way, has climbed atop a Montmartre windmill. As Jules scoots around, making signs
and ringing a bell, it seems to Ferdinand that the cripple's antics are instructions that direct the bombarding

aircraft. The indestructible imp has become a demonic artist. Ferdinand is also a beleaguered participant in his chronicle. He is knocked about by other tenants who crowd into the lobby and under a table where they soil themselves in fear. When Ferdinand is not describing the bombing, he is trying to avoid Normance, a gigantically fat tenant. Normance, who sleeps through most of the bombardment, spends his waking moments trying to force Ferdinand to give medical attention to the giant's unconscious wife. The fat man's favored method of persuasion is to throw his obese mass on top of the bruised and nearly crippled doctor. Ferdinand avenges himself when, in search of medicine, he directs a mob of tenants to use Normance as a battering ram against a locked door. In typical Célinian fashion, the giant's head is squashed.

When the bombardment is at last over, another crowd mysteriously appears, this one intent on killing the well-known traitor, Ferdinand Céline. Ferdinand hides on the floor in Normance's gore, while the crowd abuses him verbally, then disappears, and returns carrying Normance's body. They throw the huge, bloody mass down the elevator shaft, supposedly into the Montmartre catacombs. Ferdinand is rescued by Ottavio, a vigorous friend who saves him from the bloodthirsty but cowardly mob. Ottavio carries the disabled chronicler upstairs to Ferdinand's now ruined apartment. In search of water, Ottavio knocks a hole in the wall. Through it Ferdinand, his wife, and Ottavio enter the adjoining building. Here they find the famous actor, Norbert, sitting silently at a fully set table. Aside from lacking window panes, the apartment shows no sign of the recent, cataclysmic bombardment, although Ferdinand's quest for water does turn up a pair of mysterious bodies, one lying in a bath-

tub full of cooling Champagne bottles. When asked what
it all means, Norbert states that he is awaiting the Pope,
Churchill, and Roosevelt.

The novel ends on this marvelously absurd note. Before leaving the apartment, Pliny-Ferdinand replaces
his tattered clothes with a toga made of a dish towel. In
the final pages this Montmartre Roman finds himself
wandering in the street, at the same spot where in *Féerie
I* he was sick in front of Jules's studio. This circular
movement completes the absurd narration in a manner
perhaps designed to suggest mythical time, for the novel
turns in upon itself, undermining its own reality, while
the circularity shows that the hero has survived the ordeal that history has inflicted upon him. Ferdinand
wanders in the street as a mammoth deluge of his papers
fills the air and floats down to cover the ground. The
papers recall his lost novels and legends telling of his
past exploits. As they whirl about Ferdinand he again
loses consciousness and completes the cycle of catastrophes.

The world of *Normance* is described by a would-be
chronicler who is trapped within the confines of his own
delirious vision. Céline is pushing his use of a deliriously unreliable center of consciousness to its extreme
limit. Ferdinand's hallucinatory crisis opens the novel
and presumedly lasts until the novel ends and he collapses again in front of Jules's studio. This use of a constantly hallucinated narrator is the culmination of the
delirious extravaganzas that *Guignol's Band* presented.
Since the entire novel is told by a hallucinating narrator,
Céline has removed all constraints concerning what he
can narrate: anything can happen. The gratuitous absurdity and the nearly magical madness that threaten to

dominate the preceding novels are given free rein. Only
the polemic can rival *Normance* in presenting a vision
of a magical apocalypse.

With the context of the novel, Ferdinand's perspective on *Normance*'s chaos is somewhat divided. On the
one hand, he is the mock scientific observer, the natural
historian who records the unfolding of a cataclysm, even
if it takes place in his own head. On the other hand, he
is the often battered participant who seeks to survive
his own hallucination; he is the mythical hero whose
exploits the chronicler will offer to posterity. This polarity presents a narrative problem analogous to the one
Céline faced in *Voyage au bout de la nuit*, where, to
compensate for his picaro's limited vision, he used an
older narrator who could observe from a disengaged
vantage point. In *Normance* Ferdinand is both the victim
of a hostile world and the narrator who is a creator of the
myth that is necessary to encompass the dimensions of
this volcanic outburst of *délire*. In his chronicle Ferdinand is both Joinville and Saint Louis, or, in another
respect, both Pliny and Vesuvius. Even though the
chaos of the elements that Ferdinand observes comple-
ments the mad disorder in which he is ensnared, he has
difficulty playing the role of both chronicler and hero.
This confusion only serves to augment the bedlam that
makes up the narrative, for Ferdinand never really
succeeds in joining his narrative roles.

The furious bombardment that Ferdinand untiringly
observes is an appropriate decor for the absurd events
that constitute the novel's minimal plot. Its ultimate
significance, if there is any sense to this sound and fury,
is its representation on a mythical and perhaps allegorical level of the eruption of *délire* that has caught
Céline in its path. Ferdinand's fall at the beginning of

Normance appears to be Céline's bow to the semi-naturalistic conventions he sometimes respects. The fall serves as an excuse for the unleashing of *délire* in the novel, though it might also be seen as a symbolic statement of Céline's fall into the abyss of *délire*, or, more simply, as a symbol of his miserable condition. Once *délire* is unleashed, however, Ferdinand's chronicle is a record of an essentially static vision of a never-ending *féerie* of fire and explosions:

des coups de mines de trente quarante tonnes!... si la surface polke, vous pensez! si les immeubles embardent... ballottent... arrachent leur trottoirs! Hop! renfoncent!... restent là... fendus, penchés, bancals, songeux... et *tarrraboum!* d'une autre rese-cousse tout repart! l'ouragan! l'orchestre! d'autres bâtisses s'échappent, se retournent... toutes pendantes! ça va nous arriver nous-mêmes!... l'autre genre, c'est les maisons qui glissent... s'étirent!... s'élongent... en hauteur... loukoums!... partent s'emmêler plus haut chaque *braoum!* quel travail! et ça s'enroule gigote dénoue! le bacchanal plus haut que le ciel!... (p. 113.)

(explosions of mines weighing thirty, forty tons!... what a polka, you can imagine! how the buildings jump about... sway back and forth... tear up their sidewalks! Whoops! rush back!... stay there... all split open, bent over, wobbly, pensive... and *baboom!* with another re-jolt everything starts up again! the hurricane! the orchestra! other shacks take off, flip around... hanging there! that's going to happen to us!... the other kind is the houses that slide away... stretch out!... become elon-gated... in height... like soft sugar candies!... take off and get mixed with each other higher up at each *boom!* what a job! and they coil up, jerk about, come loose! an uproar that's higher than the sky!...)

These "cosmomediumic storms" that fill the skies are a projection of the madness that is "on and in the earth"

(*Féerie I*, p. 85). Yet the destruction makes no progress. It turns about itself with an unvarying fury that never seems to advance or diminish.

Ferdinand's hallucination in *Normance* may be compared in one respect to Bardamu's fascinated vision in *Voyage*. He watches endless streams of objects that expand, swell, melt, and undergo other forms of destructive distortion:

l'Académie fond... en beige... en vert... dégouline au Quai... puis à la Seine... la Coupole flotte un moment... se retourne! coule!... Ah, et la Madeleine et la Chambre!... elles ont l'air de s'envoler... gonflées montgolfières... elles s'élèvent un petit peu... balancent... passent bleu! rouge! blanc! éclatent! (p. 111.)

(the Academy melts... in beige... in green... flows down to the Quai... then into the Seine... the Cupola floats for a moment, turns over, sinks!... Ah, and the Madeleine and the Chamber of Deputies!... they look as if they're going to fly off... swollen up like lighter-than-air balloons... they rise a little... sway... turn blue! red! white! blow up!)

Bardamu, however, was fascinated with the effects of decomposition as it developed in time. There is no temporal dimension in *Normance*, for time has become a static present. Ferdinand permanently and untiringly describes a world of total disorder that cannot run down because it is not really in motion. It is a world of utter stasis, of utter immobility. In the Célinian universe the inevitable consequence of stasis is omnipresent devastation as the forces of *délire* pursue themselves in a circle.

Unending, eternal destruction is, of course, nothing less than hell. Ferdinand's hallucination has granted him the privilege of a look into the bowels of the inferno itself. Or, as Céline put it in *Féerie I*, when he screamed:

Pétrarque, Dantus, Homère, Prout Prout! bout bout! l'iniquité du fond des âges! Ils imaginaient des Enfers, nous il est là! (p. 152.)

(Petrarch, Dantus! Homer! Prout Prout! [read Proust] bout bout! iniquity from the depths of the ages! They imagined Hell, for us it's here!)

Ferdinand is a privileged observer whose *délire*, in the full poetic sense of the term, permits him to see a hell on earth of which no one else in the novel seems aware. If *Normance*'s world is hell, then there must be a demonic principle underlying it, a principle that is no longer incarnated in the Jews, but in Jules, the malicious artist:

J'ai vu des bombarderies d'autres guerres qu'étaient vraiment retourneuses du sol et des paysages, mais des déployments de fureurs volcaniques féeriques pareils demandent que l'Esprit participe!... abjure le Bien! appelle au Mal! Le Mal c'est pas tout le monde qui l'a! je le connais moi le Mal dans sa caisse! là-haut, comme il est joli... ivrogne, pissat, cochon, satyre! tronc! scélérat!... là-haut sur le moulin qu'il est! ah! (p. 27.)

(I saw bombardments in other wars that really plowed up the ground and the countryside, but such wondrous volcanic furies demand that the Spirit take part in it... abjure the Good! make call to Evil! It ain't everyone who's got Evil! I know him, Evil in his box! up there isn't he a fine one... drunkard, pisser, pig, satyr! trunk! scoundrel!... up there on the windmill he is!)

Jules, the artist who represents the gratuitous and perhaps magical creation of this inferno, is again the focal

point of Ferdinand's vision. In *Féerie I* Jules heaped
scorn and ridicule on Ferdinand with impunity. Now
he triumphs over Ferdinand's perceptions as, from the
top of the windmill, he joyfully directs and orchestrates
the multicolor holocaust that Ferdinand must try to describe. Just as Jules once cuckolded the narrating Pierrot,
now he turns Ferdinand into a ludicrous observer who
can scarcely cope with what he sees.

Albert Paraz insisted on *Normance*'s eschatological
ambitions when he wrote: "As for *Normance*, you are
wrong to try to read it like a novel. It is an apocalypse.
Take the Bible and read it; you will see that you cannot
read it all at once." [4] Seen through the eyes of a cuckolded Pierrot, however, it is a rather buffoon apocalypse,
one that finds its source in a demonic satyr. Not only is
it comic in its mechanical repetition of catastrophe, but
it is burlesque by its very arbitrariness. The entire berserk cosmos impinges on the consciousness of the clown
as though to mock him, perhaps to impose new forms of
humiliation on him, as when, for instance, a building
soars into the air after much hesitation:

Je vous disais: le palais du "16" s'envole plus, il gonfle seulement... voire! voire!... il oscille, il branle, il s'arrache! il me
surprend! ah! et il s'élève! zut! j'ai déconné... il vogue!...

(I was telling you: the palace at number 16 isn't flying away
now, it's just swelling up... indeed! indeed!... it's wavering,
it's shaking, it tears itself up! it surprises me! ah! and it's
going up! nuts! I was blathering... it's sailing!...)

It floats pointlessly for a moment and then descends:

il vogue entre les avions... les projecteurs... il se balance au-
dessus du moulin!... ah!... et juste au-dessus de son empla-

cement! entre le "12" et le "15"... il perd de hauteur... il arrive
à l'endroit exact... il hoche branquille... et il se replante!...
mais dégonflé... le voilà tout dégonflé!... tout minci!... rape-
tissé!... (p. 195.)

(it's sailing among the airplanes... the searchlights... it's swaying above the windmill... ah!... and right over its site! between
number 12 and number 15... it's losing altitude... it's coming
to the exact spot... it nods, stumbles... and it fixes itself again...
but deflated... there it is all deflated!... all small!... shrunk!...)

Ferdinand's hallucinations ridicule him by their very
indecisiveness. It is as though Vesuvius had decided to
tease Pliny before flinging molten lava on him. *Normance*
is unique in that Céline has created in it a clown's apocalypse.

As a meticulous chronicler, Ferdinand is also a self-
conscious historian whose constant reflections on his
task set off the *féerie* in all its burlesque absurdity:

Je dois tout vous noter! je vous note! ils achèteront plus tard
mes livres, beaucoup plus tard, quand je serai mort, pour
étudier ce que furent les premiers séismes de la fin, et de la
vacherie du tronc des hommes, et les explosions des fonds
d'âme... ils savaient pas, ils sauront!... un Déluge mal observé
c'est toute une Ere entière pour rien!... Toute une humanité
souffrante qu'à juste servi les asticots!... Voilà le blasphème et
le pire! Gloire à Pline! (p. 25.)

(I must make a note of everything for you! I'm noting it down
for you! they'll buy my books later, much later, when I'm
dead, to study what were the first earthquakes of the end and
of the shittiness in men's bodies, and the explosions from the
soul's depths... they didn't know, they'll find out!... a badly
observed Deluge is a whole era for nothing!... a whole suffering humanity that just helped out the maggots!... That's
blasphemy and the worst! Glory to Pliny!)

Ferdinand is comically didactic, for it hardly seems necessary to stress that "the world's harmony is not at all
what people imagine" (p. 60). This commentary on the
chronicler's art creates a type of burlesque double perspective, for the reader views Ferdinand as Ferdinand
views himself while he watches Ferdinand try to cope
with his absurd vision. The result is a comic juxtaposition of pretention and reality, though "reality" in this
instance must be seen in the delirious *féerie* that over-
whelms Ferdinand. Since the standard for comic judgment is in itself burlesque, there is established a play of
comic mirrors that, much as in *Guignol's Band,* undermines any belief in any reality, except the war's *délire.*

As a participant in his hallucination, Ferdinand is
considerably less disengaged than when he is playing
historian. Like his Ferdinand predecessors, the Ferdinand Céline of *Normance* is often embroiled in a desperate situation that threatens him with sudden annihilation, and he appears to be less in danger from the
bombing than from his fellow tenants. When Ferdinand
is not fulfilling his task as chronicler, he is usually
telling of his efforts to escape their desire to flay him
alive. Yet, because the novelistic world of *Normance*
is limited to the one created by Ferdinand's *délire,* the
other characters cannot really intervene in the novel.
We see them only as mute presences whose occasional
shrieks and shouts could either be a part of his hallucinations or voices that penetrate Ferdinand's consciousness from a world beyond the one delimited by his
délire. For example, Ferdinand shouts at Normance to
ask where the cannon fire he hears is coming from:

— Eh, Normance! Normance!
Je l'appelle... je lui hurle.

— D'ou ils tirent?
Mastodonte idiot il sait pas!...
— Quoi? Quoi?
— Les canons?
— Quoi? Quoi?
Broum! Broum!
— Hippopotame, zut!
Y a pas de conversation possible. (p. 82.)

("Hey, Normance! Normance!"
I'm calling him... I'm screaming at him.
"Where are they shooting from?"
The stupid mastodon, he doesn't know!...
"What? What?"
"The cannons?"
"What? What?"
Boom! Boom!
"Hippopotamus, nuts!"
Conversation isn't possible.)

No conversation is possible, because in *Normance* there is only one voice. Much like *Féerie I, Normance* is another form of monologue, a gigantic verbal performance in which one voice mimes a personal apocalypse. As a megalomaniacal demonstration of sheer energy, it has no equivalent in even Céline's works.

The other characters are present in this *délire* to the extent that they represent a danger the hero must overcome, and in the latter part of the novel they are increasingly ready to draw and quarter Ferdinand, the well-known traitor. When dawn comes and the bombardment ends, Ferdinand gives up his role of chronicler to take up that of the harassed hero who tells of his ordeal. Ferdinand's perspective on this demented world is then that of the disabled scapegoat, a pariah perhaps, first viewing the world from the bloody floor, and then from an upside-down position as Ottavio carries him on his shoulder. Lying on the floor, undergoing additional humiliation as he lies in blood and plaster, Ferdinand is a privileged observer of the mob that wants to slaughter him. He is an unwilling *voyeur* who sees a world in red. As an upside-down observer, he gives the reader access to a world that is precisely that—upside down. Atop Ottavio's shoulder, Ferdinand's perspective on things is reversed: he goes in quest of water and can find only a bathtub full of Champagne and a stray body. Although these curious perspectives are highly suggestive, especially with regard to Céline's portraying his constant humiliation and persecution, ultimately they do little more than vary our view of this disconcertingly absurd world.

Assuming that in the latter part of the novel Ferdinand is playing the role of the mythical hero who will survive his many trials, Ferdinand's survival and the circular return to the novel's beginning, in front of Jules's studio, suggest, much as in *Guignol's Band*, that he represents the victorious hero, broken down but victorious in Célinian terms. The fantasy events in the last part of *Normance* also confirm this interpretation. The absurd events do of course lend themselves to other interpretations. Ferdinand's role as a hero who has triumphed over madness and mob hostility is, in any case, subordinate to his role as narrator of the delirious destruction that takes up three fourths of the novel, and this is perhaps the novel's major weakness. It is very difficult to see a relationship between the plot and the novel's vision of *délire*, though it might appear that Céline is trying to grant himself nearly mythical status in an allegory about France's demise.

What is one to make of these two works when taken as a whole? In *Féerie I* Céline offers what appears to be a portrait of himself. Fictional elements are generally subordinated to his explicit purpose of depicting himself for the reader—and berating the reader. The turbulent monologue is a dramatization of Céline's plight as he wishes it to be seen. In *Normance,* although Céline has given his name to an entirely fictional Ferdinand, the novel's absurd events are set in an autobiographical framework in order to relate them to the fate of the prisoner in *Féerie I.* Yet the distinction between autobiography and fiction is blurred. The political prisoner in *Féerie I* and *Normance*'s delirious Ferdinand seem, in Céline's mind at least, to be the same, and one must recognize a fictional creation in the political prisoner as in the delirious hero; or, conversely, for Céline his fictional creation in *Normance* is as real as the political prisoner he shows himself to be. Like the Jarry who carried Ubu's pistols or the Nietzsche who signed his last letters "Dionysos," Céline seems to have fallen completely into the existential fallacy. He seems to have believed that he had become a sacrificial victim for the entire universe. Fiction and reality have merged in the hallucination that Céline seems to believe to be a truer form of reality than either.

Only the simulation of madness can convey the truth of Céline's personal catastrophe, and that truth can only be grasped, it would appear, on a mythical level. As a chronicler, Céline has attempted to create the myth of his destruction by the gratuitous forces of madness that erupted before and after the Liberation. One might prefer to speak of an allegory with regard to *Normance,* for it is possible with a little ingenuity to see an almost one to one correspondence between the events in the novel and the period's historical events. For example, as David Hayman has pointed out, Normance, the slaughtered giant, is probably to be equated with France, and one could make other, equally ponderous identifications.[5] Céline perhaps intended for the novel to have an allegorical significance, but his fervent desire to make explicit his relation to the narrative destroys its representational level.

Not only is the general symbolic level so obvious as to be trivial, but Céline constantly intervenes to force the reader to see the meaning of events. When he is hiding in Normance's gore, for instance, Céline must cry out that it is because the B.B.C. has been inciting the crowd to murder him:

"Londres" a donné mon adresse! voilà ce qu'ils racontent... et pas que Londres! aussi Brazzaville!... et que j'étais un sale pornographe... libidineux en plus de traître, le plus ou- trageant du siècle!... à faire rougir les pissotières! qu'il fallait nettoyer la France et la langue française d'un sexographe démoralisateur, dégrammeur pareil qui souillait la Patrie sacrée et son patrimoine littéraire!... que jamais ça serait plus la France si on égorgeait pas ce porc! moi, le porc! (pp. 285–286.)

("London" gave out my address! that's what they're saying... and not just London! Brazzaville, too!... and that I'm a filthy pornographer... libidinous besides being a traitor, the most outraging of the century!... enough to make the public urinals blush! that France and the French language had to be purged of such a language-destroying, demoralizing sexographer who was sullying the sacred Fatherland and its literary patri- mony!... that it would never be France again if they didn't cut that pig's throat! that's me, the pig!)

Céline's overwhelming desire to decry the injustices perpetrated against him would not allow him to achieve,

fortunately perhaps, his project of portraying his disaster
on an allegorical level.

Céline did not succeed in creating an allegory because
he was too bewildered, too astonished even, to arrive
at any real explanation of his fate. Ferdinand's cries,
"y a des forces fantastiques en branle!" ("there are
some fantastic forces in movement!") (p. 32) or "Y a des
forces de magie c'est tout!" ("there's some magic forces
that's all!") (p. 35), are the cries of a baffled man. The
word "Jew" might well be substituted for "fantastic
forces" or "magic" as an adequate means of explaining
the madness that has gratuitously persecuted Céline.
In *Féerie pour une autre fois* Céline has, of course, given
up his anti-Semitism, but he has advanced very little
beyond the polemic in his capacity to deal with his fear
of *délire*. Fascinated and repelled at the same time by
the violence he has seen at work, Céline seems to have
come to believe that only by emulating dementia could
he escape from its attractions.

In *Féerie I* Céline turned his rage against a few specific targets — Sartre, the French ambassador, the Resistance in general — that he could easily blame for his
misery. No single person or group, however, could be
held totally responsible for the catastrophe that had
befallen Céline and, in Céline's mind, France. Thus he
turned from venting his wrath on specific causes, in
Féerie I, to portraying in *Normance* the cosmic forces
that had brought him to ruin. In *Normance* the battle is
joined between Céline, the mythical hero and chronicler
of myth, and the universe's devastating powers of *délire*.
Yet the portrayal of such a conflict necessitated at least
a general comprehension of the historical and social
forces that had contrived to bring Céline to his state of
ruin. His failure to possess this understanding is, in many
respects, the failure of the novel. The riotously absurd

concatenation of events in *Normance*, however in-
triguing it may be, fails as a mythical allegory and has
no real moral or intellectual dimension, not even a consistent view of the absurd, that would elevate the narrative above the level of cosmic buffoonery.

Cosmic buffoonery, coming from Céline's pen, is still
an accomplishment that many lesser writers would envy.
His frantic slapstick and burlesque *délire* endow the
novel with a curious force. As a gratuitous verbal performance, *Féerie pour une autre fois* probably has no
equal in modern literature. Céline is visibly present in
his efforts to bend his obsessions and paranoia to fit a
mythical mold that will dramatize and explain his very
real misery. The reader is inevitably struck with admiration for the very frenzy of Céline's struggle. He sees
that Céline is grappling with a problem whose solution
can never be found through mere verbal energy, that
Céline is wrestling with a personal demon that he tries
to shout down—and Céline's volume has never been
greater. The greater the incomprehensibility of his disaster, the more Céline seems to believe that his verbal
magic can work a counter-spell against the evil that has
caused it. Yet the reader also sees that Céline's revolt
has turned into a parody of itself. His refusal has become
a series of comic obsessions that generate an incredible
amount of noise, but represent ultimately no more than
a cosmic belch of disgust. Taken together, then, *Féerie I*
and *Normance* are Céline's last expression of a visceral
refusal of the undigested and indigestible past that the
earlier novels tried to purge. They are also the first expression of his revolt against history and its collective
manifestations of *délire* that the last novels will present
on the scale of nations, if not the cosmos.

CHAPTER VI   History as *Délire*

The failure of *Féerie pour une autre fois* did not cause Céline to question his basic approach to writing. Having become the hero of his own hallucinated world, he was determined henceforth to pursue in "chronicle" form the narration of his own catastrophes. *Normance*'s failure did perhaps cause Céline to give up pretentions of raising his misfortunes to the status of myth. His final trilogy is to be taken as an exact "chronicle" of his wanderings, beginning with his flight from France to Germany and ending with the momentary illusion that he had found safety in Denmark. That the work was written in three parts, consisting of *D'un château l'autre*, *Nord*, and *Rigodon*, is undoubtedly attributable, to some extent, to the chance success Céline enjoyed with the publication of *D'un château l'autre* (*Castle to Castle*) in 1957. Just as *Voyage* had been a revelation for that generation of readers which included Sartre, Queneau, and Henry Miller, *D'un château l'autre* awakened a new generation of readers to the then nearly forgotten existence of

Céline's extraordinary style and savage sense of humour.
Julien Gracq, for example, is not alone in being able to
say: "This book struck me, then I read others, including
Journey to the End of the Night, which appeared to me
to be less good. What interests me in his writing is above
all his very judicious and effective use of this quite
artificial language—an entirely literary language—that
he has taken from spoken language." [1] Receiving favorable criticism throughout Europe and translated immediately into German, *D'un château l'autre* gave
Céline new recognition and pointed to the approach
to fiction he was to use in his last two works, *Nord* and
Rigodon.

Céline's chronicles are somewhat disconcerting if
read in the order of their appearance. *D'un château
l'autre* tells various anecdotes about Céline's stay
at Sigmaringen, the medieval village where Hitler in-
terned the Vichy government in exile. *Nord,* published
in 1960, begins with Céline's earlier flight from France
in July, 1944, and ends with his leaving Zornhof, a fictional village near Berlin, to go north.[2] *Rigodon,* written
in the last months of Céline's life and published posthumously in 1969, picks up Céline's flight as he leaves
Zornhof and traces his travels to the north and then back
to the south to Sigmaringen. In an entirely confusing
manner, perhaps because Céline did not really finish
the novel, *Rigodon* skips over the Sigmaringen period
(November, 1944, to March, 1945) and relates his later
travels north to Denmark. In their general outline these
three chronicles appear to be accurate in their presentation of Céline's journeys, though there is much confusion about specific incidents. Their principal interest,
however, lies in Céline's vision of history as delirious
farce.

One might prefer to begin with *Nord,* which initiates
Céline's odyssey in Germany to reach Denmark, where
he believed he had safely stashed away a sizable sum
of money before the outbreak of war. After leaving Paris
and probable assassination, the doctor-picaro, accompanied by his wife, his cat, and the actor Robert Le
Vigan, first stops in Baden-Baden. Here he is the astonished underground observer who reports the ludicrous machinations of the corrupt plutocrats in a Baden-
Baden luxury hotel as they scurry after pleasure and the
caviar and Champagne that are dropped by parachute
while Germany is destroyed about them. When the
Reich decides to put a stop to this scandal, Céline and
his companions must go to Berlin. The tattered travelers
arrive during a lull in the Allied bombing and manage
to find a hotel that has been only partially destroyed by
the recent aerial holocausts. Police, spies, and spy-
hunting *Hitlerjugend* seem to be everywhere, and, when
the refugees can no longer stand the tension, Céline
decides to compromise himself totally by taking refuge
with a medical acquaintance, Dr. Harras, a 100 percent
Nazi S.S. colonel. Harras graciously receives Céline
in his underground bunkers, where, in exchange for
Céline's correcting his French accent, Harras offers
all the hospitality the crumbling Third Reich can provide.

This underground holiday can hardly last, so Harras
sends the French doctor to Zornhof, where Céline is to
"collaborate" in a study of Franco-German medical re-
lations through the ages. Céline's bit of collaboration is
quickly forgotten when he discovers that Harras has
housed him in the castle of a family of Prussian aristocrats whose intrigues, hatreds, and personal animosities
make them oblivious to the disastrous advance of the

Russians from the east. Only the baron-comte Rittmeister, senile and crippled, seems conscious of the coming destruction, and his decision to set out alone on horseback to stop the Russians with his saber points up the illusions these mad aristocrats indulge themselves in. Céline, the wandering scapegoat, finds his lot to be a constant struggle in an environment where he can only expect the worst, if not from the anti-Nazi villagers, from the murderous aristocrats or the French prisoners at Zornhof. *Nord,* then, sets forth in its final episodes a microcosm that reflects the insanity of a world bent on self-destruction in its nihilistic rage.

Rigodon takes Céline from Zornhof and shifts him from one train to another going back and forth across the embers of the Third Reich. His travels are a rigadoon, a dance of madness that condenses Céline's journeys to their essence of constant flight. As much time is spent struggling with mobs in train stations as in movement. Céline's train trip, one of the longest in literature, takes him first to Rostock in the north, but he is unable to cross the Baltic to Denmark. Reluctantly he returns to Moorsburg, near Zornhof, where Harras informs him of the existence of Sigmaringen's French colony. The flight now leads south, under phosphorescent skies, through train stations filled with refugees from every corner of the New Europe, to Berlin, then to Ulm, where Céline arrives in time for Rommel's funeral and bizarre conversations with Ulm's only surviving fireman. Without warning, Céline suddenly skips over his months in Sigmaringen to find himself on a train headed north toward an unknown destination. His next stop turns out to be a trap designed for the extermination of some of the Reich's unwanted. Thanks to an advance warning, Céline, whom nobody wants, narrowly es-

capes the slaughter and hobbles north to the ruins of
Hanover. In spite of an explosion that hurls a brick into
Céline's head, he, his wife Lili, and their cat are able to
catch a train for what remains of Hamburg.

On the way north the good doctor comes into possession of a number of refugee children. Starving, slob-
bering, and speaking no recognizable language, they
become Céline's charge when a French teacher of German, a dying refugee, can no longer manage them. *Rigodon*'s high point is Céline's tale of his efforts to marshal
his herd of "slobberers" through Hamburg and its mysterious underground stores to the north. Frolicking
under the bombs, for they have never known anything
else, these hungry urchins lead Céline to Denmark. At
the frontier Céline proclaims them to be Swedish and
thus hops aboard a Swedish train that is repatriating
Swedish nationals by way of Denmark. The novel suddenly breaks off when Céline reaches Copenhagen. As
Céline's last work, it points back to *Féerie I*, with its
portrayal of Céline's Danish prison cell, and further back
to the voyage Céline's first novel recounts. In retrospect,
Rigodon's journey from one ruin to the next seems an
almost logical conclusion to those travels that started in
the night many years before. His final journey is again
a journey in darkness, for the only light Céline can find
on this last voyage is provided by bombs, by the ma-
chinery of *délire* as perfected in the twentieth century.

D'un château l'autre, the first work of the trilogy,
presents one stage in his flight from destruction and
délire. Its portrayal of the world of Sigmaringen, the
collapsing world of still optimistic Nazis and deluded
collaborators, is as insane as any of Céline's purely fictional hallucinations. After a narrator's prelude that occupies nearly one third of the novel, Céline offers the

reader some "historical tourism" in the fantasy decor of Sigmaringen's medieval castle. Here 1,142 condemned Frenchmen await the arrival of General Leclerc and his Free French troops. Yet the Vichy government and its entourage of crazy believers continue to act out their role as the French authorities in the New Europe. Céline sketches quick portraits of Pétain, Laval, and of Vichy ministers such as Bichelonne, Bonnard, and Marion. Other portraits include men who were central to the Vichy government such as the German ambassador Abetz or the writer Chateaubriant—plus a gallery of unknown collaborators whose politics had backfired in 1944.

Céline, the colony's overworked and persecuted doctor, acts out a day in the life of Sigmaringen in the best tradition of his ever-harried hero, Ferdinand. At every moment he must cope with the continual flow of refugees, impostors, and demented derelicts who arrive from all corners of Hitler's crumbling empire. As a result of the unhealthy diet at Sigmaringen traffic to the toilets is heavy, and they overflow and flood his room, though this does not prevent orgies from taking place there. Rushing through the castle's labyrinth, he must serve Vichy's elite as it needs him, without regard for his personal needs. Thus he must hurry to the train station to protect a German officer's daughter from the bacchanalia that goes on there among the refugees and soldiers. When he returns from one of his ventures, he finds a lunatic masquerading as a surgeon and preparing to operate on an unwilling patient in Céline's room. And while hurrying from one patient to another, Dr. Destouches discovers that he has been condemned to death, this time by the Germans, for having sold out to the Intelligence Service instead of, as is usual, to the Nazis.

The overworked doctor has no time to worry about one more accusation, not in a world where everyone is busy denouncing everyone else.

The work's final image of madness is perhaps epitomized by the train trip he takes with a group of ministers who travel to northern Germany to attend the funeral of another minister who has mysteriously died in an S.S. hospital. Riding in a railway car designed for a shah who once visited Kaiser Wilhelm, the group nearly starves and freezes to death. The car has no windows, only regal draperies and silks that the ministers wrap about themselves in their futile effort to stay warm as they go from one bump to the next toward their senseless destination. This baroque play of antitheses, the illusion of regal splendor and the reality of cold misery, mirrors the impending fall of the ministers while it condenses to farce the mindless *délire* in which they are ensnared.

The three chronicles of Céline's wartime journey are comparable in their narrative and thematic structures. Critics may disagree as to which one is the most powerful, the most worthy of being compared to Céline's earlier novels, but few would disagree that Céline uses essentially the same approach in each of the works. In structural terms *Nord* is undoubtedly the most unified of the three. It has also received the most laudatory critical commentary, perhaps because Céline does not spend the first third of the novel snarling and ranting as he does in *D'un château l'autre. Nord* has, however, the same angry narrator's prelude as *D'un château l'autre* and *Rigodon,* and its brevity seems to be due, as Céline suggests, to pressure from his publisher, and not to Céline's desire to cut short his vituperation.

The narrator's prelude to each chronicle, setting forth Céline's personal lament and anger with the present, is not confined to the first part of each of these works. Rather Céline continues his angry complaints throughout each work, creating a continual juxtaposition of the historical past and present misery that differentiates these works from the earlier novels. Céline's chronicles are, in fact, as much a form of polemical diatribe against the present as they are accounts of the past's *délire*.

The prelude to *D'un château l'autre* is the longest of the three and is, in one respect, a prelude to the entire trilogy. Its medley of complaints and recriminations is repeated with little variation throughout these works whenever Céline focuses his narrative spotlight on his present condition, usually in Meudon, a suburb above Paris, where he lives in poverty with his wife and his many animals. The narrative present is usually situated here, or in Paris, where the aging doctor has returned from exile to start life anew. Yet Céline rarely gives the impression that starting life again is worth the effort; for it is a very resigned, but still angry Dr. Céline who begins his lamentations at the beginning of *D'un château l'autre* and the other works:

> Pour parler franc, là entre nous, je finis encore plus mal que j'ai commencé... Oh, j'ai pas très bien commencé... je suis né, je le répète, à Courbevoie, Seine... je le répète pour la millième fois... après bien des aller et retour je termine vraiment au plus mal... (p. 7.)

> (To speak frankly, just between you and me, I'm ending up worse than I started out... Oh, I didn't start out so well... I was born, I repeat, in Courbevoie, Seine... I'm repeating it for the thousandth time... after a good many round trips, I'm ending up in the worst way...)

Though he has survived the destruction of Vichy France
and Nazi Germany, withstood the physical punishment
of prison, outlasted the rigors of a Baltic exile, the present is a time of continued degradation. Now, nearing
death, he only wishes to reestablish his medical practice
and, especially in *Rigodon,* avoid the stream of inter-
viewers who come to see why he is still alive. But he
also has some vehement opinions to offer about contemporary society: automobiles, communist-bourgeois
plutocrats, Sartre, the Bourse, publishers, and a host of
other postwar phenomena incur his wrath. It is obvious
that Céline likes the post-World War II era no more than
he liked the era after World War I.

Céline's rambling and grumbling in his prelude are
vexing. One has no idea where he is going, nor, apparently, does he. At one moment he unleashes an extraordinary moment of *délire* as he shows a riot on the freeway, the next moment he is indulging in sentimental
reflections on his childhood during the *belle époque,*
and then he becomes bitterly whimsical about the more
recent past:

depuis le *Voyage* mon compte est bon!... encore je me serais
appelé *Vlazine*... Vlazine Progrogrof... je serais né à Tarnopol-sur-Don... mais Courbevoie Seine!... Tarnopol-sur-Don
j'aurais le Nobel depuis belle! . . . je ferais moyenne deux
cents sacs par mois rien que du *Voyagski!* (pp. 59–60.)

(since the *Journey* my goose has been cooked!... if I'd been
named *Vlazine*... Vlazine Progrogrof... if I'd been born in
Tarnopol on the Don... but in Courbevoie Seine!... born in
Tarnopol on the Don, they'd have given me the Nobel years
ago! . . . I'd average 200,000 a month on the *Journeyeski*
alone!)

His mind soars freely, taking up one topic by association
with another, only to come back to those subjects that
obsess him. The narrative movement in the prelude,
and sporadically throughout the main body of each of
these novels, conveys a sense of impatient resignation.
Nothing is worth discussing at length. No goal makes
sense for a man so disgusted and so deceived. He can
only trace the meanderings of his wandering mind, back
and forth through time.

Céline thus gives the reader a dual perspective on
himself as a disgruntled, persecuted old man, for he also
portrays himself as the elderly novelist at work. He
shows himself writing the novel that the reader has before him. Céline must write his novels, he says, in order
to pay his bills and to satisfy his publisher, "Achille."
So he depicts himself taking up the pen again, un-
willingly and pointlessly, and in spite of his recent
failure:

Normance, question livre n'a été qu'un affreux four!... parce
que ceci!... parce que cela!... en plus de saboté comme!...
par Achille, sa clique, ses critiques, ses haineux "aux ordres,"
canards enragés!... les gens s'attendaient que je provoque,
que je bouffe encore du Palestin, que je renfonce au gniouf!
et pour le compte!... (p. 54.)

(Speaking of books, *Normance* was just a lousy flop!... because
of this!... because of that!... besides being sabotaged... by
Achille, his clique, his critics, his hatchetmen, furious scandal
sheets!... people expected me to be provocative, to eat up
some more Palestinians, to jump back in the cooler! this time
for good!)

Céline is not about to fall into the trap the critics lay
for him. To add to his problems another editor, whom

Céline suspects of being an anti-Semite, wants Céline's
next work. Both publishers tell the old clown to find
again his "drôlerie," the sale of which will permit them
to buy more stocks and bonds. Céline thus presents himself as a writer without a mission, without a purpose. He
should be allowed to die in peace, but the law of the
market forces him to sell his writing. This disclosure of
his motives is a form of self-parody, but it is also a way of
taking vengeance on his publishers and, more especially, on his public. A number of writers, from Sterne
to Gide, have shown the novelist at work, but few have
shown the writer vaunting his lack of interest in the
novel he is writing. Céline must wander about, looking
for a subject that will satisfy his publishers and will
make his public laugh. He is the old clown, as unwanted
as Baudelaire's *saltimbanque,* who must perform
again. He would forget the entire show if a water meter
reader, reminding him of bills to pay, were not outside
his window.

Céline's seeking vengeance is not limited to his attacks on his publisher, critics, and public, for, in a whimsical manner, he again assumes the role of racist prophet.
He is no longer anti-Semitic; rather, he now speaks as the
elderly biologist who foresees and sometimes rejoices
in the prospect of the disappearance of the white race.
Like Léon Bloy, he forecasts the arrival of the Chinese
at Brest, though for Céline it appears that the Chinese
(and occasionally the Negroes) will triumph through
genetic superiority. Nearly the entirety of *Rigodon*'s
prelude is taken up with Céline's fantasy racism, especially with how much he enjoys embarrassing even his
favorable critics with it.

When Robert Poulet, for instance, supposedly ac-
cuses Céline of liking paradoxes too much and of not

understanding that the Chinese are antiracist, the old
biologist replies:

"Bonne cette foutrie! qu'ils viennent ici seulement un an
ils baisent tout le monde! le tour est joué! plus un blanc!
cette race n'a jamais existé... un "fond de teint" c'est tout!
l'homme vrai de vrai est noir et jaune! l'homme blanc religion
métisseuse! des religions! juives catholiques protestantes,
le blanc est mort! il n'existe plus! qui croire?" (p. 9.)

(Fine bunch of bullshit! Let them come here for a year,
they'll fuck everyone! the trick is played! not a white man left!
that race never existed... a little white "foundation makeup"
that's all! the real man is black and yellow! white man
mongrelizing religion! religions! Jewish, Catholic, Protestant,
the white man is dead! he no longer exists! whom to believe?)

As some critics have pointed out, the word "Chinese"
has replaced the word "Jew" as the source of delirious
catastrophes, but Céline seems to have a great deal of
difficulty taking his version of the Yellow Peril very
seriously. At times it appears that he plays the role of
the mad racist prophet in order to give the public what it
wants to hear. At other times his racism seems to be a
wish projection by which Céline yearns for some future
holocaust that would vindicate him and his vision of
Europe's *délire*.

The preludes to the novels and the continued juxtaposition of past and present throughout the works serve
to vindicate Céline in another manner. His vision of history demands that the present's degradation be contrasted with the past's *délire* to show that the meaning of
history is essentially a continual repetition of insanity,
viciousness, and cataclysms. As he repeatedly points
out in *D'un château l'autre* "la vacherie humaine"

(human shittiness) never varies from one century to the
next:

> Toutefois, comme la nature humaine change en rien de
> rien, jamais! gamètes immuables, la dame "tourneuse"
> ménopausique assurée sociale vous fait de ces caprices et
> colères pire que la Maintenon!... (p. 63.)

> (However, human nature never changes in any way, ever!
> immutable gametes... the "changing" menopausal lady with
> social security can give you worse rages and tantrums than
> Madame de Maintenon!...)

Céline supplements his biological view of history's
cycles by frequent references to Nietzsche in *Nord:*

> "tout finira par la canaille"... pardi!... pas besoin de Nietzsche,
> vous pouviez être sûr a Zornhof... (p. 367.)

> ("everything will end up by being scum"... by God!... no need
> for Nietzsche, you could have been sure at Zornhof...)

History is the "eternal return" of disasters provoked by
man's innate propensity for *délire.* The preludes and the
authorial diatribes against the present—whole chapters
break up the chronicles' narrative to spew forth Céline's
disgust with contemporary society—are obsessively
repetitious, but they do function to create a sense of
cyclical return within the chronicles themselves.
Céline's diatribes are paranoid, and his vision of history
is often no more than a farcical maniac's lament. But in
his best moments, when creating a vision of *délire* on
the freeway, for example, Céline offers a vision of contemporary madness that does seem to represent a return
of the *délire* that erupted under the Third Reich. And
Céline is again vindicated, at least in his own eyes, for

only the repetition of the cosmos' demented hostility
could account for his continuing misery.

The preludes to *D'un château l'autre* and *Rigodon*
seem in some respects to be parodies of the narrator's
prelude he used in earlier works. In both novels Céline
describes an attack of fever that forced him to go to bed
before he could begin to write. Each of these attacks is
preceded by a ghostly apparition, perhaps symbolizing
the presence of the death Céline longs for. Preludes to
Céline's hallucinated vision, these attacks resemble
farcical repetitions of the narrator's *délire* in *Mort à
crédit*. *Rigodon*'s opening fever attack represents a
rather perfunctory repetition of this kind of prelude,
whereas the attack in *D'un château l'autre* presents an
extended metaphor for all of Céline's writing. In the
prelude to this novel Céline says that on the way home
that night he saw a real *bateau-mouche* on the Seine, a
boat like those he knew when he was a boy. Céline is
shaken, and even more so when Le Vigan, Céline's traveling companion across Germany, emerges and explains that the boat is Charon's ferry. Céline is dubious
until he notices the unmistakable odor emanating from
the boat and the giant oar on it, an oar that only Charon
could possibly handle. After learning that Charon takes
only paying customers, Céline returns home and goes
to bed, suffering from his first malaria attack in twenty
years. Here he will remain to recall the memories that
make up the rest of the novel.

Céline's encounter with Le Vigan, a farcical but symbolic encounter with the past and with death, has given
him something to write about—his experience at
Sigmaringen:

je veux remémorer!... je veux qu'on me laisse!... voilà! tous
les souvenirs!... les circonstances! tout ce que je demande!

je vis encore plus de haine que de nouilles!... mais la juste
haine! pas "l'à peu près"!... et de la reconnaissance! pardon!...
j'en déborde!... Nordling qu'a sauvé Paris a bien voulu me
tirer du gniouf... que l'Histoire prenne note!... (p. 102.)

(I want to reminisce... I want to be left alone!... that's it! all
my memories!... the circumstances!... all I'm asking for! I
live more on hatred than on noodles!... but good hatred! not
just an approximation!... and gratitude! look out!... Nordling
who saved Paris wanted to get me out of the can... History,
take note!...)

Turning to confront his past and History, Céline finds
that malaria gives him access to time past. Fever is the
source of his writing:

je visionne! . . . après 39° vous voyez tout!... la fièvre doit
servir à quelque chose!... j'ai la nature jamais rien perdre!...
jamais! (p. 111.)

(I'm having a vision! . . . above 102° you see everything! fever
must be good for something!... it's my nature never to forget
anything!... ever!)

If *délire* again gives the Célinian narrator access to the
past, the past from which he can never escape, it also
offers the reader another perspective on the writer at
work. Only when hallucinated, Céline implies, can he
find anything to write about. Moreover, he must write
even if he is going to die, for he too will have to find the
fare to pay Charon, a venal merchant much like his
publisher.

In short, the preludes to each of the chronicles
establish Céline as the aging picaro, the Ferdinand who
is ready to die, but who must return to a past that is
somehow responsible for his present anguish. He is,
as he says at the beginning of *Nord,* a voluntary galley

slave, one for whom the future and its "H, Z, and Y bombs" have no importance. The chronicles' narratives themselves are gratuitous acts that the old doctor does with disdain, and yet with the passion of a man who could never cease playing the prophet. Many critics have regretted that Céline could not stop himself from punctuating his tales with his paranoid haranguing, but his pariah complex seems to be the necessary pre-condition for the creation of these chronicles of Germany's madness. It is a madness seen from the underground by the persecuted picaro as he wanders from catastrophe to catastrophe.

Unlike *Normance*'s repetitive and static narrative, the narrative structure of these novels is based on a constant movement forward. The unifying principle is found in the picaresque flight through episodic experience, though the picaro's flight does not become a metaphysical one, as in *Voyage*. It remains a physical voyage through a *délire* that is a reflection of history. The narrative is founded on constant movement from one castle to the next, from one trap to the next, from one group of smoking ruins to the next. Most episodes are brief, and the long stay at Zornhof in *Nord* is not really an exception. Within the context of Zornhof's microcosm, Céline's journey continues with unabated rapidity. At the center of this constant flight is the lucid pariah who often suffers from physical infirmities, but who strives to see clearly from his vantage point as an outsider. Nearly crippled by his sickness, suffering from head troubles, Céline is nonetheless able to guide us through a world of cataclysmic insanity as he scurries for safety. Being a pariah, Céline claims, he even has advantages:

Vu de l'autre bord c'est assez chouette... vous avez plus à bavarder perdre votre temps à être aimable, le statut de paria

a du bon... quand je vois de Gaulle chez Adenau... Adolf et
Philippe à Montoire... Charles-Quint chez Elizabeth... que de
salamalecs, rouges à lèvres, poudres de riz, pour rien!...
"l'Intouchable" a plus à se farder, un peu plus de merde, et
c'est tout, du haut en bas, tout ce qu'on lui demande! (*Nord,*
pp. 368–369.)

(Seen from the other side it's pretty swell... you don't have
to chat, waste your time being friendly, the status of pariah
has its good moments... When I see De Gaulle with Adenau...
Adolf and Philippe at Montoire... Charles V with Queen
Elizabeth... what a bunch of bowing and scraping, lipstick,
face powder for nothing!... the "Untouchable" doesn't have to
put on makeup anymore, just a little more shit, and that's all,
from top to bottom, all they ask of him!)

Plunged into existence's excrement, but stripped of all
pretense, this galley slave can look topside and watch
the masters' delusions as they destroy themselves. Especially in *D'un château l'autre* and *Nord* Céline's
sociology is again simplified to allow him to sink to the
bottom of the underworld and, from that vantage point,
show up the ridiculous antics of those who think they
run the ship.
    Though Céline is isolated by the forces that contrive
to persecute him, he hardly ever finds himself alone.
His flight is doubled by the movement of the hordes who
sweep across Germany in delirious panic. His chronicles
are, in one respect, the tale of their flight, of their mass
délire, as seen through the eyes of the doctor-picaro:

Dans les vieilles chroniques on appelle les guerres autre-
ment: voyage des peuples... terme encore parfaitement
exact. . . . (*Nord,* p. 17.)

(In the old chronicles they name the wars differently: voyage of peoples... a term that's still perfectly accurate. . . .)

Examples of crowds caught up in war's madness abound
throughout these chronicles: the swarms of refugees
who come to Sigmaringen, the berserk crowds in *Nord*'s
Berlin, its group of homicidal prostitutes wandering
across Germany, the innumerable travelers seeking
refuge in *Rigodon*'s interminable train rides, all are
victims of history's unleashing of the powers of dementia. Trapped in Germany's "nihilistic fury" (*Rigodon,* p. 82), these crowds storm through these chronicles as projections of *délire* at the same time they try to
flee it. The mob's *délire* expresses itself in many ways:
in attacks on German soldiers, in panics on bombarded
trains, in countless orgies. Railway stations, for example,
are a favorite locale for the mob's sexual *délire.*

pour une cigarette... pour un blabla... le chagrin, l'oisiveté le
rut font qu'un!... pas que les gamines!... femmes faites, et
grand-mères! évidemment plus pires ardentes, feu au machin,
dans les moments où la page tourne, où l'histoire rassemble
tous les dingues, ouvre ses Dancings d'Epopée! . . . il faut la
faim et les phosphores pour que ça se donne et rute et sperme
sans regarder! total aux anges! Famine, cancers, blennor-
ragies existent plus!... l'éternité plein la gare!... (*D'un château
l'autre,* p. 168.)

(for a cigarette... for a little blah blah... sadness, idleness, and
female heat go together... and not just kids!... grown women
and grandmothers! obviously the hottest ones, with fire in
their twats, in those moments when the page turns, when
History brings all the nuts together and opens its Epic Dance
Halls! . . . you've got to have phosphorus and hunger so
they'll rut and sperm and get with it without paying attention!
pure happiness! no more hunger, cancer, or clap!... the station packed with eternity!...)

Though he is hardly a theorist in mass psychology,
Céline captures as have few other writers the sense of
violent instinctual energy that is released by the stresses

of dislocation, concentration camps, and flight from disaster.

This world of flight resembles in many ways that world of cosmic violence Céline portrayed in *Normance.* In *Normance* unceasing bombardment signified the *délire* of the cosmos. In the trilogy the constant aerial holocaust constitutes the exterior limit of the pariah's vision. The bombings are a constant presence, though usually removed at a distance; often they comically mock those who think they are in charge of their destiny. The bombings are arbitrary manifestations of violence that, as Céline rather accurately observes, do little to hinder the plutocrats' scurrying after pleasure or the Reich's industrial production, although they do shatter entire cities. At other times the falling bombs are distant, rhythmic reminders of how *délire* may explode at any time and destroy the picaro. The bombs can even be a source of hallucinatory enchantment, like flowers of evil:

ce qu'est joli surtout ce sont les explosions, les mines qui viennent s'écraser là en géantes fleurs vertes... rouges et bleues... contre les pierres des deux remparts de chaque côté... à éclore du haut en bas et à travers le canal... rouges bleues vertes... des fleurs de dix mètres de large... au moins... il faut avoir vu... je ne peux pas vous faire entendre ces *broum!* ... (*Rigodon,* p. 254.)

(what's really pretty are the explosions, the mines that crash down there, in giant green flowers... rose and blue... against the stones of the two ramparts on each side... blossoming out from top to bottom, and across the canal... red, blue, green... flowers thirty feet wide... at least... you've got to have seen it... I can't make you hear the *booms!*...)

Related to the bombs are the fleets of aircraft that fill the skies. For the pariah the R.A.F. bombers are not merely

mechanical means of warfare. Rather they seem to be the
irrational messengers of *délire* and are not really associated with any particular army. Thus airplanes, in a
role as autonomous beings, appear to be inspecting the
earth, as when, for example, they fly pointlessly over
Pétain and his entourage on their walks. The airplanes
bring the bombs that lay waste to whole cities, but they
also seem to come on missions whose only goal can be
to propagate waves of dementia and wreak mental havoc.

Another key example of Céline's exacerbated sense
of history's rage is found in his images of cities and the
aftermath of countless bombardments. Cities are all
reduced to smoldering ruins, converted into the stark
decor through which the pariah must flee. Berlin, Hanover, Hamburg, and most of the other cities are lifeless
piles of rubble, inhabited only momentarily by fleeing
refugees. Berlin's devastation presents a bizarre *trompe-
l'œil:*

cette ville a déjà bien souffert... que de trous, de chaussées
soulevées! drôle, on n'entend pas d'avions... ils s'intéressent
plus à Berlin?... je comprenais pas, mais peu à peu j'ai saisi...
c'était une ville plus qu'en décors... des rues entières de
façades, tous les intérieurs croulés, sombres dans les trous...
(*Nord*, p. 43.)

(that city had already suffered a lot... what a lot of holes and
heaved-up paving!... funny, no airplanes to be heard... they
aren't interested in Berlin anymore?... I didn't understand,
but I slowly figured it out... it wasn't a city any longer except
in stage decors... whole streets of façades, all the insides col-
lapsed, in gloomy holes...)

Cities have always fascinated Céline, and for his estranged picaros they stand forth as stark, menacing

forms, endowed poetically, at times, with unknown dangers. Céline's discovery of a Berlin that exists only as façades is much like Bardamu's discovery of New York:

Figurez-vous qu'elle était debout leur ville, absolument droite. New York, c'est une ville debout. On en avait déjà vu nous des villes bien sûr, et des belles encore, et des ports et des fameux même. Mais chez nous, n'est-ce pas, elles sont couchées les villes, au bord de la mer ou sur les fleuves, elles s'allongent sur le paysage, elles attendent le voyageur, tandis que celle-là l'Américaine, elle ne se pâmait pas, non, elle se tenait bien raide, là, pas baisante du tout, raide à faire peur. (*Voyage*, p. 184.)

(Imagine, their city was standing up, absolutely straight. New York is a city standing up. Sure, we'd already seen some cities, and fine ones at that, and ports, and famous ones, too. But at home the cities are lying down, along the seacoast or on the banks of the rivers, they stretch out in the countryside, waiting for the traveler, but that American one, it wasn't swooning at all; no, it stood up there really stiff, not ready for screwing, stiff enough to make you afraid.)

A city standing up or a city in façades, both promise new possibilities of destruction for the wandering underground hero. For Bardamu, New York is the capital of new forms of pustulence and isolation. For Ferdinand Céline, Berlin sets forth another image of the coming apocalypse. The difference between the cities is one of relative violence, of the way in which *délire* manifests itself. And in both cases the city is a way station in the picaro's flight from fear.

Perhaps the greatest difference between the chronicles, especially *Nord* and *Rigodon*, and novels such as *Mort à crédit* and *Guignol's Band* is the picaro's relation to the other characters. In the chronicles Dr. Céline is not overwhelmed by the others' *délire*, nor does he project his own hallucinations onto the world of the novel. Rather, he is a reasonably lucid observer who tries to make sense of what others do and is often baffled by the events that occur. Especially in the last two chronicles is he a helpless observer who points out absurdities and mysteries for which neither he nor, apparently, anyone else can give an adequate explanation. In *D'un château l'autre*, on the other hand, he is often aghast when confronted with the *délire* that has seized the notables of the Vichy regime, but in this work he frequently plays the role of a comic foil, pointing up the comic illusions of men who still believe they have a future.

In fact, *D'un château l'autre* is an extraordinary comic work to the extent that it portrays political madness in a way that few history books could match. Take, for example, the comedy created when Céline plays comic foil at a dinner given by Otto Abetz, the German ambassador to France. Céline, as is often the case in *D'un château l'autre*, is a passive listener who reports whatever absurdities he hears. Abetz, who supposedly detested Céline, has his reasons for inviting the famous "pornographer" to a hypocritical austerity dinner:

il pérorait pour que je l'écoute et que je répète... pour ça qu'il m'avait invité!... on nous sert un rond de saucisson, un rond chacun... alors mon Dieu, qu'on s'amuse!... (p. 241.)

(He was perorating so that I'd listen and repeat it... that's what he'd invited me for!... we're served a slice of sausage, one slice each... O.K. by God, let's have some fun!...)

Abetz, living in well-stocked comfort, begins a speech
after Céline pointedly asks him what he will do when
General Leclerc's army arrives:

"Oh! vous exagérez Céline! vous exagérez toujours! tout!...
toujours! la victoire?... mais nous l'avons dans la main!...
Céline! l'arme secrète?... vous avez entendu parler?... non?...
mettons Céline, je vais dans votre sens, je vais exagérer avec
vous!... défaitiste! j'admets que nous soyons vaincus! là!
puisque vous y tenez!... il restera toujours quelque chose du
National-Socialisme! nos idées reprendront leur force!...
toute leur force!... nous avons semé, Céline! semé! répandu
le sang!... les idées!... l'amour!" (p. 241.)

("Oh! you're exaggerating, Céline! you always exaggerate!
about everything! always! why we have victory in the palm of
our hand!... Céline! the secret weapon?... you've heard of it?...
no?... suppose, Céline, I'll take your point of view, I'll exaggerate with you!... as a defeatist! I'll suppose we're defeated!
so there! since you insist... some part of National Socialism
will always remain! our ideas will regain their vigor!... all
their vigor!... we have sowed, Céline! sowed! spread blood!...
ideas!... love!")

To set this madness in perspective, Céline need only
comment, "Le confort fait bien déconner." ("Comfort
really makes you run off at the mouth.") (p. 242.) Abetz's
délire reaches even more extravagant heights when he
envisages their victorious return to Paris and the great
statue of Charlemagne that will be built in honor of the
Axis. Céline's irony was never more concise as he pic-
tures this madness to himself:

Je voyais Charlemagne et ses preux... Gœbbels en Roland...
(p. 242.)

(I could see Charlemagne and his valiant knights... Goebbels decked out as Roland...)

As the pariah, looking up from the muck, but knowing where the truth lies, Céline's vision forces this delusion to stand out in its hyperbolic absurdity. The chronicler of *D'un château l'autre* may be suffering from a persecution complex, but his picaro realism lets him know when the game is up.

In *Nord* and *Rigodon* the pariah must deal with what one character calls "fous baroques" (*Nord*, p. 20), who mystify Céline as much as they do the reader. An atmosphere of pervasive mystery is created when he confronts, for example in *Nord*, multiple murders at Zornhof, or, in Berlin, the strange Doctor Faustus who has come into possession of a painted fan once given to Céline's wife, and who also suffers from hallucinations when he salutes Hitler on an empty square before the Chancellery. Faustus' insanity is obvious, but his role in the novel is considerably less so. At Zornhof characters go berserk for no particular reason; so does Céline's friend Le Vigan, who proclaims he is the murderer of two aristocrats whose death cannot be explained. The aristocrats themselves are "baroque madmen" in their obsessions with caste and privilege. Céline never enters their demented world, for his only interest is to remain as far from them as possible. Their blindness to the destruction that is racing toward them can only threaten to bring the pariah to ruin. In *Nord* and *Rigodon* the pariah is related to what we might call the surface of events. Since he does not enter into this world of *délire*, he can only speculate on the characters' hallucinations and delusions. In these novels the pariah appears more isolated and estranged from the menacing

world that surrounds him. Wandering in a strange
climate of calamity, devastation, intrigue, and incon-
gruity, he rarely does more than suggest what madness
might lie beneath the surface.

His estrangement is both a weakness and a strength in
these chronicles of flight. On the one hand, the vertigi-
nous interplay between the picaro's lucidity and the
other characters' *délire* has virtually disappeared, and
the dimensions of the novelistic world are considerably
reduced. On the other hand, Céline's isolation in his
own pseudohistorical world conveys a powerful sense
of the tension and bewilderment to which the pariah
is always subjected. Mystery is everywhere, and history's unfolding of madness manifests itself in bizarre
calamities that constantly surprise Céline himself. In
Nord and *Rigodon* he is no longer the self-assured
picaro who saw defeat and the coming tribulations well
before the deluded collaborators at Sigmaringen. He is
another estranged wanderer, going from cataclysm to
cataclysm, expecting only the worst from a world of
unpredictable hostility that exceeds even Céline's
expectations.

Many critics have been less than favorable to these
bizarre chronicles that, to paraphrase Gide, do not depict
history, but the hallucination that history provokes.[3]
What Maurice Nadeau says about *D'un château l'autre*
summarizes much of what critics have said about the
trilogy: "The heart of what makes up the great works
has disappeared. The *délire* that animated the author
of *Journey* . . . has been transformed into petty rage, into
ridiculous hatreds whose exaggeration makes one smile,
and into an abject desire to be pitied."[4] This judgment
is perhaps true if one compares this trilogy to Céline's

first three novels, and it could be argued that his last
works are less interesting than the extravagant experiment Céline attempted in *Féerie pour une autre fois.*
Whatever the chronicles' weaknesses, it is perhaps
unfair to reproach Céline for not having written another
Voyage or *Mort à crédit.* Taken on their own merits,
the chronicles are both extraordinary testimonies to the
frightful dislocations worked by the historical contradictions of the twentieth century and a paradigmatic
revelation of the limitations of Céline's revolt.

What gives these novels their greatest power, yet
makes them extremely irritating, is Céline's bewildered
sense of the historical contrasts and contradictions that
the war has created and that the present perpetuates.
The constant juxtaposition of the narrator's past and
present creates a sense of history's delirious accelera-
tion, as do the series of temporal antitheses set within
the narrative itself. A medieval castle is juxtaposed with
fleets of modern bombers. Parks designed by Mansard,
symbols of the order France once imposed upon Europe,
are contrasted with wandering refugees, living symbols
of the New Europe's collapse. The luxury of a shah's
private train is set against the present misery in which
ministers nearly freeze to death. In other terms, Céline's
childhood, from an era that possessed a sense of order
and duty, is contrasted with the rage that destroys all
order and unleashes all forms of demented passion.
Moreover, Céline's hatred of the opulent present, of
the postwar overfed consumer society, creates another
set of antitheses between the past's violence and the
present's forgetful preoccupation with its stomach. The
contrast is all the more startling since this same European society, only a few years earlier, was bent on destroying itself. Céline may have no intellectual grasp of

Europe's "economic miracle," but he is all too aware that this miracle cannot mask the *délire* that shook Europe so very recently.

These chronicles also reveal a Céline who is still a *moraliste*, though a comic *moraliste* who has little interest in integrating his observations into the fabric of the narration itself, as he did in *Voyage*. This lack of integration can be disconcerting, but Céline's virtuoso performances in *D'un château l'autre* and *Nord* (*Rigodon* is a much weaker work in this respect) are often hilarious displays of the old clown's gift for discerning *délire* in its most hyperbolic forms. Consider, for example, the constant arrival of "phoney doctors" at Sigmaringen, a curious phenomenon that provides Céline with no little food for thought:

les bougres avaient la manie d'opérer! n'importe quoi, n'importe comment, hernie, otite, verrues, kystes!... trancher qu'ils voulaient, tous!... chirurgiens!... (*D'un château l'autre,* p. 226.)

(these bastards had a mania for operating! anything, any way, hernia, otitis, warts, cysts!... they all wanted to cut, every one of them!... surgeons they were!...)

The portrait of quacks at Sigmaringen immediately suggests parallels with the quacks who practice under normal conditions:

c'est bien à remarquer, même dans la vie ordinaire que, les dingues, illuminés, rebouteux, chiropracts, fakirs, sont pas satisfaits du tout de donner juste des petits conseils, pilules, fioles, gris-gris, caramels... non!... le Grand Jeu qui les hante!... Grand Guignol!... que ça saigne!... (p. 226.)

(it's worth noting that even in ordinary life, the screwballs, faith-healers, bone-setters, chiropractors, fakirs, aren't at all

satisfied to dish out a little advice, pills, phials, good-luck
charms, caramels... oh no!... the Big Show haunts them!...
Grand Guignol! it's got to bleed!...)

And it is only a step further to describe the normal surgeon's art:

la chirurgie ordinaire, bien impeccable, bien officielle,
tient plus qu'un peu du Cirque Romain!... sacrifices humains
bien tartufes!... (p. 226.)

(normal surgery, even the most flawless and most official, is
related more than a little to the Roman Circus!... hypocritical
human sacrifices!...)

Leaping from one association to the next, Céline joy-
ously offers the crowning observation:

vous avez un fils qui se destine?... se sent-il réel assassin?...
inné? le vieux fond anthropopithèque? décerveleur, trépaneur,
cro-magnon?... bon! bon! excellent!... des Cavernes? qu'il se
lance! qu'il le proclame! il a le don!... la Chirurgie est son
affaire! il a l'étoffe du "Grand Patron"!... les dames, connes et
sadiques comme pas! pâmeront rien que de lui voir les
mains... (p. 227.)

(you have a son who's going into it?... does he feel he's a real
assassin?... innate? the old anthropopithecus instinct? loboto-
mizer? trepanner? Cro-Magnon?... fine! fine! excellent!...
right out of the cave? let him get on with it! let him proclaim it!
he has the gift!... Surgery is his game! he has the stuff of a
"Great Doctor"!... the ladies, dumb asses and sadistic to beat
the band! they'll swoon just at the sight of his hands...)

These verbal extravaganzas are unlike anything found in
Voyage or the earlier novels. This narrative flight is
only loosely rooted in the "chronicle" itself, though this

kind of slapstick continues the parody of the act of
writing. It shows Céline's capricious disdain for maintaining a single narrative thread or a coherent structure.
Moreover, these antics reflect the rage and astonishment
of a writer who cannot offer enough insights into man's
innately vicious *délire*. Any example is a good one, and
seemingly no amount of repetition can do justice to the
task of cataloguing the madness he has seen. The
scattering of *moraliste* performances throughout *D'un
château l'autre* and *Nord* enriches these novels even as
it shatters the linear narrative development. What might
be a monotonous stream of Céline's personal catastrophes is broken up by the comic volleys. *Rigodon*
suffers from precisely this kind of monotony. Céline,
perhaps dying as he wrote this last work, appears not to
have been able to muster the strength to engage in such
narrative pirouettes, and *Rigodon*'s continuous narration of perilous train rides seems belabored in comparison with the staccato movement of *D'un château l'autre*
and *Nord*.

In more general terms Céline's pseudohistorical narratives again present an essentially comic vision, though
this one is grounded in a view of history. The kind of
comedy varies considerably throughout these novels.
The historical personages in *D'un château l'autre* may
be likened to Céline's fictional creations in their delirious pretentions. The collaborator Chateaubriant, for
instance, is demented in a way reminiscent of Courtial
des Pereires or Sosthène when he declares that he is
going to the Tyrol region to perfect a "moral bomb"
that will seize a victory for fascism from the invading
Allied armies. Illusion born of *délire* is the key to
comedy in *D'un château l'autre* as in *Mort à crédit*.

D'un château l'autre is the only novel in the last

trilogy in which Céline attains the mad rhetoric of his earlier works, for simulation of the characters' *délire* demands the kind of verbal energy he displayed in *Mort à crédit* and *Guignol's Band*. In *Nord* and *Rigodon* a language in which violence is attenuated accompanies Céline's rejection of high comedy of character in favor of a vision of history as a bloody farce. The constant and mechanical recurrence of calamities, bombardments, assassinations, and close escapes produces a farcical series in which Céline, in spite of his persecution complex, plays a role comparable to Buster Keaton's in one of his chase sequences. In these two novels the picaro himself is often another guignol figure in a world of unending destruction. The blows he periodically receives, in spite of their historical seriousness, are mock epic gestures that reduce this pariah to another clown running madly in an absurd show. Or, to offer another comparison, the obsessive repetition of Céline's disasters transforms them into the same order of misfortunes that beset the unhappy clown. He is always squirted with Seltzer water when he is least expecting it.

Céline's comic vision is again a way of exorcizing and negating the past he despises. It is perhaps in his revolt against the past and the misery it has caused in the present that Céline's real weakness is to be found. Céline continues to refuse *délire*, but his revolt is not an all-encompassing negation of the manifold forms of destruction that *délire* works on men, things, and nations. His visceral refusal has subsided—nausea has virtually disappeared from this trilogy—and in its place the reader encounters a powerful but absurdly egocentric view of the ravages of history. Céline's outcry against the incomprehensible unfolding of events that has led to his downfall is, ultimately, grounded in a paranoid clown's view of history as a personal apocalypse:

je peux me vanter d'être dans le droit fil, aussi haï par les gens d'un bout que de l'autre... je peux dire, sans me vanter, que le fil de l'Histoire me passe part en part, haut en bas, des nuages à ma tête, à l'anu... (*Nord*, p. 242.)

(I can boast of being on the right track, hated as much by the people on one side as by those on the other... I can say, without boasting, that the thread [cutting edge] of History goes right through me, from top to bottom, from the clouds to my head, through the anus...)

One can accept Céline's performance as a pariah to the extent that this role endows him with an angle of vision that throws in relief the madness of the Third Reich and the Vichy regime. Yet Céline's refusal to go beyond his own misfortunes reduces his revolt against *délire* and its eviscerating agent, History, to a sterile caricature. Moreover, in spite of Céline's often brilliant pyrotechnics, in spite of the comic angle of vision his pariah complex gives him, one must regret that Céline's paranoia, seemingly founded on an obstinate will to perceive only what pleased him, appears to be a defense mechanism by which he shields himself from knowledge that could destory him. Céline could never have been called an intellectual; he always wrote from beneath the solar plexus. But it is more than regrettable that his obsessive revolt could not have been tempered, if not by understanding, at least by compassion. In the trilogy of chronicles Céline has lost that sense of compassion that was one of the most admirable sides to the negation he expressed in his earlier works. It is this narrowness that makes these works oppressive, though at the same time it intensifies their comedy. Céline's work ends, then, with a paradox much like the one that began it in *Voyage:* the very source of the strength of his vision makes it intolerable.

CHAPTER VII The Célinian Novel

Céline's legacy to European literature consists of seven uneven novels. Bombastic and obscene, long and repetitive, infuriatingly incoherent, they nonetheless force the reader to confront great comic revelations of the abysses of human misery and disgust. Of the seven, only one, *Voyage au bout de la nuit,* has really entered the European literary consciousness. There remains, therefore, a great body of work to be recognized, explored, and assimilated. Not that everyone can assimilate Céline's often intolerably strident outcry. It may well be that his work, by its very nature, is destined to remain an example of underground literature, surrounded by legend and obscurity, open only to those who are willing to subject their sensitivity to Céline's violent discourses in delirium. This has been Céline's fate until recently, and perhaps the work itself, more than Céline's political vicissitudes, accounts for the neglect.

To enter into Céline's work demands more than an

acceptance of his capacity for insane politics. It demands cohabitation with a mind whose excess of lucidity borders on madness, whose hatred of delirium turns upon itself in simulation of the closed world of the paranoid. In *Voyage* Céline gave an almost prophetic résumé of the dangers he faced when he put the following outburst in the mouth of Dr. Baryton:

"Retenez bien ceci Ferdinand, ce qui est le commencement de la fin de tout c'est le manque de mesure! La façon dont elle a commencé la grande débandade, je suis bien placé moi pour vous le raconter... Par les fantaisies de la mesure que ça a commencé! . . . Alors au néant tout le monde? Pourquoi pas? Tous? C'est entendu! Nous n'y allons pas d'ailleurs, on y court! C'est une véritable ruée! je l'ai vu moi, l'esprit Ferdinand, céder peu à peu de son équilibre et puis se dissoudre dans la grande entreprise des ambitions apocalyptiques!" (pp. 414–415.)

("Remember this well, Ferdinand, what is the beginning of the end of everything is the lack of moderation. The way the great stampede started, I'm well placed to tell you about it... By fantasies going beyond all bounds, that's how it started! . . . So everyone down the abyss? Why not? Everyone? Of course! Besides we're not just headed there, we're running toward it! It's a real rush! I've seen the mind, Ferdinand, give up little by little its equilibrium and then dissolve itself in that grand enterprise of apocalyptic ambitions!")

Céline's legacy is, in one sense, both a monument to the destruction worked by a fascination with madness that went beyond all bounds and the debris of his own apocalyptic ambitions.

In another sense his legacy is what one can call the Célinian novel, for it is obvious that, for all the variations found in his works, Céline approached the novel in a consistent manner. Whether transposing his personal experience on a fictional level or fictionalizing his biography, he conceived the novel as a form of revolt whose essential function was to negate time past. The past that Céline insisted never to have forgotten weighed upon him as an unbearable burden, and his first novels were a symbolic effort to rid the past of its vitriolic content.

In *Voyage* the story is told by an older narrator who looks back "from the other side of time" on the debacle of his youth and middle age. The novel's journey through time past ends in a revolt that protests against the limits of existence, though this suicidal revolt is in contradiction with Céline's own hatred of death. The narrator in *Mort à crédit* looks back on childhood as he approaches death, and his tale is a vomiting forth of a poisoned past he can no longer stomach. Though it opens with a vision of war's insane holocaust and contains moments of extravagant lyricism, *Guignol's Band* is also an effort to purge, through ritualistic means, the older narrator of a delirious and death-obsessed past. All of Céline's narrators are situated on the brink of annihilation, and their stories are attempts to shake off the weight of the past's accumulated, detested experience before they fall into "the hole," or as *Voyage*'s narrator puts it:

Quand on sera au bord du trou faudra pas faire les malins nous autres, mais faudra pas oublier non plus, faudra raconter tout sans changer un mot, de ce qu'on a vu de plus vicieux chez les hommes et puis poser sa chique et puis descendre. Ça suffit comme boulot pour une vie tout entière. (pp. 27–28.)

(When we've come to the hole's edge, we mustn't show off, but we mustn't forget either, we'll have to tell everything, without changing a word, about the most vicious things we've seen in men and then kick off and go on down. That's enough of a job for a whole lifetime.)

The structure of the later works also turns on this desire to tell everything that is vicious, but the past to be exorcized is more immediately Céline's own. Having become his own hero in *Féerie pour une autre fois,* Céline first goes through his ritual of the dying narrator—and perhaps he believed he was going to die in his Danish prison cell—and then turns to an apocalyptic destruction of his past, one whose hyperbolic dimensions create the usual comic exorcism. In each of his chronicles Céline also posits himself as the elderly narrator whose only desire is to find death in peace but who is supposedly obliged by present misery to go in search of the past's madness. The chronicles seek to raise time past to the level of history, but the exorcism that comedy works aims essentially at emptying Céline's own past of the inexplicable *délire* that has persecuted him and brought about his downfall.

This consistent narrative polarity established by the narrator's static present and the picaro protagonist's chaotic past points to Céline's view of temporality as a form of *délire.* The picaro, Ferdinand, is engaged, usually catastrophically engaged, in the temporal duration that is, in effect, time past for the older narrator. Yet the sense of duration and the sense of insane destruction worked through time are preserved in the novels. Ferdinand's acts and outcries are not fixed by the passing of time in a series of historical moments. His perception is fluid, deliriously confronted with an ever unfolding present time. Céline's language is most extraordinary perhaps in its emulation of the temporal flow that engulfs the protagonist. Ferdinand's sense of time is an intuitive openness to an immediate present that besieges him with waves of *délire.* Take a random example:

Y a un dragon qui les croque tous!... qui leur arrache à tous
le derrière... la tripaille... le foie... je vois tout!... Ah! les
pauvres viandes!... que ça dégouline saigne! que ça me gicle
dans l'œil! (*Guignol's Band*, p. 192.)

(There's a dragon that's biting into all of them!... that's tearing
away their rear... their guts... their liver... I see it all!... Oh!
that poor meat!... it's dripping everything, bleeding! it's spurt-
ing up into my eye!)

Taken from context, Ferdinand's description of one of
his hallucinations surges forth as an obviously immediate vision of madness that explodes into the present and
orders the flow of immediate duration. It is not simply
the use of the French narrative present tense that
creates this sense of immediacy, for Céline often
achieves the same effect using past tenses. The violent
disarticulation of language and the images of destruction convey Ferdinand's immediate *délire* as he lives it,
as it shatters his consciousness with its comic powers of
distortion.

On the other hand, Céline's narrators, all nearing
death and final quiescence, if they are not yet on the
other side of time, are in a static situation that serves to
orient the reader toward the disordered mass of past experience Ferdinand woefully undergoes. The narrator's
presence imposes a structure on these novels, if only as
a limit to the protagonist's experience. This is especially
true in the first novels, whereas the narrator of the later
chronicles often fractures his tales by his constant intervention with his present lament. Yet even in these
later works the narrator's presence serves to guide the
reader into a past that is essentially chaos and flight, a
past that by its nature is nearly formless.

Time past is the process of *délire's* unfolding in its
myriad forms: violence, putrescence, disease, hallucination, persecution, cosmic apocalypse. Time is thus
raised to the level of an immediate psychic duration,
ordered only by extraordinary emotional patterns set in
a world in constant flux. The protagonist's self is a point
of interaction between this world and the inner autonomy he seeks to preserve, even when, as in the above
passage, he is struggling with his own hallucinations.
Délire is often too powerful, and when it is, the picaro
is submerged by those forces from which he would flee.
Therefore, the older narrator must be in a static present,
seemingly removed from time, if he is to escape *délire's*
onslaught. In one respect Céline always narrates in the
present tense, dividing his narration only in terms of
the madness that besieges Ferdinand and the death that
promises his narrator both tranquillity and escape from
délire. *Féerie pour une autre fois* might seem an exception to this pattern, for the narrator in prison finds no
peace whatsoever. Yet, even in *Féerie pour une autre
fois*, with its mad monologue that serves as the narrator's prelude, the narrator finds himself in a place of
detachment, far from the chaotic cataclysms that *Normance* sets forth as time past.

The world of Céline's ubiquitous Ferdinand, the
picaro and pariah caught in the unbearable immediacy
of constantly unfolding madness, is the heart of Céline's
original vision. It is a world of absolute flux, of chaos
and violent upheaval, that is much like a dramatized
vision of the chaos Western mystics since at least Plato
have tried to flee. But Ferdinand never really succeeds
in fleeing or in finding a refuge. He is unendingly
trapped. His obscene humor is the only defense he
possesses, the only salvation he can find, to alleviate

his disgust and misery. The Célinian hero has a divided consciousness that can neither escape from the immediacy of its distress nor give in to it. The division is reflected in the polarities of *délire* and lucidity and, structurally, in the dichotomy between the younger protagonist and the older narrator. Ferdinand's consciousness is divided against itself and is as unstable as the flux that makes up its psychic life. His consciousness presents the first part of a dialectic that can never resolve its conflict in any form of synthesis. The dissonance, as Trotsky called it, never ceases. Instability and astonishment are constants, for Ferdinand can never stop being surprised by his turmoil and agony. The opposition between Ferdinand's need for some transcendent relief and his unending anguish could seemingly be resolved only in acquiescence to death or madness—both of which are temptations throughout Céline's work.

Perhaps it was this same intolerable tension that drove Céline, in an existential sense, to identify with his own fictional creation. Undoubtedly his fictional Ferdinand was initially a projection of Céline's deepest consciousness. The identification of creator and created was almost enough to destory Céline's later work. Only a strong comic sense, deriving from Céline's one-sided lucidity, kept his work from sinking into a morass of subjective nightmares. Yet, it cannot be denied that his confusion of reality and literature worked to the detriment of the latter.

Neither Céline's relation to his works nor the torn consciousness that is found throughout them obscures the fact that he achieved a great comic creation. Without the redeeming grace of comedy, Céline's vision would undoubtedly be insufferably narrow. In *Voyage* he be-

gan with a virulent satire that frequently blended with
genuine comedy. Céline then developed in *Mort à
crédit* and *Guignol's Band* a form of high comedy in
which language became the mark of comic deviation,
though the comedy is far more than verbal. Ferdinand's
divided consciousness reflects a world view that can
transform a world of delirious flux into a world of hilarious comic mechanisms. The horror of the present is reduced through laughter to dimensions the isolated self
can deal with. In *Féerie I* the clown-narrator screams a
bizarre monologue with comic antics that are ultimately
a form of slapstick directed against prison walls. And
Normance's apocalyptic destruction turns into an arbitrary, repetitive mechanism, comic by its very futility.
The last trilogy is a fundamentally comic work. The
historical caricatures in *D'un château l'autre* are
devastating bits of comedy by which Céline savagely
smashes mad pretentions in the face of the certain defeat
reality promises. *Nord* and *Rigodon* are alternately
scenes of farcical calamities, set in history's demented
rages, and the ritual comedy of Céline's own efforts to
survive.

One should not suppose that either the temporal chaos
or the misery of the Célinian hero confronting existence
precludes a comic world view. The Greeks, who were
among the first to elaborate a philosophical doctrine of
absolute flux, supposedly made laughter a divine
privilege — for the gods were the detached and privileged spectators of the comedy man acts out in the
world. By the same token Céline's withdrawn narrator
offers a detached view on the absolute flux the protagonist must face. And absolute flux can be nothing more
than a hyperbolic, repetitive mechanism, which, as
Bergson showed, is a fundamental condition for comedy.

Existence's prolonged *délire* is comic by its very nature as a cyclical, repeating disorder. Moreover, *délire* is a privileged metaphor Céline used to characterize existence because it is a metaphor that expressed his revolt while transforming it into a comic ritual. Céline's comedy is, throughout his works, both a form of negation and an antidote for that negation. Comedy in Céline, after *Voyage*'s cry of impossible revolt, is a continual form of exorcism that seems to have allowed Céline to coexist with his horrible awareness and refusal of what that awareness forced him to see.

Perhaps we must finally attribute Céline's decline as a writer to his failure to find a ground for an affirmation that would have permitted him to maintain the force of his revolt; for a more logical conclusion to his revolt would have been silence, not interminable cosmic farce. Favorable critics, usually overlooking Céline's anti-Semitic crisis, have attempted to find a positive principle in his works, one that might mitigate the starkness of his absolute refusal or even justify the paranoia of his last works. Salvation through eros, through physical perfection, through art and dance — these and other motifs have been suggested as a source of light in Céline's underworld. True, these motifs are scattered through Céline's novels, like so many unrealized promises, but it is difficult to see that Céline ever gave any lasting consideration to these themes of salvation, any more than he seriously thought about the mystique he speaks of in his polemic and in letters. One American critic, Erika Ostrovsky, has called Céline's vision an inverted humanism, by which we might understand a humanism of negation in which the absence of values pleads for their creation. The Célinian novel is more than a little instructive, then, for few if any modern writers have carried a negative revolt so far, so persistently to its bitter conclusions.

Finally, Céline's legacy is his use of language. Language, *délire*, comedy, and revolt are inseparable in Céline. It is through his blend of argot, neologisms, popular expressions, and obscenities, through his blend of fractured syntax and popular speech patterns, and through his furious, rhythmic punctuation that Céline emulates chaos, emotional distress, and madness. It should be stressed again that neither his originality nor his stylistic force resides in his use of argot and slang. One has only to compare Céline's works with some contemporary novels whose authors seem to believe that a clever imitation of popular speech can suffice to create a jazzy style (as in a work as interesting as Queneau's *Le Chiendent*). Céline's "music," as he was well aware, goes far beyond such a simplistic dependence on a single device. Consider, in this respect, the epic scene of seasickness in *Mort à crédit* when the child Ferdinand and his parents cross the English channel:

L'écume emporte, mousse, brasse, tournoye entre nous toutes les ordures... On en ravale... On s'y remet... A chaque plongée l'âme s'échappe... on la reprend à la montée dans un reflux de glaires et d'odeurs... Il en suinte encore par le nez, salées. C'est trop!... Un passager implore pardon... Il hurle au ciel qu'il est vide!... Il s'évertue!... Il lui revient quand même une framboise!... Il la reluque avec épouvante... Il en louche... Il a vraiment plus rien du tout!... Il voudrait vomir ses deux yeux... Il fait des efforts pour ça... Il s'arc-boute à la mâture... Il essaye qu'ils lui sortent des trous... Maman elle, va s'écrouler sur la rampe... Elle se revomit complètement... Il lui est remonté une carotte... un morceau de gras... et la queue entière d'un rouget... (p. 611.)

(The foam sweeps up all the garbage, makes it lather, stirs it up, spins it around among us... We again swallow some of

it... We get it back out... At each plunge your soul takes
off... at every swell you get it back in a reflux of mucus and
stink... It oozes out your nose, all salty. It's too much! One
passenger begs forgiveness... He screams out to heaven that
he's empty... He strains... And he comes up with a raspberry
after all!... He stares at it with fright... He's goggle-eyed...
He really has nothing left... He'd like to vomit his two eyes...
He's really making an effort... He braces himself against
the mast... He's trying to get them to come out of their holes...
Mama, she goes and collapses on the rail... She vomits herself
up again... She got a carrot up... a piece of fat... and the whole
tail of a mullet...)

This scene of massive vomiting, a visceral projection
of all the misery in Ferdinand's childhood, is both an expression of revolt and a scene of delirious comedy.
Céline's language accumulates organic images of disgust
that convey a symbolic expression of his refusal of this
misery. Yet, the hyperbole, especially the detailed
images of the vomit, and the rhythmic expression of
mock astonishment create a sense of hallucination that
presents the comedy of *délire.* In this passage Céline
uses neither argot nor direct obscenity to create *délire,*
his only verbal invention being the neologistic exaggeration "se revomir," which expresses nausea's total
permeation of this world. The insistence on verbs, the
accumulation of disgusting but comic images, and the
well-spaced punctuation simulates the immediacy of
the *délire* that has erupted here. Céline's language has
the symbolic function of representing meaning, but also,
through its torrential form and violent dislocation, it *is*
meaning. The form of Céline's language is *délire.*

The Célinian novel is then, if only through the immediate force of language, one of the most naked revelations of the tormented self in modern literature. Its hero,
Ferdinand, is forever crying out in bewilderment as

he struggles to cope with existence' dementia. Yet we remember his lament with an ironic smile, often with great laughter. Ferdinand is the prototype of the bumbling a-heroic hero, striving ineffectually and for no good reason to survive against the cosmos' accumulated hostility. In spite of the odds, he does survive, perhaps because he enjoys his profane vituperation too much to allow a mere catastrophe to quiet him. Language mimics madness and destruction in Céline. It also mimics a riotous joy, the joy of shouting down all the misery and injustice with which life can crush a man. It is this exuberance that will not allow us to abandon Céline.

EPILOGUE   Who Was Céline?

The writer who chooses to hide behind a pseudonym prefers to confront his public with a mask. In turn the public feels challenged and invariably tries to strip away the mask and peer into the reality the writer has concealed. It is perhaps the supreme irony of "Céline," the feminine name that Dr. Louis-Ferdinand Destouches offered his public, that this mask should have come to fuse with the reality that Dr. Destouches sought to hide behind it. From *Voyage au bout de la nuit* to the last chronicles, Céline's journey is one that leads from literary disguise to ensnarement in the mythical identity he invented.

The difficulty in finding the "real" Céline or Destouches appears even more complex when one recognizes that the legends that surround Céline's life are largely a product of his own mind, though the hatred and adulation he inspired are the source of some of these legends. Especially after "Céline" was no longer an effective mask, after the mask had become synonymous with the man both in his own mind and in the public's, the doctor seems to have taken advantage of every opportunity to adopt defensive stances that would throw the public, the homicidal public, off his tracks. With all this in mind, I shall attempt to give an interpretative sketch of Céline's life that may facilitate an understanding of his novels, with their mixture of fiction and reality.[1]

Feeling compelled perhaps to set forth a biography that was in agreement with his literary identity, Céline often depicted his childhood in the following gruff terms:

> Je suis né à Courbevoie, 12, Rampe du Pont, en 1894, la Seine a gelé, ma mère crachait le sang . . . de misère il faut le dire, elle a vécu 74 ans. Elle était ouvrière dentellière. Elle est morte aveugle. On a toujours été bien travailleur dans ma famille. Et bien cons.[2]

> (I was born in Courbevoie, 12, Rampe du Pont, in 1894, the Seine froze over, my mother was spitting blood . . . from misery, it must be said, she lived 74 years. She was a lacemaker. She died blind. We were always really hard workers in my family. And damned stupid.)

Born under the sign of misery, Céline would have us believe he came into a world of poverty and sickness. First the newly industrialized Parisian *banlieue* and then the stinking gaslit and glass-covered Passage Choiseul behind the Boulevards were the scenes of his childhood. He supposedly spent much of his childhood running about Paris as he helped his mother sell her lace. Such an unremunerative occupation was done in the name of making ends meet in the Destouches household. His father, though he had a university diploma, was a minor bureaucrat with an insurance company; probably the post made up for its small salary with white collar status. Trapped in the senseless misery of the petty bourgeois urban economy, Céline's family supposedly lived with one preoccupation — escaping the threat of hunger.

Like many young Parisians, Louis-Ferdinand went to the primary school in his commune. After he had won his primary school certificate, his parents had enough ambition for their son, as Céline often pointed out, to send him abroad for short periods of time so that he might learn languages. Louis-Ferdinand perhaps acquired his taste for travel during his early trips to Germany and England. His parents hoped that foreign languages would enable their son to go into business. His mother must have seen commerce as the key to escaping from the Passage:

C'était l'idéal pour elle. Et mon père le pensait aussi. Parce que lui il avait réussi si mal dans la licence ès-lettres! Et mon grand-père agrégé!... Ils avaient réussi si mal qu'ils disaient: lui il réussira dans le commerce.[3]

(That was her ideal. And my father thought so, too. Because he'd done so poorly with the bachelor's diploma stuff! And my grandfather with his doctorate!... They'd done so poorly that they said: he'll make it in business.)

Life was a continual quest for security, and the trappings of academic achievement had little to offer when one needed to eat. Money was the only thing that offered freedom from anguish. All his life Céline never ceased repeating this lesson.

Céline's sketch of his childhood supplements the vision of childhood as an epic in mindless destruction

that one finds in *Mort à crédit*. One can only conjecture
what reality lies behind this self-portrait. Often it seems
to be a defensive mask of the kind that Céline later
adopted to justify his literary vision. At least one of
Céline's friends contests his portrayal of his childhood
deprivation. Marcel Brochard insists that his parents
were devoted to him, were respectable people, and
made a very good family.[4] Perhaps we must interpret
Céline's vision of his childhood in terms of the class
contradictions from which it springs, for his mother was
not a worker, but rather a *petite commerçante*, a margi-
nal merchant who was a prototype of the Parisian *petite
bourgeoisie*. His father no doubt resented being confined to this class, and perhaps his frustration is one of
the keys to Céline's outlook on his childhood. As an
educated man, coming from a family whose aspirations
were oriented by bourgeois cultural values, Céline's
father must have suffered a sense of failure and misery
that can best be explained in terms of alienation rather
than of physical hardship or hunger. Having interiorized his father's sense of frustration and degradation and
identifying through normal filial bonds with his mother
and her unrewarding toil, Céline came to view with
horror the suffering and deprivation of the Parisian working class. His mother was also an artisan, and her sense
of work molded Céline's mind as did few other single
influences. If he himself did not lack the bare necessi-
ties of life, he came to fear the meanness of a life constantly threatened by hard poverty. And it was this
threat, measured in terms of greater aspirations, that was
more damaging, more destructive, than would have been
been real destitution. His reaction to the misery he saw
around him undoubtedly sensitized him to the multiple
forms of destruction the city contains.[5]

After finishing elementary school, it appears that the young Louis-Ferdinand did join the ranks of commerce, though in a rather desultory manner. He took a variety of odd jobs, which usually entailed running about Paris as an errand boy. At the same time he prepared on his own for the first part of the *baccalauréat* examination. Céline's feverish thirst for knowledge and his ability to learn quickly enabled him to pass the first part of the examination in 1912. The army was Céline's next teacher, for he enlisted in the army, just as his Bardamu would later do in the same precipitate way. Céline's life in a boot camp for cavalrymen was the source of another novel, *Casse-Pipe*, of which only a few fragments remain.

Then the war came. Under heavy fire on the Flanders front, Céline volunteered for a liaison mission. He was severely wounded during the mission and spent nearly a year recuperating from his injuries. He was awarded a medal for bravery and had his picture placed on the cover of a popular illustrated magazine. The best-known part of Céline's legend concerns his war injuries. According to that legend, he was wounded in the arm and head, and the head wound supposedly necessitated trepanation. Given Céline's head injury, it has been only too easy for critics to reduce his work to the expression of a deranged mental condition and to infer that his later "instability seems to come from a damaged brain." [6] Of course, Céline himself, often as though to justify himself, seemed to take a curious pleasure in mentioning his head injury. "On m'a cassé le crâne" ("They've broken my skull"), Céline said in 1932 to explain to a friend why he could rarely sleep.[7] In later years he referred to his head wound more frequently, though after his outburst of anti-Semitic polemic, it might appear that he was attempting to find another defensive pose. As he put it during an interview in 1957:

J'ai une balle dans la tête et j'ai le bras en morceau. Je suis invalide à 75%. Alors ça suffit.[8]

(I've got a bullet in the head and my arm is in pieces. I've got a 75 percent disability rating. So that's enough.)

His friend Marcel Brochard, denies that Céline was ever wounded in the head, though Céline may have suffered an ear injury. For Brochard the story of the trepanation was only one of the many fantasies that Céline invented.[9] The critic Jean A. Ducourneau, after having examined Céline's medical records, also denies that Céline ever suffered a head injury. Multiple arm injuries, which entitled Céline to a 70 percent disability rating, are all that his medical records list. Ducourneau's statement is quite categorical: "And the trepanation, the scar, the bump? And the steel plate that some people have touched? One must fortunately accept the evidence, for none of that existed. Through their immutable presence and unpoetic reading, the authentic documents build history and take apart legend. No head wound was recorded. . . ."[10] Yet Céline's compulsive references to his head, to his insomnia, and to the buzzing in his ear are too compelling to be so quickly dismissed. What is one to make of the image of the injured or smashed head that recurs like an obsessive leitmotif throughout Céline's novels? It is at this point that the critic realizes how difficult it is to separate Céline's masks from the novelistic nightmares he offers his public. Céline probably never underwent trepanation, but the question of his obsession remains, as well as the question of his belief in his own fantasies, whatever defensive use he may have made of a fictitious wound at a later date.

The biographer in search of a real Céline encounters
more difficulties in the period of Céline's life that immediately followed the war. Most sources, nearly all
dependent on his inventive memory, contradict each
other. It would appear that after his convalescence,
perhaps in 1916, Céline was sent to fill a bureaucratic
post in the Cameroons and that, sick with malaria and
dysentery, he returned shortly afterwards to France.
The following year, having passed the final part of his
baccalauréat, he went to London. However, according
to his friend Georges Geoffroy, Céline took a job with
the French passport office in 1915 before going to
Africa. Later tales of Céline's intrigues in London would
appear to be more fantasy he invented to surround himself with an aura of mystery. Céline and his friend
Geoffroy seem to have led a very carefree existence
and made a good many friends in the "French milieu"
of London's Soho area: According to Geoffroy: "Some
days we had money, other days we were completely
broke! Things always worked out in Soho. The French
pimps and their protégées were nice to us, always ready
to offer us a meal." [11] Céline's main interests in London,
aside from wandering in the city, were the ballet—or,
more precisely, the dancers—and, if we can believe his
friend, German philosophy. Geoffroy recalls that
Céline often awakened him early in the morning when
he would start reading, sometimes aloud, passages
from Hegel, Fichte, Nietzsche, and Schopenhauer.
Céline's life in London's rollicking underworld of pimps
and whores provided him, of course, with the experience
for *Guignol's Band.*

After a year or so in London, Céline returned to France
to begin his medical studies at Rennes in 1918. During
this time he delivered a series of lectures in Brittany on
the prevention of tuberculosis. He quickly courted and

married Edith Follet. Mlle Follet was an excellent choice for a future doctor, since her father was both a prosperous doctor and the director of the medical school in Rennes. That a successful medical career promised both wealth and status no doubt provided more than an unconscious motivation for Céline's rather sudden marriage.

In 1924 Céline, *lauréat* of the medical school that year, defended and then published his thesis, *La Vie et l'œuvre de Philippe-Ignace Semmelweis*. This thesis topic seems, in retrospect, more than fortuitous, for it is a tale of catastrophe that reveals an early predilection in Céline for self-destruction. Semmelweis, a nineteenth-century gynecologist who discovered a prophylaxis for puerperal fever, destroyed himself in his fight to have his discovery accepted. Thousands of women would not have died in childbirth, had Semmelweis, who was finally driven to madness, been able to prevail against the combined forces of ignorance and medical orthodoxy. There have been a number of interpretations of the importance of this thesis for an understanding of Céline. Renato Barilli offers one that is worth quoting at length:

Henceforth it is clear that, being in love with life, filled with anguish at the thought of the disease and death that strike humanity, dedicated to the medical profession and to its moving certainties, from the beginning Céline glimpsed in Semmelweis an emblematic image of himself. An emblem that was good not only for the radiant days in which some hope to bring an authentic contribution to salvation could subsist, but also for those dark days in which incomprehension and persecution would be given back to him by his beneficiaries. For humanity, blinded by the narrow circle of its miseries, is ungrateful toward the figure of the Saving Doctor, it rejects the way of the raw and implacable "truth" he shows it, and places a cross on his back until he can be expelled from his own community. When Semmelweis denounced the dangers of puerperal fever and proposed appropriate prophylactic measures, he was derided and opposed in every manner. This makes the emblematic figure an obligatory stopping place in the Célinian biography: through an atrocious irony, he who started out in life with a warm love of a healthy and balanced life will be constrained by the obstacles he encounters to deviate from these values and to take up the path of madness. The usury of repeated, crushing daily afflictions obliged him to seek compensation in a fictitious world of dreams and shadows. The great mythomaniacal heroes of the Célinian novels will know something of the same, for they, too, are crushed, although in different conditions from those of the doctor from Prague, beneath the weight of a reality that has become unbearable.[12]

One senses immediately the attraction Céline must have felt for Semmelweis, both for the magnanimity of his struggle and for the futility of a self-defeat that ended in death. Moreover, Céline concluded his lyrical thesis in a strangely prophetic way, saying that the ultimate cause of Semmelweis' misfortunes was that his discovery went beyond the strength of his genius. It would be difficult to find a more concise way of describing the cause of Céline's own, later misfortunes.

Semmelweis was not Céline's only medical publication. In 1925 he wrote *La Quinine en thérapeutique.* This technical work, which testifies to Céline's very serious interest in medical science, became something of a standard text in the field and was translated into Spanish and Italian. Céline's dedication is made quite explicit as he calls upon his profession not to forget that its final goal is to cure and to combat suffering:

Par malheur les physiologistes ont souvent perdu de vue
précisément que la fin de leurs études était la pratique
journalière qui soulage et qui sauve et travaillé comme
s'ils étaient hors de la vie courante. Au lieu d'expérimenter
dans les conditions où le médecin se trouve chaque jour,
des conditions de science dite pure les séduisent davantage.
(p. v.)

(Unfortunately physiologists have often overlooked the fact
that the goal of their studies was the daily practice that
relieves pain and saves lives and have worked as if they were
removed from daily life. Instead of experimenting in those
conditions where the doctor finds himself everyday, they
have been more enticed by the problems of so-called pure
science.)

Céline's view of medicine and pure research as shown
in *Voyage* completes our view of his commitment to
medical practice whose only justification is to bring
relief to the suffering. It is not an exaggeration to say
that at the beginning of his career Céline even looked
upon his profession as a secular or positivistic form of
sacerdotalism. Céline was also interested in social
questions that medical practice raises. In 1928 he published his essay, "Les Assurances sociales et une
politique économique de la santé publique." [13] This
essay shows conservative doubts about the efficacity
of social security, but it calls nonetheless for a revolution
in the practice of medicine. Céline would have nurses
made available for office consultation and would send
doctors into homes and factories. The essay presents a
curious example of Céline's way of thinking, for he
poses here as Disraelian neo-conservative and yet will
accept nothing less than a radical solution to a social
problem. Céline's essay probably received little attention.[14]

The next period of the doctor's life began with a sudden rejection of the secure existence his medical career promised him. It is difficult to imagine Céline at ease in the smug atmosphere of the provincial middle class and therefore not altogether surprising that he suddenly left his wife and baby daughter to take a position with the League of Nations. The new freedom enabled him to visit several foreign countries. On a boat for Africa, he learned of his divorce. After a stay in the colonies, where the doctor observed what French civilization meant for both the colonizer and the colonized, Céline went to the United States. Here for six months, perhaps in 1926, he studied medical problems at a Ford plant. His experiences during this period caused him to write a medical article on working conditions and, far more important, inspired the vision of modern industrialism he recorded in *Voyage*. Further travel led him to Canada and Cuba. Travel was Céline's vice before it became Bardamu's.

Just as Bardamu's peregrinations came to an end in Paris, Céline terminated his wanderings, briefly at least, by returning to Paris in 1928 and setting up a private medical practice in Clichy. His days he devoted to patients, his nights to literary composition. Though he had been a voracious reader, nothing in Céline's past had indicated that he was interested in writing. His first work was a play, *L'Eglise*, a satire in which a Dr. Bardamu shows up the political machinations of the League of Nations. The play has little interest today, except to the extent that it foreshadows some of the themes Céline developed in *Voyage*. Céline gave up his private medical practice in 1931 and took a position in a municipal clinic in Clichy. Continuing his nocturnal writing, he started on *Voyage*, though it seems he was not en-

tirely a slave to this project. He was never without female companionship. *Voyage* carries a dedication to
Elisabeth Craig, an American dancer who was Céline's
favorite until she left him to return to the United States.
She was neither the first nor the last dancer in Céline's
life.

After some four years of composition, *Voyage* was put
in final form. Jeanne Carayon, a friend of Céline's in
Clichy, tells that he came unexpectedly to her apartment
one night and gave her a typewritten copy of *Voyage* to
correct.[15] In the meantime he sent copies of the novel to
the publishers Denoël and Steele and to Gallimard.
Robert Denoël, after a night of intensive reading, was
quick to accept and became Céline's publisher until the
Liberation. The fever of writing having consumed itself, the nightly toil having come to an end, Céline refused to have anything further to do with his manuscript
and left all final corrections to his friend. Given Céline's
minute method of composition, it is difficult to understand this aloof attitude toward what the printer might
do to his work. Perhaps the novel must be seen as a
form of catharsis for Céline. Once completed, it could
no longer interest him.

It was at this moment that Dr. Destouches took on the
mask "Céline." Always minimizing the importance of
his decision to hide his identity behind a female name,
he offered various, usually financial, reasons for hiding
his identity:

Moi, à ce moment-là, j'avais un mal énorme à payer mon loyer,
justement... C'était pourtant pas brillant, je vous assure...
Alors, comment en sortir... Et je m'suis mis à écrire... Et j'ai
pris le nom de ma mère, qui s'appelait Céline. . . . Sans rien
lui dire, évidemment... Parce que, comme ça, je gagnerais, je
mettrais des sous d'côté... Et puis alors, je paierais... j'achè-

terais peut-être un appartement... je resterais avec ma mère... Et comme ça personne n'en saurait rien. On n'viendrait pas m'chercher sous un prénom féminin... Et puis voilà toute l'histoire de Céline...[16]

(Right at that time, I was having a lot of trouble paying my rent... And it wasn't much, I assure you... So, how to work it out... And I started to write... And I used my mother's name, which was Céline... ...Without telling her anything obviously ... Because that way I'd come out ahead, I'd put a little cash aside... And then I'd pay off... Maybe I'd buy an apartment... I'd stay with my mother... And that way no one would know anything. No one would come looking for me behind a feminine name... And that's the whole story of Céline.)

This explanation brings up at least two problems. First, if we are to believe Henri Mahé, Céline had already moved into a very comfortable apartment in Montmartre in 1931, a year before he published *Voyage* under the name Céline: "Bourgeois decor, country doctor style, or a priest's perhaps? Rustic table, polished, shining Breton armoires, period armchairs, a wide divan, a tall tapestry screen, rugs well laid out on the floor, on the wall a little pastel of dancers signed by Degas, two or three decorative trifles, and, through the studio's bay window, what a view of Paris!"[17] This description seems to indicate that Céline knew a degree of prosperity at the time. Reducing his decision to write and to hide behind a feminine name to a mere financial question is perhaps another defensive device Céline used, though there can be no doubt that Céline hoped his work would sell. All his life he was obsessed with a fear of finding himself without money.[18] The second problem is related to Céline's dismissing his writing as a financial venture, for the question immediately comes up: who was, as he implies, going to hunt him out behind a feminine name? The name seems to presuppose the need to hide from vague dangers in the world. Céline foresaw himself as a possible victim of the world's hostility even before he published his first novel.

Voyage, arriving in the heart of the Depression, caused an immediate furor. Céline, supported by Léon Daudet and Lucien Descaves, almost received the Prix Goncourt that year. The literary prize finally went to Guy Mazeline for his novel *Les Loups,* and Céline had to content himself with the Prix Renaudot, the traditional consolation prize. Not everyone was willing to accept the ribald genius that animated *Voyage,* the work Céline later blamed for all his misfortunes. With the advent of literary fame, Céline continued his medical practice, though he made occasional gestures toward Parisian literary life. In 1933 he published an article in defense of *Voyage.*[19] And, in the same year, he delivered his "Hommage à Zola," the only public speech Céline ever made on literature.[20] In this speech he recognized Zola's importance but refused any affiliation with the naturalistic writer. Truth, in Zola's sense, after the near-suicide of nations in the last war, had become impossible. For the truth was, according to Céline, that the European masses were guided by a profound death instinct which, at the least shock, would plunge them again into murderous convulsions. In his speech Céline rejected all explanations that current ideologies then offered for European malaise, including his own view of exploitation. In making these remarks, perhaps Céline had his next novel in mind, *Mort à crédit,* another long novel in which the death instinct is pervasive. It may be noted that although "Hommage à Zola" contains a few of the themes of Céline's later polemic, nothing in it foreshadows his coming anti-Semitic crisis. In fact,

The text of this book was set in Caledonia Linofilm and printed by Offset on P & S Special Book manufactured by P. H. Glatfelter Co., Spring Grove, Pa. Composed, printed and bound by Quinn & Boden Company, Inc., Rahway, N.J.

"Hommage à Zola" contains insulting references to Hitler and to nationalism in general.

Céline's personal life at this time was not as quiet as has been supposed. His correspondence shows that he made frequent trips, often to see friends, though perhaps more often from a need to be in movement, to satisfy his curiosity, to escape from Paris and the daily drudgery he encountered as a doctor. It would appear that he came to the United States in 1934 and in 1937, the first time in search of Elisabeth Craig and perhaps to see about the possibility of doing a Hollywood version of *Voyage*. He also visited Russia (of which *Mea Culpa* was the result), as well as England, Denmark, Belgium, and various parts of France. Brittany was his favorite vacation site, with its interesting coast, ports, and sailing vessels. The imaginary journey Céline set forth in his first novel had its parallel in the writer's life. Until his disgrace after World War II he could never stop traveling.

The correspondence of the thirties depicts a man who is often generous and, at times, naïvely opportunistic. Letters to such men as Eugène Dabit, Léon Daudet, Lucien Descaves, and Elie Faure, as well as to a host of other friends, show a Céline who had a great zest for life—especially where eroticism was concerned—as well as an attitude of permanent revolt. Perhaps the most revealing letter of this period is one he wrote to the great art historian Elie Faure. Explaining his refusal to adhere to any party or group, he declared:

Je suis anarchiste depuis toujours, je n'ai jamais voté, je ne voterai jamais pour rien ni pour personne. Je ne crois pas aux hommes. Pourquoi voulez-vous que je me mette à jouer du bigophone soudain parce que douze douzaines de ratés m'en

jouent? Moi qui joue pas trop mal au grand piano? Pour me
mettre à leur toise de rétrécis, de constipés, d'envieux, de
haineux, de bâtards? C'est plaisanterie en vérité. Je n'ai rien
de commun avec tous ces châtrés—qui vocifèrent leurs sup-
positions balourdes et ne comprennent rien. . . . Ils la reculent
la révolution au lieu de la faciliter. . . . Ils me fusilleront
peut-être les uns ou les autres. Les nazis m'exècrent autant
que les socialistes et les communards itou . . . Ils s'enten-
dent tous quand il s'agit de me vomir. Tout est permis sauf de
douter de l'homme—alors c'est fini de rire. J'ai fait la preuve;
mais je les emmerde aussi tous.[21]

(I've always been an anarchist, I've never voted, I'll never
vote for anything or anyone. I don't believe in men. Why do
you expect me to start all of a sudden playing a paper whistle
because twelve dozen lousy writers play it for me? When I
don't play the grand piano so badly myself? So I can cut myself down to their size of constipated, envious, hateful bastards? That's really a joke. I have nothing in common with
these castrated flops—who scream out their clumsy supposi-
tions and don't understand anything. . . . They're delaying
the revolution instead of facilitating it. . . . They'll put me in
front of the firing squad, one group or the other. The Nazis
despise me as much as the socialists or the commies, too . . .
They can all get together when it's a question of loathing me.
Anything is permitted except *doubting man*—then the laughing is over. I've tried it out, but I keep giving them hell.)

This letter, written probably in 1934 and before Céline
had written any anticommunist or anti-Semitic polemic,
shows that Céline's sense of isolation had its roots in an
almost willful desire to be persecuted. He accepts full
responsibility for his uncompromising revolt and seems
to rejoice in the destruction it promises. The revolution,
and it is dubious that Céline has any precise idea in
mind, cannot be accomplished in any case. Perhaps the

only true revolution would be the one that would abolish man's despicable nature. So while waiting for the
firing squad—and Céline was nearly a prophet in that
respect—he will continue to play his "grand piano,"
to create that music of revolt he knows will be his ultimate undoing.

In 1936, the same year as the publication of *Mort à
crédit,* Céline went to the Soviet Union to spend his
author's royalties after Louis Aragon and Elsa Triolet
had translated *Voyage* into Russian. The result of this
trip was a ferocious little pamphlet, *Mea Culpa,* attacking Soviet Communism. The diatribe's explosive language demonstrated what a virulent polemist Céline
was. In *Mea Culpa* Céline assailed the new forms of
human exploitation that the Soviet Union had developed, and, at the same time, he pursued his doubting
of man to new extremes:

La supériorité pratique des grandes religions chrétiennes,
c'est qu'elles doraient pas la pilule. Elles essayaient pas
d'étourdir, elles cherchaient pas l'électeur, elles sentaient
pas le besoin de plaire, elles tortillaient pas du panier. Elles
saisissaient l'homme au berceau et lui cassaient le morceau
d'autor. Elles le rencardaient sans ambages: "Toi, petit
putricule informe, tu seras jamais qu'une ordure... De nais-
sance tu n'es que merde... Est-ce que tu m'entends? C'est
l'évidence même, c'est le principe de tout!..." (pp. 17–18.)

(The practical superiority of the great Christian religions was
that they didn't coat the pill. They didn't try to astonish anyone, they didn't seek out the voter, they didn't feel the need
to please, they didn't beat around the bush. They grabbed
hold of man in the cradle and broke the bad news to him
right away. They let him in on the secret without messing
around: "You little amorphous particle of putrescence, you'll

never be anything except garbage. By birth you're just shit...
Do you hear me? It's obvious, it's the first principle of everything!...)

Man's nature condemns him to the rubbish heap. Céline's ironic remarks about the church might appear to
suggest that only authoritarian structures can keep man
from giving into his penchant for dissolution, but it is
doubtful that Céline had anything so precise in mind.
Rather, man's innate propensity to turn sour and decay,
like existence itself, makes the hope for democracy,
socialism, communism, or any form of just social organi-
zation an illusion. The Soviet Union is only one more
example of man's incapacity to transcend his nature. Of
course, one should not look for consistency in Céline's
comments on politics and society, for he later declared
himself a communist in his pamphlets, and his attitude
during the Occupation showed that he wanted some
form of revolution that would abolish injustice and social
privilege — all this in spite of his refusal to believe in
man.

Mea Culpa has been viewed as the outcry of a man
who became violently disenchanted with the socialist
hope of the thirties; the title is certainly suggestive in
this respect. Nothing in Céline's past, however, indicates that he ever seriously envisaged any form of social
collectivism as a solution to man's exploitation of man
or as a solution to the problem of human suffering. His
medical article on social security shows that he even
mistrusted this rather innocuous form of social planning.
It would seem that Céline, while remaining in revolt
against the inhumanities of capitalist democracy, had
seized the opportunity to denounce the Soviet Union's
new forms of dupery and enslavement. Following the

logic of his total revolt, however, Céline had left himself no outlet, and, when he could no longer bear the strain, he fell prey to a good many of the absurd platitudes of the fascist right.

The following year, in 1937, after a few weeks of frenzied writing, Céline launched his first attack against the Jews, a decadent France, the coming war, and a good many other targets in *Bagatelles pour un massacre.* Though written in Céline's virulent, original style, this work of insane anti-Semitism echoed most of the clichés that were then current with the French extreme right and the Nazi propaganda machine. *Bagatelles* astounded the French literary community. André Gide believed that it was a monstrous satire, a parody that by its very grotesqueness and exaggeration was intended to discredit anti-Semitism.[22] Céline quickly dispelled any such illusions when, in 1938, he wrote another vituperative piece of anti-Semitism, *L'Ecole des cadavres.* This work not only attacked the Jews but, pursuing Céline's pacifist logic, called for a Franco-German alliance to prevent a second episode of mutual carnage. Despised by the left, unwanted now by the right, Céline had succeeded in bringing about the isolation he had foreseen in his correspondence.

The doctor's medical career suffered at this moment. In 1938 he was dismissed from his clinic. In later years Céline offered the following explanation for his dismissal:

J'ai été viré par la municipalité communiste aux ordres du Dr ... émigré juif lithuanien, et pas du tout MEDECIN: imposteur, mais dont le frère était rédacteur à la PRAVDA, imposé à Clichy par la PRAVDA... dès son arrivée *nommé* médecin-chef ... en dépit de toutes les Lois françaises,

parlant à peine le français, a entrepris de virer tout ce qui
n'était pas *juif*, et *surtout* moi! [23]

(I was fired by the communist municipal government which
was taking orders from Dr. ——, a Jewish Lithuanian emigrant,
and not at all a DOCTOR: an impostor whose brother was a
writer for PRAVDA, who was imposed on Clichy by PRAVDA
... the moment he arrived, barely speaking French, he was
named head doctor . . . in spite of all the French Laws and
attempted to fire everyone who wasn't *Jewish*, and *especially*
me!)

Some critics have seen this incident as one of the
sources of Céline's anti-Semitism; however, Céline had
already published *Bagatelles pour un massacre* when
he was dismissed. The story, perhaps invented by
Céline himself, is more indicative of his way of interpreting his misfortunes than of anything else. A second
attempt at private practice was a failure. Céline then
moved into his mother's apartment, perhaps for financial reasons, since in 1939 he was also condemned for
libel in *L'Ecole des cadavres*.

With the outbreak of the war Céline tried to reenlist,
but was refused. Determined to see action, he then
became the head doctor of the *Chella*, an armed merchant ship. Almost immediately afterward, the *Chella*
collided with a British vessel. According to Jean
Ducourneau, the *Chella* was set afloat, only to be sunk
a second time, this time by the Germans. Céline, probably having had enough maritime action, returned to
Paris, where he replaced the head doctor of the Satrou-
ville municipal clinic. Disaster was quick to catch up
with him. Céline was soon forced to join the exodus of
refugees fleeing the German invasion. Driving an ambulance, he made his escape by transporting to La

Rochelle two infants, an octogenarian, and a dancer from the Opéra-Comique. Céline had good reason to flee. "Je ne voulais avoir à aucun prix l'air d'attendre les Allemands" ("At no price whatsoever did I want to appear to be waiting for the Germans"), he later wrote to Albert Paraz, for Céline knew that a good many people already looked upon him as a potential agent for the Nazis.[24] In his capacity as doctor, he stayed two weeks at La Rochelle, where he was supposedly offered the opportunity to escape to England. In October of 1940, however, he returned to Paris to take a position as head doctor of the clinic at Bezons.

Céline's activity during the Occupation years is surrounded by a cloud of accusations and denials. When the Communist press, among others, charged him with being an important German secret agent, Céline did little for his defense when he asserted that the Jews should erect a statue in his honor for having abstained from doing them any further harm.[25] Nothing, however, indicates that Céline was ever involved in any form of collaboration. After his return to Paris, he took an apartment in Montmartre, where, it appears, he gave refuge to a Jew at the beginning of the war.[26] Later he was quite aware that a Resistance group held frequent meetings in the apartment beneath his. A friend of the group, who had been tortured by the Gestapo, received medical aid from Céline. In return for his aid the group kept Céline informed on the war's developments.[27] Céline's contacts with the Germans, other than those necessitated by his medical practice, seem to have been limited to some activity with the Institut Allemand, which, under the direction of Karl Epting, translated some German poetry into French. Epting himself has made clear that Céline had little to do with the Germans: "He

never solicited anything for himself except paper in
order to have his works printed. But in that Céline was
treated very shabbily by the propaganda services of the
Militärbefehlshaber. The representatives of the Party
and of the National Socialist state never took him into
account. . . . Most of the "Propaganda" representatives . . . moreover were not able to understand Céline's
French." [28] Céline was later charged before the French
courts, however, with having collaborated with the
Office Central Juif; nothing substantiates this accusation.[29] One anecdote would even indicate that Céline
went out of his way to disrupt this kind of organized
anti-Semitism. According to Lucien Rebatet, Céline
once attended a meeting of the Institut de Questions
Juives. While listening to a long harangue against the
"Judeo-Marxist tyranny," Céline began to ask, "Et la
connerie aryenne, dis, t'en causes pas?" ("What about
Aryan stupidity, you got anything to say about it?").[30]
Céline's disturbances provoked a fight between a member of the audience and a member of the speaker's
committee, and supposedly won over the audience and
disrupted the meeting. The story is perhaps apocryphal
but certainly indicative of Céline's anarchism, of his
refusal to accept any institutionalized solution to any
problem.

Céline's writing brings up other questions when con-
sidering his attitude during the Occupation. His last
work of polemic, *Les Beaux Draps,* did appear during
the Occupation in 1941 and could perhaps be con-
strued as giving aid to the enemy. This small book,
though much abated in tone, was still anti-Semitic. It
contained, moreover, such a violent attack on French
institutions—notably the army—that it provoked a
protest from one of the collaborationist newspapers.[31]

Céline also compromised himself by some letters he wrote. These appeared, sometimes on the front page, in such collaborationist newspapers as the *Emancipation Nationale, Au Pilori,* and the *Révolution Nationale.* A letter written to *La Gerbe* best illustrates Céline's attitude during the first part of the Occupation. Writing to explain why he was no longer writing, Céline attacked those writers who were just then rallying to Vichy; he wanted them to explain themselves on the Jewish question:

Cent mille fois hurlés "Vive Pétain" ne valent pas un petit "vire les youtres" dans la pratique. Les juifs sont-ils responsablent de la guerre ou non? Répondez-moi noir sur blanc, chers écrivains acrobates.[32]

(Yelling "Vive Pétain" one hundred thousand times isn't worth one little "Kick out the kikes" in practice. Are the Jews responsible for the war or not? Answer me black on white, dear acrobat writers.)

More telling than Céline's smug repetition of his anti-Semitism was his expression of disappointment in the course of events since the Occupation had begun. There had been no revolution:

C'est ça votre révolution? Aux fous! Vous accourrez me réveiller quand on abolira les trusts. Pas avant! De grâce! (p. 1.)

(That's your revolution? Nuts! You'll come running to wake me up when the trusts are abolished. Not before! Please!)

Céline's attitude toward collaboration can be explained, in part, by his scorn for the Vichy government's politics, for his radical imagination could conceive of no improvement of society that would entail less than a total transformation of France. Céline's politics were in fact a rejection of politics, as he made clear when he discussed the remaking of France in an interview given to *Emancipation Nationale:*

Il faut des hommes; alors une autre vie recommencera. Il y a une idée conductrice des peuples. Il y a une loi. Elle part d'une idée qui monte vers le mysticisme absolu, qui monte encore sans peur, et progresse. Si elle file vers la politique, c'est fini. Elle tombe dans la boue et nous avec.[33]

(We must have men; then another life will start anew. There is a guiding idea of peoples. There is a law. It starts with an idea that ascends toward an absolute mysticism, that still ascends without fear and progresses. If it heads for politics, it's finished. It will fall into the mud, and us with it.)

These remarks again suggest Péguy's distinction between "politique" and "mystique," though one might well suspect that the mysticism Céline speaks of is only a negation of all he detests. "Remaking France" might well be read as "remaking human existence." His quest for "another life," for a "law," is another side of what we have seen in the polemic, the positing of a principle of light that can illuminate the darkness. Yet it is hard to believe that Céline had anything precise in mind, apart from an undefined desire for a transforming apocalypse. His groping for a mystique is too amorphous to be given any name, though one can see that his irrationalism mimics certain aspects of fascism.

Céline married again during the Occupation. His choice of a wife was, inevitably, a dancer, Lucette Almanzor, or the "Lili" of the last chronicles. Having abandoned his polemic, he began work on *Guignol's*

Band, the first part of which he published in 1944. The future also preoccupied Céline during this time, for he knew the Occupation could not last. In the company of several French doctors, Céline made a trip to Berlin in 1942 for the purpose of visiting some hospitals. Presumedly this trip was only an excuse for him to get in touch with a friend who was to arrange for him to go to Denmark. Before the war, perhaps in 1938, Céline had sent some gold ingots to Denmark, thus preparing what he believed would be a secure refuge in the event of war. Evidently circumstances for such a move were not favorable in 1942, and Céline was obliged to return to France. According to Céline's own testimony, he then attempted to establish himself in Brittany, but the Germans refused him the necessary permission.[34] Perhaps Céline thought Brittany was safer for him than Paris, for as the Resistance grew stronger, the notorious anti-Semite found himself a marked man. One of Céline's friends has commented, "Repeatedly, the London radio reminded listeners of the death sentence against Ferdinand that the Resistance had pronounced." [35] Thus in July, 1944, he finally decided it was time to leave Paris. Accompanied by the actor Robert Le Vigan, his wife, and his cat, Céline went to Germany, giving as an excuse that he was going to a medical convention. Denmark was undoubtedly their destination, but the German authorities did not allow the group of refugees to cross the Danish frontier for nearly a year.

It is true that Céline's wanderings in Germany are rather well if apocalyptically documented in his last three works, but Céline offered other versions of his travels to those who asked for them. The biographical introduction to the Pléiade edition of *Voyage* and *Mort à crédit* tells us, for example, that he and his companions

were first detained in Baden-Baden for three months
and that after Céline refused to aid the Nazi propaganda
services they were sent to Berlin, only to be detained in
a camp for "freethinkers." One can easily imagine
Céline's motivation for portraying himself as a victim of
the Nazi regime. Lucien Rebatet, one of the exiles at
Sigmaringen, offers another version of Céline's travels,
this one having the advantage of being confirmed by
his account of his travels in *Nord*. According to Rebatet,
Céline left Baden-Baden and went to Berlin, where his
presence embarrassed his friend Dr. Haubolt, an important medical functionary in the Reich. Haubolt then
sent Céline and his companions to Kräntzlin, near Neu-
Ruppin. Here they lived in a small castle: "There was
nothing punitive or anything like a concentration camp
in the retreat, which hardly turned out to be fun, but
which fitted in with Louis-Ferdinand's schemes." [36]
After learning of the existence of a French "colony" in
Germany, Céline requested to be sent to Sigmaringen.
His stay there and his views on the chaotic life of the
Vichy government in exile were the basis for his first
chronicle, *D'un château l'autre*.

In 1945, as Germany was being destroyed in the last
spasms of the war, the long-awaited permission to enter
Denmark was granted, and Céline began the train ride
through the Inferno that was at least partially the basis
for *Rigodon*. Taking the last train that crossed the frontier, he arrived in Denmark in March, but remained in
hiding until the Germans left. In December, on the
request of the French legation in Copenhagen, the
Danish authorities arrested Céline. He spent the next
fourteen months in prison, perhaps most or all of that
time in solitary confinement. The French government
failed to take any definitive action in his case, so the

Danish authorities released Céline. His health seriously undermined, he spent some time recuperating in a hospital. Céline's persecution complex began to find some objective justification at this time, for he was imprisoned again on the request of the French legation. Finally, after he had given his word not to leave the country and in view of the inertia of the French government, the Danish allowed Céline to live with his wife. She, too, had been imprisoned, though the authorities released her after two months so that she could undergo an operation. Suffering as an exile in the harsh Baltic climate, Céline spent the next five years waiting for a final disposition of his case. From a strictly juridical point of view, it would appear that there was no case against him. His publisher, Robert Denoël, was in fact acquitted of all charges of collaboration, and it was Denoël who had possessed all rights for the republication of Céline's works, including the polemic—which perhaps accounted for Denoël's assassination on the Esplanade of the Invalides.

The French government finally convicted Céline, by default, in 1950. The court sentenced him to one year in prison, a fine of fifty thousand francs, and the confiscation of one half of his property. In light of the sentences given others accused of collaboration, this sentence seems something like a smack on the wrists. Céline had already replied to the accusations made against him with a point-by-point refutation, and this now provoked a rebuttal by Maurice Vanino, a member of the Resistance, in his *L'Ecole du cadavre, l'Affaire Céline*. While Vanino was accusing Céline of having used his anti-Semitism to give the French a dose of Pan-Germanism in order to facilitate the Nazi enterprise, the military court of Paris gave Céline amnesty. Céline was thus able to return to

France in 1951, but it can hardly be said that he returned
to a country that had forgiven him for his polemic before
the war. Indeed, Vanino's accusations were published
shortly after Céline's return to France.

Contrition, however, was far from Céline's mind, especially after the harsh punishment of prison and exile.
His postwar behavior—performance is perhaps the better word—shows that he was convinced his enemies
were merely using his writings as an excuse to destroy
him. A letter to Albert Paraz, an unfailing friend throughout Céline's exile, makes clear that Céline saw himself
as the victim of a plot whose only goal was to destroy
him:

> . . . Il semble impossible, inimaginable à mes ennemis
> (tellement grand en est leur désir), que je me sois abstenu de
> toute collaboration.
> Cette abstention leur parait monstrueuse, impensable. Il
> faut, pour leurs fins, que j'aie collaboré. A n'importe quel prix.
> Ils comptent sur cette collaboration pour me faire condamner
> et exécuter, si ce n'est légalement, par assassinat. . . .[37]

> (It seems impossible, unimaginable, to my enemies (so
> great is their desire of it) that I abstained from any form of
> collaboration.
> This refraining appears monstrous and unthinkable to them.
> To accomplish their goals it's imperative that I have collabo-
> rated. At any price. They are counting on this collaboration
> to have me condemned and executed, if not legally, then by
> assassination. . . .)

But Céline did not lose his paradoxical sense of humor.
Ever ready to turn his rage against his persecutors, to
disavow the past and to march again on the attack, in
another letter he wrote:

Question Juifs, il y a beau temps qu'ils me sont devenus
sympathiques: depuis que j'ai vu les Aryens à l'œuvre, fritz
et français.

Quels larbins! Abrutis, éperdument serviles. Ils en rajoutent.
Et putains! Et fourbes! — Quelle sale clique — Ah j'étais fait
pour m'entendre avec les Youtres. Eux seuls sont curieux,
mystiques, messianiques à ma manière. . . .[38]

(Speaking of Jews, I took a liking to them a long time ago:
since I saw Aryans at work, both Krauts and French.

What flunkeys! Stupid, and infinitely servile. They overdo
it. Whores! And cheats!—What a lousy clique—Ah I was
meant to get along with the Kikes. They're the only ones
who are curious, mystical, messianic in my way.)

If Jews were no longer the cause of Western decadence,
Céline was not slow in finding another one. What is
perhaps most amazing about this writer after the war is
that he quickly set about fabricating another mask and
began again to play the role of the prophet who forecasts
cataclysms.

Chinese hordes arriving at Brest became Céline's next
prognostication. Reaching back to turn-of-the-century
racist mythology, he decided to revive the Yellow Peril.
One can hardly believe that Céline took seriously his
new predictions of catastrophes. Rather, it would appear
that he decided to play to the hilt his role of madman, to
assume entirely the insanity that had been his before
the war. In any case, by 1950, and several years before
D'un château l'autre made his new racism public,
Céline was writing letters such as the following one he
sent to his traveling companion Le Vigan:

Question grand avenir. Toute la terre aux *Jaunes*. Ils sont
dominants dans les mélanges. Leurs gamètes gagnent. Tout
est là. Ils avaleront Ruskos, Boches, Francailles, Yankees, à

coups de sperme. Dominants, dominants. Ni juifs, ni Noirs,
ni Blancs, ni Indiens n'existent devant le métissage jaune.
Mais c'est pas nos oignons! C'est pour dans un siècle ou deux,
et c'est le prochain achat de raviolis qui m'angoisse... Je suis
trop vieux, je ne la verrai pas, et trop malade, l'arrivée des
Chinois à Paris. Je ne crois pas aux Russes! Chrétiens comme
nous, suceurs de doigts de pieds, ils sont faits pour s'entendre
avec Mauriac! Vive Chou en Lai, un vrai raciste! L'avenir du
monde: jaune! La question juive n'existe plus! [39]

(Looking at the long run. The whole earth belongs to the
Orientals. They're dominant in crossings. Their gametes win
out. Everything is in that. They'll swallow Russkies, Krauts,
Frenchies, Yankees, with shots of sperm. Dominant, dominant.
Neither Jews, nor Blacks, nor Whites, nor Indians can last in
yellow crossbreeding. But that's not our kettle of fish. It'll happen in a century or two, and it's the next purchase of ravioli
that makes me fearful... I'm too old, and too sick, I won't see
the Chinese arriving in Paris. I don't believe in the Russians.
Christians like us, they suck their toes; they're made to get
along with Mauriac! Long live Chou-En-lai, a real racist!
The world's future: yellow! There's no longer any Jewish
question!)

Having leaped once into the public arena as a racist
prophet, Céline seemed determined to follow this role
to its most absurd conclusions, to become a clown whose
ill humor is an expected ritual. Yet one can also see that
his racism offered him another mask; it gave him some
defense against the past while it allowed him to vent his
disgust with contemporary society. Céline's new racism
was not so much anti-Chinese as it was a wish to see
European society suffer some cataclysm that would
justify Céline's view of its essential insanity.

Céline poured forth his vituperation in several kinds
of writing. In the sixteen years that remained for him to
live after the war he wrote the two-volume *Féerie pour*

une autre fois, his three chronicles, plus some smaller
pieces, a remarkable feat of endurance given his poor
health. In 1948, for example, after learning that Sartre
had accused him of being paid by the Germans, he wrote
a short pamphlet, *A l'agité du bocal,* which bitterly attacked "tartre," who was to remain one of Céline's
favored polemical subjects for the rest of his life. In
1948 also appeared *Foudres et flèches,* a "mythological
ballet" which reveals that Céline never stopped thinking about the dance, even in his most trying moments.
Two years later *Scandale aux abysses,* a cartoon scenario,
again demonstrated Céline's whimsical side. *Féerie*
and *Normance* were published in 1952 and 1954, though
by this time Céline was practically a forgotten name.

Thus in 1955 he picked up the challenge of modern
publicity and published his own *interviowe* in the form
of his *Entretiens avec le professeur Y...* This comic ad-
vertisement for himself is more than a diatribe, for it
sets forth Céline's defense of emotivity as the basis for
aesthetics. Defending himself as an inventor, Céline
claimed that he had discovered how to transcribe the
emotion of spoken language into written form. And in a
paradoxical about-face he disclaimed any intent to have
ever wanted to play the oracle:

J'ai pas d'idées moi! aucune! et je trouve rien de plus
vulgaire, de plus commun, de plus dégoûtant que les idées!
les bibliothèques en sont pleines! . . . (p. 19.)

(I don't have any ideas! none! and I find nothing more
vulgar, more common, more disgusting, than ideas! libraries
are full of them!)

Céline wanted, understandably enough, to be recognized for nothing more than his "emotive rails," his
points of suspension that guide his emotive subway

through his works. That, according to Céline, was enough for the world to accord him genius. Céline continued to put his theory into practice, and in 1957 the publication of *D'un château l'autre* marked his first step toward regaining a public. *Nord*, a second chronicle of Céline's stay in Germany, followed in 1960, one year after *Ballets sans musique, sans personne, sans rien* had made all of Céline's whimsical and fantasy ballet scenarios available in print. Only death on July 1, 1961, prevented Céline from giving the printer a third wartime chronicle, *Rigodon*, the manuscript of which required eight years of deciphering before it could be published in 1969, five years after the deciphering of the lost, concluding manuscript of *Guignol's Band* made that work available in its entirety, in 1964. Thus the full scope of Céline's work has been known for only a few years.

The pariah remained faithful to his medical profession until the end. Upon his return from exile he and his wife moved into a house in Meudon, a Parisian suburb overlooking the bend in the Seine where a Renault factory covers one of the islands. Surrounded by animals of all sorts, especially a pack of dogs who barked at anyone's approach, Céline attempted to resume his practice. Undoubtedly this was a practical necessity, for his wife gave lessons in the dance to help make ends meet. One may suppose that patients were not very anxious to come to this doctor who was poorly dressed, often went unshaved, and lived in a bestiary. If Céline can be believed, however, he did have a small practice among the poor — and a steadily increasing flood of visitors who came armed with tape recorders to interview him. Céline's life was his work, both in literature and in medicine, and as his last interview makes clear,

he was willing to give his life to accomplish the tasks
he had set for himself:

j'écris pas pour les mêmes raisons, ni pour l'Académie, ni
pour les fesses du jardinier: ça s'est vu, ça se voit... J'écris
tout simplement pour les rendre illisibles, Mme Valéry, M.
Colette ça s'imite, y a une façon: du tricot main, si on veut,
de la broderie de demoiselle, mais pas de la tapisserie qui
vous prend la vie d'un homme... Pas des cathédrales de
dentelle, mais de pierres arrachées aux carrières de la vie. Ce
boulot-là, ça vous grignote tout le temps, il en reste plus que
pour se coucher le soir.[40]

(I don't write for the same reasons, neither for the Academy,
nor for the gardener's buttocks: that's been done, it's still
done... I write quite simply to make the others unreadable,
Mme Valéry, M. Colette; that can be imitated, there's a way:
knitting, if you like, or a spinster's embroidery, but not a
tapestry that consumes a man's life... Not cathedrals in lace,
but in stones torn from life's quarries. That job eats away all
your time, there's just enough left to go to bed in the evening.)

Even though he was near death, Céline remained the
cantankerous and sardonic polemist he had always been.
In spite of the bravado, or perhaps because of it, this is
the final image of Céline that seems most appropriate.
It is the image of a man who, remaining unrepentant to
the end, refused to assuage the violence of the contradictions he had lived.

Notes

Introduction

1. *Cahiers de L'Herne*, III (1963), 92.

CHAPTER ONE: *The Picaro's Flight into Darkness*

1. R.-M. Albérès, *Histoire du roman moderne* (Paris: Albin Michel, 1962), p. 299.

2. Germaine Brée and Margaret Gulton, *An Age of Fiction: The French Novel from Gide to Camus* (New Brunswick, N.J.: Rutgers University Press, 1957), p. 165.

3. David Hayman, *Céline* (New York: Columbia University Press, 1965), p. 20.

4. Milton Hindus, *L.-F. Céline tel que je l'ai vu*, trans. André Belamich (Paris: L'Arche, 1951), p. 94.

5. Louis-Ferdinand Céline, "Correspondance à Milton Hindus," *Cahiers de L'Herne*, V (1965), 99.

6. Alex Jacquemin, "Voyage avec Céline," *La Revue Nouvelle*, May 15, 1962, p. 476.

7. Michel Beaujour, "Temps et substances dans *Voyage au bout de la nuit*," *Cahiers de L'Herne*, V (1965), 185.

8. Cf. Alvin Greenberg, "The Novel of Disintegration,"

Wisconsin Studies in Contemporary Literature, VII (Winter-Spring, 1966), 103–104.

9. Alain, *Système des Beaux-Arts* (Paris: Ed. de la N.R.F., 1926), p. 319.

10. See Leo Spitzer, "Une Habitude de style, le rappel chez Céline," *Cahiers de L'Herne*, V (1965), 153–164.

11. Eliseo Vivas, *Creation and Discovery* (New York: Noonday, 1955), pp. 112, 116.

12. Wayne Booth, *The Rhetoric of Fiction* (Chicago: University of Chicago Press, 1961), pp. 382, 383.

13. George Bernanos, *Le Crépuscule des vieux* (Paris: Gallimard, 1959), pp. 341–346.

14. Nicole Debrie-Panel, *Louis-Ferdinand Céline* (Paris: Vitte, 1961), p. 155.

CHAPTER TWO: *The Delirium of Childhood*

1. *"Métro émotif"* is the expression Céline often used to describe his style. In later years he asserted that his only interest in literature was to create a style that would transpose the emotion of spoken language into written language. Cf. his hilarious *Entretiens avec le Professeur Y...* (Paris: Gallimard, 1955). With regard to his punctuation, in this work Céline also says that the "trois points sont indispensables! . . . Pour poser mes rails émotifs!..." ("the three dots are indispensable! . . . In order to lay my emotive rails!...") (p. 115).

2. Céline's *Hommage à Zola* is reprinted in *Cahiers de L'Herne,* III (1963), 169–172.

3. Erika Ostrovsky, "Céline et le thème du roi Krogold," *Cahiers de L'Herne,* V (1965), 202.

4. Pol Vandromme, *Céline* (Paris: Ed. Universitaires, 1963), p. 30.

5. Michel Beaujour, "La Quête du délire," *Cahiers de L'Herne,* III (1963), 284.

6. Henri Bergson, *Le Rire* (Geneva: A. Skira, 1945), pp. 16–17.

7. Northrop Frye, *Anatomy of Criticism* (Princeton, N.J.: Princeton University Press, 1957), p. 284.

8. George Meredith, *An Essay on Comedy* (London, 1905), p. 82.

CHAPTER THREE: Délire *as Ritual Farce*

1. In Germaine Brée and Margaret Guiton's *An Age of Fiction* (New Brunswick, N.J.: Rutgers University Press, 1957) *Guignol's Band* is placed somewhere between literature and psychotherapy (p. 168). V. S. Pritchett in "Cellar Rats," *The New Statesman and Nation*, XLVIII (October 2, 1954), dismissed the first part of the novel as a nightmare composed of a series of knockabout farces (p. 412). Most critics have had much the same opinion, though a more favorable critic, Nicole Debrie-Panel, in her *Louis-Ferdinand Céline* (Paris: Vitte, 1961), tried to salvage the unfinished novel by calling it a "transitional work" (p. 154).

2. *Guignol's Band*, the first volume, will be cited as *G.*, and *Le Pont de Londres*, the second volume, as *L.* It should be stressed that *Le Pont de Londres* is not a sequel to the first volume. They are one novel. The first paragraph of *Le Pont de Londres* continues the last paragraph of *Guignol's Band.*

3. According to Robert Poulet, who did the final editing of *Le Pont de Londres*, there are three copies of the manuscript, only one of which was in an approximately final state. Poulet states that his editing consisted in correcting the obvious typing errors or lapses and in reestablishing Céline's punctuation in those cases where it had been forgotten (*L.*, p. 6). For various versions of the history of the manuscript, see Erika Ostrovsky, *Voyeur Voyant: A Portrait of Louis-Ferdinand Céline* (New York: Random House, 1971), pp. 296–297.

4. Northrop Frye, *Anatomy of Criticism* (Princeton, N.J.: Princeton University Press, 1957), pp. 63–64.

5. Pol Vandromme, *Céline* (Paris: Ed. Universitaires, 1963), p. 43.

6. The distinction between reliable and unreliable narrators belongs to Wayne Booth. In his *Rhetoric of Fiction* (Chicago: University of Chicago Press, 1961), he develops at length the advantages and disadvantages the novelist and the reader

encounter when dealing with narrators who are to be taken at their word and with narrators who do not, for various reasons, tell the truth.

7. Pritchett, "Cellar Rats," p. 412.

8. Robert Poulet, *Entretiens familiers avec L.-F. Céline* (Paris: Plon, 1958), p. 99.

9. Jean Tortel, "Roman populaire," *Histoire des littératures*, Vol. III, ed. Raymond Queneau (Paris: Bibliothèque de la Pléiade, 1958), pp. 1590–1591.

CHAPTER FOUR: *Political Delirium*

1. Sartre's "Portrait de l'antisémite" was first printed in *Les Temps Modernes*, III (December, 1945), 462.

2. Cf. J. Morand, "Les Idées politiques de L.-F. Céline: L'Accusation de fascisme," *Revue Politique et Parlementaire*, 751 (December, 1964), 48–55, an excellent study that should convince any open-minded critic that Céline can be called a fascist only by using the term in so wide a sense that it loses all meaning.

3. John R. Harrison, *The Reactionaries* (New York: Schocken Books, 1967), p. 29.

4. André Gide, "Les Juifs, Céline et Maritain," *Nouvelle Revue Française*, 295 (April, 1938), 630–634. Reprinted in *Cahiers de L'Herne*, V (1965), 335–337.

5. The French fascist Lucien Rebatet offers a revealing anecdote in this respect: "I must say, to be precise, that if we fascists did a pyrrhic dance around *Bagatelles pour un massacre* in 1938, *L'Ecole des cadavres*, a year later, knocked us flat. Hitler had just entered Prague, and that was the moment that Céline chose to call for a total economic, political, and military alliance with Germany. It was impossible, even for us, to print a single word about such a maniac. . . . Céline was still exaggerating." From "D'un Céline l'autre," *Cahiers de L'Herne*, III (1963), 45.

6. Peter Viereck, *Conservatism* (Princeton, N.J.: Van Nostrand, 1956), pp. 16–17.

CHAPTER FIVE: Délire *as Myth*

1. Nicole Debrie-Panel, *Louis-Ferdinand Céline* (Paris: Vitte, 1961), p. 148.

2. It is quite possible that parts of *Féerie I* were written while Céline was in prison. On June 11, 1947, Céline wrote to Milton Hindus that he was writing a work in which he was dealing with a bombardment of Montmartre by the R.A.F. See "Correspondance de Céline à Milton Hindus," *Cahiers de L'Herne,* V (1965), 79. Céline is here describing *Normance.* Does this mean that the entire first volume, which precedes the bombardment, was then completed? If so, it must surely have been written in part while Céline was in prison.

3. Céline will repeat this defense of his anti-Semitism for the rest of his life. For example, he wrote Albert Paraz the following lines in a letter that was later published: "Vivent les Youtres! Les Fritz n'ont jamais été pro-aryens, seulement anti-sémites, ce qui est absolument idiot. J'en voulais à certains clans juifs de nous lancer dans une guerre perdue d'avance. Je n'ai jamais désiré la mort du Juif ou des Juifs. Je voulais simplement qu'ils freinent leur hystérie et ne nous poussent pas à l'abattoir." ("Long live the Kikes! The Krauts were never pro-Aryan, just anti-Semitic, which is absolutely idiotic. I was angry at certain Jewish clans for wanting to throw us into a war that was lost before it started. I never wanted the Jews to be killed. I just wanted them to put a brake on their hysteria and not push us into the slaughterhouse.") Reprinted in Paraz's *Le Gala des vaches* (Paris: Editions de l'Elan, 1948), p. 94.

4. "Extraits de lettres d'Albert Paraz à Pierre Marcot sur Céline," *Cahiers de L'Herne,* V (1965), 297.

5. David Hayman, *Louis-Ferdinand Céline* (New York: Columbia University Press, 1965), p. 36.

CHAPTER SIX: *History as* Délire

1. In "Pourquoi Céline... 8 Ecrivains répondent," *Arts,* December 22, 1965, p. 12.

2. There are two editions of *Nord*. In the first Céline used the names of real persons, and this involved him in legal difficulties. Quotations in the chapter are from the second edition or the "édition définitive" in which fictional names have been given to the characters and to some of the places. A comparison of the two editions shows that the changes Céline made are slight. Mme von Seckt becomes Mme von Dopf, Dr. Hauboldt becomes Dr. Harras, Kräntzlin becomes Zornhof, etc.

3. André Gide, "Les Juifs, Céline et Maritain," *Nouvelle Revue Française*, 295 (April, 1938), 630–634. Reprinted in *Cahiers de L'Herne*, v (1965), 337.

4. Maurice Nadeau, "En marge: Céline," *Lettres Nouvelles*, LVII (September, 1957), 348.

EPILOGUE: *Who Was Céline?*

1. For a semifictional biography, see Erika Ostrovsky, *Voyeur Voyant: A Portrait of Louis-Ferdinand Céline* (New York: Random House, 1971). This work has much useful documentation. Dominique de Roux has written a work, *La Mort de L.-F. Céline* (Paris: Christian Bourgois, 1966), which is in part a biography, though it is more a work of polemic and meditation based on Céline's life. For chronological outlines of Céline's life, one may consult the one that Jean A. Ducourneau has established in the first volume of the *Œuvres de Louis-Ferdinand Céline* (Paris: André Balland, 1966), or the one in the latest edition of Marc Hanrez's *Céline* in the series Pour une Bibliothèque Idéale. Earlier outlines, including the one in Hanrez's *Céline* (Paris: Gallimard, 1961), are not accurate.

2. In Albert Paraz, *Le Gala des vaches* (Paris: Editions de l'Elan, 1948), p. 111.

3. Jean Guénot and Jacques Darribehaude, "Des pays où personne ne va jamais," *Cahiers de L'Herne*, III (1963), 188.

4. Marcel Brochard, "Céline à Rennes," *Cahiers de L'Herne*, III (1963), 14.

5. In an interview Céline said, however, that he became conscious of social injustice only after World War I: "C'est

venu, vous savez, avec les mercantis, comme on appelait alors. Des embusqués, qui gagnaient du pognon pendant que les autres crevaient." ("That came, you know, with the *mercantis*, as we called them. Shirkers, who made money while the others were getting killed.") In Guénot and Darribehaude, "Des pays où personne ne va jamais," p. 187.

6. V. S. Prichett, "Down the Drain with M. Céline," *The New Statesman*, June 17, 1966, p. 883.

7. Erika Landry, "Céline et une jeune étudiante allemande," *Cahiers de L'Herne*, v (1965), 36.

8. *L'Express*, June 14, 1957. Reprinted in Madeleine Chapsel, *Les Ecrivains en personne* (Paris: Julliard, 1960), p. 79.

9. Brochard, "Céline à Rennes," p. 15.

10. Jean A. Ducourneau, "Céline n'a jamais été trépané," *Le Figaro littéraire*, October 27, 1966, p. 4.

11. Georges Geoffroy, "Céline en Angleterre," *Cahiers de L'Herne*, iii (1963), 11.

12. Renato Barilli, "Vitalità patologica di Céline," *Verri*, xxvi (February, 1968), 43.

13. Céline's article on social security was first printed in *La Presse Médicale*, November 24, 1928; reprinted in *Cahiers de L'Herne*, v (1965), 12–18.

14. Céline later wrote an article, "La Médecine chez Ford," which was printed in *Lecture 40* in 1941; reprinted in *Cahiers de L'Herne*, iii (1963), 173–180. In this article Céline recognized the benefits to be gained from keeping the sick at their work under medical supervision. The article throws a curious light on the episode involving the Ford plant in *Voyage*.

15. Jeanne Carayon, "Le Docteur écrit un roman," *Cahiers de L'Herne*, iii (1963), 21.

16. In Jean Guénot, "Voyage au bout de la parole," *Cahiers de L'Herne*, v (1965), 252.

17. Henri Mahé, *La Brinquebale avec Céline* (Paris: La Table Ronde, 1969), p. 24.

18. Mahé came to know how obsessed Céline was with

making money. When Mahé asked him to do a preface for some sketches, Céline first agreed, but then refused to do his friend this favor for less than 25,000 francs. See *La Brinque-bale avec Céline*, p. 76.

19. First printed in *Candide*, March 16, 1933, reprinted by Jean Ducourneau as "Céline: Je m'explique," *Les Nouvelles littéraires*, November 3, 1966, pp. 1, 4.

20. Reprinted in *Cahiers de L'Herne*, III (1963), 169–172.

21. In "Louis-Ferdinand Céline à Elie Faure," *Cahiers de L'Herne*, V (1965), 55.

22. André Gide, "Les Juifs, Céli1e et Maritain," *Nouvelle Revue Française*, 295 (April, 1938), 630–634. Reprinted in *Cahiers de L'Herne*, V (1965), 335–337.

23. In "Louis-Ferdinand Céline à Albert Paraz," *Cahiers de L'Herne*, III (1963), 148–149.

24. Albert Paraz, *Valsez, Saucisses* (Paris: Amiot-Dumont, 1950), p. 235.

25. Louis-Ferdinand Céline, "Réponses aux accusations," *Cahiers de L'Herne*, V (1965), 321–322.

26. Robert Chamfleury, "Céline ne nous a pas trahis," *Cahiers de L'Herne*, III (1963), 66.

27. *Ibid.*, p. 65.

28. Karl Epting, "Il ne nous aimait pas," *Cahiers de L'Herne*, III (1963), 57.

29. The charge is repeated in Maurice Vanino, *"L'Ecole du cadavre," l'Affaire Céline* (Paris: Créator, 1952). It is based on a letter from the German ambassador, Abetz, recommending Céline as a collaborator. As such, the letter is of dubious significance. See the reprint in "Extraits de *L'Ecole du cadavre*," *Cahiers de L'Herne*, V (1965), 331.

30. Lucien Rebatet, "D'un Céline l'autre," *Cahiers de L'Herne*, III (1963), 48.

31. See "Louis-Ferdinand Céline répond au *Pays Libre*," *Pays Libre*, April 5, 1941, p. 3. It is also worth noting that the Vichy government banned *Les Beaux Draps*, which in turn prompted a rather compromising protest from Céline. See "Lettre de Céline au capitaine Sezille," the secretary of the

Institut d'Etude de Questions Juives. First reprinted in Vanino, *L'Affaire Céline*, then in *Cahiers de L'Herne*, v (1965), 329.

32. Louis-Ferdinand Céline, "Acte de foi," *La Gerbe*, February 13, 1941, p. 1.

33. In "Entretien avec Céline," *Emancipation Nationale*, November 21, 1941, p. 2.

34. Céline, "Réponse aux accusations," p. 321.

35. André Pulicani, "Chez Gen Paul, à Montmartre," *Cahiers de L'Herne*, iii (1963), 39.

36. Rebatet, "D'un Céline l'autre," p. 50.

37. Paraz, *Le Gala des vaches*, p. 238.

38. *Ibid.*, p. 213.

39. In *Le Monde*, February 15, 1969, p. v of the literary supplement.

40. Pierre Audinet, "La Dernière Invective de Céline," *Arts*, November 24, 1965, p. 14.

Selected Bibliography

After the novels the important sources for a study of Céline are the two *Cahiers de L'Herne* (Paris), III and V (1963 and 1965), which are devoted to him. These two reviews contain many letters and pieces by Céline that are difficult to find. They also offer a varied selection of critical articles and *témoignages* dealing with Céline and his work, as well as very complete bibliographies. In the following bibliography I have not listed correspondence, biographical essays, and critical articles on Céline that are in the *Cahiers de L'Herne*, though I have cited them in the chapter notes whenever I have made specific use of them.

Works by Louis-Ferdinand Céline

A l'agité du bocal (pamphlet). Paris: P. Lanauve de Tartas, 1948. Reprinted in *Cahiers de L'Herne*, V (1965), 22–27.

Bagatelles pour un massacre. Paris: Denoël, 1937. New edition with photographs, 1943.*

Ballets sans musique, sans personne, sans rien. Paris: Gallimard, 1957.

* Editions quoted in this book.

Les Beaux Draps. Paris: Les Nouvelles Editions, 1941.

Casse-Pipe (fragment). In *Entretiens familiers avec Louis-Ferdinand Céline* by Robert Poulet. Paris: Plon, 1958.

Casse-Pipe (fragment). In *Cahiers de L'Herne*, III (1963), 167–168.

D'un château l'autre. 43d ed.* Paris: Gallimard, 1957. Trans. Ralph Manheim as *Castle to Castle.* New York: Dell, 1968. London, Holt-Blond.

L'Ecole des cadavres. Paris: Denoël, 1938. New edition with preface, 1942.*

L'Eglise, comédie en 5 actes. Paris: Denoël et Steele, 1933.

Entretiens avec le professeur Y... Paris: Gallimard, 1955.*

Féerie pour une autre fois I. 57th ed.* Paris: Gallimard, 1952.

Guignol's Band. Paris: Denoël, 1944. Also, 10th ed.* Paris: Gallimard, 1952. Trans. Bernard Frechtman and Jack T. Nile. New York: New Directions, 1954.

Mea Culpa. (Followed by *La Vie et l'œuvre de Semmelweis.*) Paris: Denoël et Steele, 1936.* Trans. and introd. Robert Allerton Parker. New York: Little, 1937.

Mort à crédit. Paris: Denoël et Steele, 1936. Also, Bibliothèque de la Pléiade, Paris: Gallimard, 1962.* Trans. Ralph Manheim as *Death on the Installment Plan.* New York: New Directions, 1966. Also trans. John H. P. Marks. New York: New Directions, 1938. London, The Bodley Head.

Nord. Edition définitive.* Paris: Gallimard, 1960. Trans. Ralph Manheim as *North.* New York: Delacorte, 1971. London, The Bodley Head.

Normance: Féerie pour une autre fois II. Paris: Gallimard, 1954.*

Le Pont de Londres: Guignol's Band II. Paris: Gallimard, 1964.*

La Quinine en thérapeutique. Paris: Doin, 1925.*

Rigodon. Paris: Gallimard, 1969.*

La Vie et l'œuvre de Philippe-Ignace Semmelweis. Paris: Imprimerie Francis Simon, 1924. Also, Paris: Gallimard, 1952.*

Voyage au bout de la nuit. Paris: Denoël et Steele, 1932. Also, Bibliothèque de la Pléiade, Paris: Gallimard, 1962.* Trans. John H. P. Marks as *Journey to the End of the Night.* New York: New Directions, 1934. London, Chatto and Windus.

It should also be noted that in the 1960's the publisher André Balland brought out the *Œuvres de Louis-Ferdinand Céline,* ed. Jean A. Ducourneau, in an edition that includes much critical and biographical information. Unfortunately these are not the complete works, and Céline's anti-Semitic pamphlets will remain difficult to find.

ARTICLES, INTERVIEWS, AND CORRESPONDENCE BY CÉLINE

"Acte de foi," *La Gerbe,* February 13, 1941, p. 1.

"Céline: Je m'explique," *Les Nouvelles Littéraires,* November 3, 1966, pp. 1, 4. Presented by Jean Ducourneau.

"Céline nous écrit," *La Révolution Nationale,* April 5, 1942, p. 1.

"Entretien avec Céline," *Emancipation Nationale,* November 21, 1941, pp. 1–3.

"Epilogue," *Histoire de Vichy* by Robert Aron. Paris: Fayard, 1960. P. 729.

"Excerpts from His Letters to Milton Hindus," *Texas Quarterly,* V (1962), 22–38. Translation of letters in *Cahiers de L'Herne,* V (1965).

Letters to Henri Mahé in his *La Brinquebale avec Céline.* Paris: La Table Ronde, 1969.

Letters to Albert Paraz in his *Le Gala des vaches.* Paris: Editions de l'Elan, 1948.

Letters to Albert Paraz in his *Le Menuet du haricot.* Geneva: Connaître, 1958.

Letters to Albert Paraz in his *Valsez, saucisses.* Paris: Amiot-Dumont, 1950.

"Lettres d'exil," *Ecrits de Paris,* 197 (October, 1961), 103–110. Presented by Robert Poulet.

"Louis-Ferdinand Céline répond au *Pays Libre*," *Pays Libre*, April 5, 1941, p. 3.

"Voyage au bout de la haine" (interview), *L'Express*, June 14, 1957. Reprinted in *Les Ecrivains en personne* by Madeleine Chapsul. Paris: Julliard, 1960.

SECONDARY SOURCES: BOOKS

Albérès, R.-M. *Histoire du roman moderne*. Paris: Albin Michel, 1962.

Arland, Marcel. *Essais et nouveaux essais critiques*. Paris: Gallimard, 1952.

Beauvoir, Simone de. *La Force de l'âge*. Paris: Gallimard, 1960.

Bernanos, Georges. *Le Crépuscule des vieux*. Paris: Gallimard, 1959.

———. *Les Grands Cimetières sous la lune*. Paris: Plon, 1960.

Boisdeffre, Pierre de. *Histoire vivante de la littérature d'aujourd'hui (1938–1958)*. Paris: Ed. Universitaires, 1958.

Brasillach, Robert. *Les Quatre Jeudis*. Paris: Les Sept Couleurs, 1943.

Brée, Germaine, and Guiton, Margaret. *An Age of Fiction: The French Novel from Gide to Camus*. New Brunswick, N.J.: Rutgers University Press, 1957.

Debrie-Panel, Nicole. *Louis-Ferdinand Céline*. Paris: Vitte, 1961.

Dominique, Pierre. *Les Polémistes français depuis 1789*. Paris: La Colombe, 1962.

Drieu La Rochelle, Pierre. *Le Français d'Europe*. Paris: Balzac, 1944.

———. *Sur les écrivains*. Paris: Gallimard, 1964.

Hanrez, Marc. *Céline*. Paris: Gallimard, 1961. New edition in the series Pour une Bibliothèque Idéale, n.d.

Hayman, David. *Louis-Ferdinand Céline*. New York: Columbia University Press, 1965.

Hindus, Milton. *The Crippled Giant*. New York: Boar's Head Books, 1950. Trans. André Belamich as *L.-F. Céline tel que je l'ai vu*. Paris: L'Arche, 1951.

Howe, Irving. *A World More Attractive: A View of Modern Literature and Politics.* New York: Horizon, 1963.

Jamet, Claude. *Images mêlées de la littérature et du théâtre.* Paris: Ed. de l'Elan, 1947.

Kaminski, H.-E. *Céline en chemise brune.* Paris: Nouvelles Ed. Excelsior, 1938.

Nadeau, Maurice. *Littérature présente.* Paris: Corréa, 1952.

Ostrovsky, Erika. *Céline and His Vision.* New York: New York University Press, 1967.

——. *Voyeur Voyant: A Portrait of Louis-Ferdinand Céline.* New York: Random House, 1971.

Picon, Gaëtan. *Panorama de la nouvelle littérature française.* Paris: Gallimard, 1951.

Poulet, Robert. *Entretiens familiers avec L.-F. Céline.* Paris: Plon, 1958. New ed. *Mon Ami Bardamu,* 1971.

——. *La Lanterne magique.* Paris: Debresse, 1956.

——. *Partis-pris.* Brussels and Paris: Les Ecrits, 1943.

Roux, Dominique de. *La Mort de L.-F. Céline.* Paris: Christian Bourgois, 1966.

Sérant, Paul. *Le Romantisme fasciste.* Paris: Fasquelle, 1959.

Vandromme, Pol. *Céline.* Paris: Ed. Universitaires, 1963.

Vanino, Maurice. *"L'Ecole du cadavre," l'Affaire Céline.* Paris: Créator, 1952.

Vivas, Eliseo. *Creation and Discovery.* New York: Noonday, 1955.

SECONDARY SOURCES: ARTICLES

Audinet, Pierre. "La Dernière Invective de Céline" (partly an interview), *Arts,* November 24, 1965, pp. 14–15.

——. "Dernières Rencontres avec Céline," *Les Nouvelles Littéraires,* July, 6, 1961, pp. 1, 4.

Beaujour, Michel. "Céline, artiste du laid," *French Review,* XXXVIII (December, 1964), 180–190.

Bertherat, Y. *"Le Pont de Londres"* (book review), *Esprit,* XXXII (July, 1964), 176–178.

Boisdeffre, Pierre de. "Louis-Ferdinand Céline," *Revue de Paris,* LXVII (October, 1960), 131–135.

Bourniquel, Camille. "La Fin du voyage," *Esprit*, IX (September, 1961), 336–337.

Brenner, Jacques. "Céline et *Féerie*," *Nouvelle Revue Française*, I (April, 1953), 721–723.

Cousteau, P.-A. "M. Céline rallie le fumier (doré) du système," *Rivarol*, 336 (June 20, 1957), 5.

Descaves, Pierre. Book review of *Nord*. *La Table Ronde*, October, 1960, pp. 183–184.

Ducourneau, Jean. "Céline n'a jamais été trépané," *Le Figaro Littéraire*, October 27, 1966, pp. 1, 4.

Erk, Jules Van. *"D'un château l'autre* by L.-F. Céline," *The European*, LV (September, 1957), 57–58.

Fitch, B. T. "Bardamu dans sa nuit à lui," *Bulletin des Jeunes Romanistes*, VIII (December, 1963), 31–36.

Frazer, John. "The Darkest Journey: Céline's *Death on the Installment Plan*," *Wisconsin Studies in Contemporary Literature*, VIII (Winter, 1967), 96–110.

Frohock, W. M. "Céline's Quest for Love," *Accent*, II (Winter, 1942), 79–84.

Glicksberg, Charles I. "Nihilism in Contemporary Literature," *Nineteenth Century and After*, 144 (October, 1948), 214–222.

Greenberg, Alvin. "The Novel of Disintegration," *Wisconsin Studies in Contemporary Literature*, VII (Winter-Spring, 1966), 103–124.

Hahn, Pierre. "Pourquoi Céline?... 8 Ecrivains répondent," *Arts*, December 22, 1965, pp. 12–13.

———. "Sur Céline," *Marginales*, November-December, 1961, pp. 71–74.

Hindus, Milton. "Céline: A Reappraisal," *The Southern Review*, Winter, 1965, pp. 76–93.

Jacquemin, Alex. "Voyage avec Céline," *La Revue Nouvelle*, May 15, 1962, pp. 473–481.

Marteau, R. Book review of *Nord*. *Esprit*, XXVIII (December, 1960), 2137–2138.

Matthews, J. H. "Céline's *Journey to the End of the Night*," *Contemporary Review*, 1095 (1957), 158–161.

Mondor, Henri. "Voyage au bout de la colère," *Les Nouvelles Littéraires,* March 29, 1962, p. 3.

Morand, Jacqueline. "Les Idées politiques de L.-F. Céline: L'Accusation de fascisme," *Revue Politique et Parlementaire,* 751 (December, 1964), 48–55.

Nadeau, Maurice. "En marge: Céline," *Lettres Nouvelles,* LVII (September, 1957), 345–352.

————. "Une Nouvelle Littérature," *Mercure de France,* 308 (March, 1950), 499–503.

Orlando, Walter. "Grandeur et misères de Bardamu," *La Table Ronde,* LVII (September, 1952), 171–173.

Pinette, G. L. Book review of *D'un château l'autre, Books Abroad,* XXXII (1958), 21–22.

————. "Louis-Ferdinand Céline: The Fury of Truth," *Books Abroad,* XXXIII (1959), 397–400.

Porquerol, Elizabeth. "Céline, il y a trente ans," *Nouvelle Revue Française,* IX (September, 1961), 550–557.

Poulet, Robert. "*Nord,*" *Rivarol,* July 28, 1960, p. 13.

————. "Présentation *D'un château l'autre,*" *Rivarol,* June 13, 1957.

————. "Un Article posthume de L.-F. Céline: 'Vive l'amnistie, Monsieur!'," *Rivarol,* December 20, 1962, p. 3.

Pritchett, V. S. "Cellar Rats," *The New Statesman and Nation,* XLVIII (October 2, 1954), 412–414.

————. "Down the Drain with Monsieur Céline," *The New Statesman,* June 17, 1966, pp. 883–884.

Reck, Rima Dell. "Céline and the Aural Novel," *Books Abroad,* XXXIX (Autumn, 1965), 404–406.

Richard, Jean-Pierre. "La Nausée de Céline," *Nouvelle Revue Française,* X (July, 1962), 33–47; continued in X (August, 1962), 235–252.

Saint-Paulien. "Céline," *Revue des Deux Mondes,* July-August, 1961, pp. 470–473.

Saurès, André. "A propos de Céline," *Nouvelle Revue Française,* IX (August, 1961), 326–329.

Sénard, Philippe. "L.-F. Céline: *Le Pont de Londres: Guignol's Band II,*" *La Table Ronde,* 197 (June, 1964), 133–134.

Slochower, Harry. "Satanism in Céline," *Books Abroad*, XVIII (1944), 332–337.

Sperber, Manès. "Céline," *Preuves*, 127 (1961), 18–22.

Steel, Eric M. "The French Writer Looks at America," *Antioch Review*, IV (Fall, 1944), 414–431.

Thiher, Allen. "The Yet To Be Salvaged Céline: *Guignol's Band*," *Modern Fiction Studies*, XVI (1970), 67–75.

———. "Sartre and Céline," *Philological Quarterly*, L (April, 1971), 292–305.

Trotsky, Leon. "Céline – Novelist and Politician," *Atlantic Monthly*, 156 (October, 1935), 413–420.

Truc, Gonzague. "L'Art et la passion de L.-F. Céline," *Revue Hebdomadaire*, VII (July 30, 1938), 550–565.

Vandromme, Pol. "Céline, la guerre et le pacifisme," *Ecrits de Paris*, 210 (December, 1962), 111–116.

———. "Louis-Ferdinand, un lyrique de la catastrophe," *Revue Générale Belge*, August, 1961, pp. 23–31.

Verri, XXVI (1968). Special issue devoted to Céline. Several very good articles.

Vial, Fernand. "French Intellectuals and the Collapse of Communism," *Thought*, XV, No. 58, pp. 429–444.

Woodcock, G. "Céline at the End of the Night," *Encounter*, X (May, 1958), 76–79.

OTHER SOURCES

Alain. *Système des Beaux-Arts*. Paris: Ed. de la N.R.F., 1926.

Aron, Robert. *Histoire de la Libération de la France*. Paris: Fayard, 1959.

———. *Histoire de Vichy*. Paris: Fayard, 1954.

Barthes, Roland. *Le Degré zéro de l'écriture*. Paris: Ed. du Seuil, 1953.

Bergson, Henri. *Le Rire*. Geneva: A. Skira, 1945. First published in *Revue de Paris* (1899).

Booth, Wayne. *The Rhetoric of Fiction*. Chicago: University of Chicago Press, 1961.

Burke, Kenneth. *The Philosophy of Literary Form.* Baton Rouge: Louisiana State University Press, 1941.

Camus, Albert. *L'Homme révolté.* Paris: Gallimard, 1951.

Cobban, Alfred. *A History of Modern France.* Vol. II. Baltimore: Penguin Books, 1961.

Duhamel, Georges. *Essai sur le roman.* Paris: M. Lesage, 1925.

Frye, Northrop. *Anatomy of Criticism.* Princeton, N.J.: Princeton University Press, 1957.

Goodman, Paul. *The Structure of Literature.* Chicago: University of Chicago Press, 1954.

Hyman, Stanley Edgar. *The Armed Vision.* New York: Knopf, 1948.

Lubbock, Percy. *The Craft of Fiction.* New York: Scribner, 1955. First published in 1921.

Luethy, Hébert. *France Against Herself.* Trans. Eric Mosbacher. New York: Praeger, 1955.

Meredith, George. *An Essay on Comedy.* London, 1905. First published in the *New Quarterly Magazine* (1877).

Michaud, Guy. *Connaissance de la littérature: L'Œuvre et ses techniques.* Paris: Nizet, 1957.

Paulhan, Jean. *Petite Préface à toute critique.* Paris: Ed. de Minuit, 1951.

Pouillon, Jean. "Les Règles du je," *Temps Modernes,* XII (April, 1957), 1591–1598.

Poulet, Georges. *Etudes sur le temps humain.* Paris: Plon, 1950.

Rader, Melvin (ed.). *A Modern Book of Esthetics.* rev. ed. New York: Holt, 1952.

Raimond, Michel. *La Crise du roman.* Paris: José Corti, 1966.

Sartre, Jean-Paul. *Réflexions sur la question juive.* Paris: P. Morihien, 1946.

———. *Situations I.* Paris: Gallimard, 1947.

Scholes, Robert (ed.). *Approaches to the Novel.* San Francisco: Chandler, 1961.

Scholes, Robert, and Kellogg, Robert. *The Nature of Narrative.* New York: Oxford University Press, 1966.

Sutton, Walter. *Modern American Criticism.* Englewood Cliffs, N.J.: Prentice Hall, 1963.

Thibaudet, Albert. *Physiologie de la critique.* Paris: Ed. de La Nouvelle Revue Critique, 1930.

Tortel, Jean. "Roman populaire," *Histoire des littératures.* Vol. III. Raymond Queneau (ed.). Paris: Bibliothèque de la Pléiade, 1958. Pp. 1579–1603.

Viereck, Peter. *Conservatism.* Princeton, N.J.: Van Nostrand, 1956.

Warren, Austin, and Welleck, René. *Theory of Literature.* 2d. ed. New York: Harcourt, Brace, 1955.

Index

ABOUT THE AUTHOR

Allen Thiher is a Texan by birth (a native of Fort Worth), but he sometimes considers himself more a Midwesterner than a Texan, perhaps by reason of his graduate education. At the University of Texas, where he earned both a Bachelor's degree and a Phi Beta Kappa key, he had his first exposure to French literature. At the time, he was planning to become a writer. This plan was unexpectedly shortcircuited by the receipt of a graduate fellowship to study twentieth-century French literature at the University of Wisconsin.

Arrived at Madison, Mr. Thiher found his decision rewarding: "Two years of intensive course work did teach me a great deal. . . . Somewhere along the way Germaine Brée introduced me to Céline, and that gave me an entirely new French language to learn, one they do not speak in the classroom or in polite society." Although he was on the point of receiving his Ph.D., he decided to take a year in Paris as a Fulbright scholar.

He returned to Wisconsin from residence in Paris and travels in Spain and Italy to finish his doctorate. He brought back with him a deep affection for Paris, to which he returns as often as possible. After two years of teaching at Duke University, Mr. Thiher became an assistant professor at Middlebury College, where this volume was largely written. It is his first book, but he has published articles in *Modern Fiction Studies*, *Romance Notes*, and *Modern Drama*.

L